Introduction to Old Testament Wisdom

Introduction to Old Testament Wisdom

A Spirituality for Liberation

Anthony R. Ceresko, O.S.F.S.

ORBIS BOOKS
Maryknoll, New York 10545

The Catholic Foreign Mission Society of America (Maryknoll) recruits and trains people for overseas missionary service. Through Orbis Books, Maryknoll aims to foster the international dialogue that is essential to mission. The books published, however, reflect the opinions of their authors and are not meant to represent the official position of the society. To obtain more information about Maryknoll and Orbis Books, please visit our website at www.maryknoll.org.

Library of Congress Cataloging-in-Publication Data

Ceresko, Anthony R.
    Introduction to Old Testament wisdom : a spirituality of
liberation / Anthony R. Ceresko.
        p.   cm.
    Includes bibliographical references and indexes.
    ISBN 1-57075-277-X (pbk.)
    1. Wisdom literature Introductions.   2. Sociology, Biblical.   3.
Liberation theology.   I. Title.
    BS1455.C47   1999
    223'.061—dc21   99-31688
                                                                CIP

Contents

Preface

This Introduction to Old Testament Wisdom results from my experience of teaching courses on the Old Testament wisdom writings at St. Michael's College, Toronto, and at St. Peter's Pontifical Institute, Bangalore. I have learned much from reading and studying both earlier scholars and my contemporaries. To them all I owe a debt of gratitude, as well as to the many students through the years whose interest and insightful questions have encouraged and helped me to deepen my understanding of this literature.

Thanks are due in a number of other quarters as well: first of all to the Board of Administration of St. Peter's Pontifical Institute, and especially the president, the Rev. John Manthadam, for granting me study leave in 1998 to write this book. The staff at Orbis Books also deserves my thanks, especially the editor-in-chief, Robert Ellsberg, for his enthusiastic acceptance of the manuscript, and editor Susan Perry for her careful shepherding of the book through the publication process.

The Oblate community south of Bangalore, "Samarpanaram," provided a congenial ambience during the months of my study leave. I shall always be grateful for their hospitality and support, especially to the Rev. Josef Költringer, O.S.F.S., the superior, and to the two brothers who did much of the initial typing, Benny Palliparambil and Maichael Mathew. It is to my brother Oblates at Samarpanaram that I affectionately dedicate this book.

Anthony R. Ceresko
Oblate of St. Francis de Sales

Easter 1999
St. Peter's Pontifical Institute
Malleswaram West
Bangalore, India

1

Introduction

WISDOM AND EXPERIENCE

In few places in our world today can one find a more brutal juxta-position of the riches of ancient wisdom and the complexities of modern life than in a country like India. Bustling factories turning out the latest technological wonders stand side by side with the appalling human misery of the slums. From the midst of the noise and confusion rise the temples, mosques, and churches, with their centers for teaching the timeless wisdom accumulated through thousands of years. The great leader and "guru" (teacher) of modern India, Mahatma Gandhi, was steeped in that ancient wisdom. At the same time he fearlessly confronted the contradictions that plagued his native land. At one point in the struggle for freedom from foreign domination, he articulated his vision of what his country can and should become:

> I work for an India, in which the poorest shall feel that it is their country in whose making they have an effective voice; an India in which there shall be no high class and low class of people; an India in which all communities live in harmony. . . . Women shall enjoy the same rights as men, since we shall be at peace with all the rest of the world, neither exploiting, nor being exploited. We shall have the smallest army imaginable. All interests not in conflict with the interests of the voiceless millions will be scrupulously respected, whether foreign or indigenous. . . . This is the India of my dreams. (*Young India*, September 10, 1931)

This remarkable leader often demonstrated his profound insight by urging his followers to turn to their own *experience* as a source of wisdom and as a guide in making decisions about the right course of action:

> I give you a talisman. Whenever you are in doubt . . . apply the following test. Recall the face of the poorest and weakest man

1

whom you may have seen, and ask yourself if the step you contemplate is going to be of any use to him. Will he gain anything by it? Will it restore him to a control over his own life and destiny? In other words, will it lead to liberation (*swaraj*) for the hungry and spiritually starving masses? Then you will find your doubts . . . melting away. (*Collected Works*, 89:125)

JESUS AND WISDOM

Some two thousand years earlier, another great wisdom teacher also counseled his followers to consult their own *experience* if they would be wise and adopt the correct course of action. Jesus of Nazareth taught his contemporaries, "Love your neighbor." When someone asked, "Who is my neighbor?" he replied with a parable that skillfully led his listeners back to their own experience to discover the answer. The story of the Good Samaritan in chapter 10 of Luke's Gospel tells how robbers attacked and beat "a certain man" going from Jerusalem to Jericho. A priest and a levite both passed the man by. They paid no attention to his plight. But an unlikely Samaritan, a stranger and member of a rival community, stopped and cared for the wounded man by the wayside. Jesus ends the story with the question, "Which of these three, do you think, was a neighbor to the man who fell into the hands of the robbers?"

The answer to the question is obvious: the Samaritan did what was right. How do we know? We have only to imagine ourselves as the victim by the roadside to understand what the situation demanded. Our own encounters with need and rescue provide the pointer. As with Gandhi, the listener's own experience and common sense confirm the authority and truthfulness of the teaching.

Notice that neither teacher, Gandhi or Jesus, refers to the sacred writings of the Jews or Hindus. Nor does either one call upon the authority of earlier teachers—Moses or the prophets, for example, in the case of Jesus. We know that both men were thoroughly immersed in their scriptures and the ancient traditions of their people. These all lie in the background. But for the practical, everyday decisions and guidance on how to live faithfully according to those traditions, the key for both, Jesus and Gandhi, is wisdom drawn from daily life.

WISDOM SPIRITUALITY

Gandhi and Jesus in their common appeal to *experience* both serve as examples or models of what we mean by a wisdom "spirituality." Jon Alexander describes spirituality as "the beliefs, values and practices that unify and orient our lives in respect to God as the origin and goal of human existence" (p. 253).

As we study the wisdom writings of the Old Testament we will learn what "beliefs, values and practices" the wisdom teachers taught and lived. In the process, it will become clear why we would consider Gandhi and Jesus among those who embody a "wisdom spirituality." Already we can point out two features of the kind of spirituality that the wisdom writings foster.

First, the wisdom teachers believed that directing one's life toward God was not limited to specifically religious activities and places. Rather, the wisdom writers understood the realm of divine–human encounter to be ordinary human life. Thus, Kathleen O'Connor proposes the image of the marketplace as a key to understanding wisdom spirituality. In the towns and villages of the ancient Near East, the marketplace acted as the center of public life:

> Besides serving as places of exchange for ordinary foods and products necessary for daily survival, the market place also functioned as the gathering spots for the community. There friends met, news was exchanged and legal and political decisions were made. Bustling, crowded spaces filled with noises and smells, the market places contained life at its most promising and its most mundane. In them deals were made, fortunes won and lost and people struggled to survive. (*Wisdom Literature,* p. 13)

O'Connor thus concludes:

> As a poetic and theological image the market place expresses the fascination of the wisdom thinkers with ordinary human existence. It represents the area where humans struggle to cope with the chaos of daily life . . . where the divine and the human meet. (*Wisdom Literature,* pp. 13-14)

An emphasis on the centrality of *relationships* forms a second feature of the kind of spirituality we will find in the wisdom writings. In one's day-to-day encounter with other human beings certain attitudes and actions are commended by these writings while other actions and attitudes are discouraged. How can one deal successfully and fairly with family, friends, business partners, civil leaders, the young, the elderly, the stranger, the fool? Questions like this form much of the subject matter of the sage's advice and reflection. Discerning the values and beliefs that inform and guide the sage's counsel will enable us to understand something of what wisdom spirituality is all about.

A SPIRITUALITY FOR LIBERATION

The story of the Exodus has exercised a powerful hold on the imagination of biblical writers and of Jewish and Christian thinkers down through the ages. The story tells of a poor and powerless group of slaves persecuted and exploited by a cruel and ruthless pharaoh, and it recounts their miraculous escape and liberation from the pharaoh's oppression. After covenanting with the God Yahweh, who freed them, they follow Moses on a pilgrimage through the wilderness to the safety and security of the promised land.

The importance of the Exodus in the memory of the biblical writers is obvious in parts of the Bible such as the Pentateuch and the prophets. By contrast, the Exodus finds little place in the wisdom writings. In fact, it does not figure at all in the three wisdom books of the Hebrew Bible—Proverbs, Job, and Ecclesiastes. Only with the two later writings, the Wisdom of Ben Sira and the Wisdom of Solomon, do references to the event occur explicitly.

Nonetheless, lack of explicit mention does not mean that the significance of the Exodus story, and its companion theme of covenant, was absent. On the contrary, one cannot read and interpret the wisdom writings, especially in their final canonical form, without understanding them against the background of this foundational event that helped to determine the identity and destiny of this people.

Consciousness of their origins as exploited and oppressed slaves continued to have a decisive impact on the outlook and mind-set of this people. What today we call the "option for the poor" finds its roots in this outlook and mind-set. Thus, in their laws and institutions, their way of organizing their life together, resistance to domination and care for the poor and vulnerable in their midst played a central role. Not only do these represent prominent "beliefs and values" of biblical spirituality. They are also central to a wisdom spirituality and provide the reason why we can refer to it as a "spirituality for liberation."

Recall our two examples of people who embody elements of such a wisdom spirituality, Jesus and Gandhi. Gandhi's "talisman" or touchstone in decision making is "the poorest and weakest person we have ever seen." And in Jesus' parable about the Good Samaritan, the "neighbor" whom we are commanded to love is the half-dead stranger lying helpless on the roadside, the powerless victim of the brutal violence of his fellow human beings.

For the people of Israel, covenant served as the way for organizing their society and setting out the social, economic, and political arrangements that would ensure a just and life-giving community. Above all, covenant put forth the principles and concrete steps for establishing and maintaining relationships within the community—husband and wife, parents and children, worker and employer, and so forth. Again and again we see how the "option for the poor" determines the expression of the "beliefs, values, and practices" that inform a covenant spirituality, a covenantal way of living day by day. A good example comes from the twenty-fourth chapter of Deuteronomy:

> When you reap your harvest in your field and forget a sheaf in the field, you shall not go back to get it; it shall be left for the alien, the orphan, and the widow, so that the LORD your God may bless you in all your undertakings. When you beat your olive trees, do not strip what is left; it shall be for the alien, the orphan, and the widow. . . . Remember that you were a slave in the land of Egypt; therefore I am commanding you to do this. (Deut 24:19-22)

Here we see an example of how Israel's laws and customs institutionalize that "option for the poor" and serve to block the tendency to greed and selfishness.

The covenant and law codes propose the basic principles. The Exodus story provides the motivation and continuing point of reference. The wisdom literature, especially a practical work like Proverbs or Ben Sira, looks to day-to-day life and provides a guide for dealing with the entire gamut of personalities and situations that life can bring.

It is thus that we can refer to Israel's wisdom literature as offering a liberating spirituality, a program for daily life oriented toward God and grounded in the history and experience of God's chosen people—the people of the Exodus and the people of the covenant. It is against this background and within this context that these books, especially in their final form and as part of the larger canon, find their most authentic reading and interpretation.

A PERSONAL LIBERATION

The wisdom writings provide a further dimension to the meaning of "liberation" in the Bible. On the one hand, Israel's historical traditions tell of the struggle to create a human community free from domination and exploitation, a society in which men and women live together as brothers and sisters under God's just and loving rule. These historical traditions stress a political and socioeconomic liberation.

The wisdom writings, on the other hand, work toward a personal liberation, a liberation that frees the individual from the psychic sources of personal or societal bondage—greed, lust, or inordinate pride and aggressiveness, for example. Wisdom, rather, sets out to motivate and educate the individual in the virtues that lead to life—the full, joy-filled life of one who is humble, diligent, prudent, in control of the emotions, faithful in relationships, compassionate, and God-fearing—in contemporary language, a mature, whole human being, able to love and to be loved.

Both aspects are essential to bring about a true and total liberation. A socioeconomic and political liberation looks toward the institutions and structures that foster justice and fairness among its members. A personal liberation ensures that the members of that society are personally and spiritually free and can work for and support such structures and institutions.

THE PURPOSE OF THIS INTRODUCTION
TO OLD TESTAMENT WISDOM

This book proposes to initiate the reader into the wisdom writings of the Old Testament. It presumes some familiarity already with Old Testament history and thought (see, for example, my *Introduction to the Old Testament: A Liberation Perspective*). The first six chapters provide background and preliminary notions about the wisdom movement in general. Then each of the five "wisdom books"—Proverbs, Job, Ecclesiastes (Qoheleth), the Wisdom of Ben Sira (Sirach), and the book of Wisdom—is treated in more detail.

One chapter gives a general overview of each book's themes, structure, and historical background. Another chapter looks more closely at key texts in each work. Review questions help the reader focus on the more important points and a bibliography for each section provides both source materials on the book and more in-depth discussion of the issues raised.

Our purpose is to provide an up-to-date and uncomplicated introduction to this rich and important part of our biblical heritage. The book stresses especially the liberation themes in these writings. Each book presents an aspect of that spirituality that nourished the liberating vision of life in a community under God's rule in ancient times. It is our hope that the readers discover for themselves that liberating vision and find guidance and support in their struggle to build a just and compassionate human community in our own day.

SUGGESTED BIBLE READINGS

Chapters 8, 10, 12, 14, and 16 comment on particular passages of the five wisdom books. These chapters provide generous quotations from the particular texts being studied. As background for the discussions that follow, however, we suggest that the reader go through at least the following parts of the five wisdom books. This would prove especially helpful prior to reading the specific chapters on each of these biblical books:

> Proverbs, chapters 1-9, 10-15, 22-24, 30-31
> Job, chapters 1-14, 22-33, 38-42
> Ecclesiastes (Qoheleth), chapters 1-7, 11-12
> Wisdom Ben Sira (Ecclesiasticus), chapters 1-4, 14-18,
>   24, 31-32, 36-38, 44-51
> Wisdom, chapters 1-11, 16-19

REVIEW QUESTIONS

1. Find two or three other parables or sayings of Jesus in which he makes use of common human experience as the basis of his teaching.

2. How does Jon Alexander describe "spirituality"? How would you define "spirituality"?

3. What are two features of the kind of spirituality that the wisdom writings foster?

4. Why is the *context* of the wisdom writings, their historical context and their present context in our Bible, important for their interpretation?

5. Describe the two aspects of "liberation" in the Bible, a socio-economic and political liberation and a personal liberation. Why are both aspects essential for a true and total liberation?

2

Wisdom in the Ancient World

FAMILY AND CLAN WISDOM

As communities formed in ancient times and struggled to survive, they would gather the fruits of reflection on their experience. The results of this reflection eventually took two forms. First, with regard to the life and good order of the wider community, the fruits of this reflection issued in the drawing up of law codes and the fixing of customs to regulate and guide the life of the society and the people as a whole.

Second, with regard to individuals and daily life in the home and family, reflection on experience developed into what we call a kind of "wisdom." The formalizing of this wisdom into a coherent set of assumptions and conclusions about life and the world evolved spontaneously out of the necessities of rearing and educating the new generation.

We have evidence even from the most primitive times of the great energy that both the older parenting generation and the new generation expended as the new generation equipped itself with "wisdom": that knowledge and those skills necessary to cope with life in the world. This process of preparing the young produced a rich store of parables and proverbs and narratives, both oral and written, to instruct the younger generation. This body of "wisdom" and the practical advice it offers reflect the values and beliefs of that culture, whether it be a culture of the past or of the present.

SCRIBES AND SAGES

By the late fourth and early third millennium, the city-state system of societal organization had developed in the great river valleys of southern Mesopotamia (ancient Sumer) and Egypt. It was imitated and spread and eventually came to dominate life in the ancient world. An elite ruling minority (1 to 5 percent) of the population, living in the large walled urban centers, controlled the population and economy of the surrounding countryside. The *scribal school* evolved out of the needs of this centralized and bureaucratic power structure.

The scribal school provided training first of all in the most fundamental skills for the ancient bureaucrat—reading and writing, skills that demanded long hours of study and practice. This was due particularly to the complex and cumbersome nature of the first writing systems, Mesopotamian cuneiform and Egyptian hieroglyphics.

In addition to writing, the school inculcated the fundamentals of administration as well as a kind of "survival ethic" for security and for successful maneuvering within the royal establishment. It was on that royal establishment that the members of the scribal schools depended for their livelihoods and for the life and welfare of their families. They were well aware of how often their lives were at the mercy of the whims of autocratic rulers. Thus, the earliest products of these schools, both in Mesopotamia and Egypt, reflect the "social location" of these scribes and stress a pragmatic, opportunist, and uniformist attitude. A good example of this attitude can be seen in the Egyptian text, *The Instruction of the Vizier Ptah Hotep,* which dates from the middle of the third millennium (ca. 2450 B.C.E.):

> If thou art one of those sitting at the table of one greater than thyself, take what he may give, when it is set before thy nose. Thou shouldst gaze at what is before thee. Do not pierce him with many stares. . . . Let thy face be cast down until he addresses thee, and thou shouldst speak (only) when he addresses thee. Laugh after he laughs, and it will be very pleasing to his heart and what thou mayest do will be pleasing to the heart. (*ANET,* p. 412)

Despite the generally pragmatic and success-oriented tone, these texts often demonstrate considerable psychological insight. This comes as the result of the keen method of observation and evaluation in which these men were trained. We see this insight, for example, in the following passage from that same Egyptian *Instruction:*

> If thou art one to whom petition is made, be calm as thou listenest to the petitioner's speech. Do not rebuff him before he has swept out his body or before he has said that for which he came. A petitioner likes attention to his words better than the fulfilling of that for which he came. . . . It is not (necessary) that everything about which he has petitioned *should* come to pass, (but) a good hearing is a soothing of the heart. (*ANET,* p. 413)

POETRY AND PROPAGANDA

The scribal schools produced administrative documents and texts for education and instructional purposes. But the leisure that the ancient sages enjoyed because of their privileged status also allowed them to pursue literary activity in the higher cultural sense. Thus, in addition to administrative, commercial, and diplomatic correspondence, they also composed and copied literary works: collections of proverbs and fables, epics, myths, and early history-like material such as the chronicles of kings' deeds.

Early on, those in the royal establishment—the king, members of the royal family, nobles—must have recognized the ideological and propaganda potential of such works. The monarch would have supported and encouraged production of favorable accounts of his exploits. Records of a king's successes in battle, his impressive building projects, and the favor shown to him by the gods represent some of the examples of this kind of literary activity. The king and his advisors obviously knew how to make good use of the skill of the scribes in order to enhance their prestige and power.

This excerpt from the annals of Tiglath Pileser I (1114-1076 B.C.E.), king of Assyria in northern Mesopotamia, provides a good example of this kind of writing from a scribal school:

> Tiglath-pileser, the legitimate king, king of the world, king of Assyria, king of (all) the four rims (of the earth), the courageous hero who lives (guided) by the trust-inspiring oracles given to him by Ashur and Ninurta, the great gods and his lords, and who thus overthrew (all) his enemies . . . .
>
> At the command of my lord [the god] Ashur I was a conqueror [lit.: my hand conquered] from beyond the lower Zab River to the Upper Sea which (lies toward) the West. Three times I did march against the Nairi countries. The widespread Nairi countries I conquered from the country Tumme as far as Daiaeni, Himua, and even as far as Paiteri and Habhi. I made bow to my feet 30 kings of the Nairi countries, I took hostages from them. I received as their tribute horses, broken to the yoke. I imposed upon them (regular) tribute and *tamartu*-gifts. (*ANET*, pp. 274-75)

PROBLEM QUESTIONS

The scribal schools imbued the students with the practical and ethical values needed to perform their official, professional functions successfully and well. They also aimed at helping the students achieve well-being and satisfaction in their daily existence. However, these scribes were also aware of the ambiguous, ambivalent nature of the human condition. There were aspects of life and questions that the knowledge and skills which they were learning could not answer. To prepare the students to cope with possible disillusionment and frustration, the instruction also dealt with the paradoxical character of human nature and the ambiguities of human existence. Thus, among their literary works we find proverbs, stories, and reflective pieces that address some of the perennial human issues such as innocent suffering, the meaning of life, and human mortality. Here we see the ancestors of the biblical wisdom books of Job and Qoheleth, both of which address similar themes.

A good example of this kind of literature is the famous *Epic of Gilgamesh,* composed shortly before or after 2000 B.C.E. This great achievement of ancient Mesopotamian culture tells the story of an early Mesopotamian king, Gilgamesh of Uruk. Early in the story his bosom companion, Enkidu, is killed by the jealousy of a goddess. Gilgamesh is so overwhelmed by his friend's death and by his confrontation with the reality of his own mortality that the rest of the epic is taken up with Gilgamesh's search for the secret of immortality. His search would end in failure, not a despairing and anguished failure but a resigned and peaceful acceptance of human fate. The words of the wise woman Sidaru, the alewife (supplier of drinks) to the gods, sum up the message:

> Gilgamesh, whither rovest thou?
> The life thou pursuest thou shalt not find.
> When the gods created mankind,
> Death for mankind they set aside,
> Life in their own hands retaining.
> Thou, Gilgamesh, let full be thy belly,
> Make thou merry by day and by night.
> Of each day make thou a feast of rejoicing.
> Day and night dance thou and play!
> Let thy garments be sparkling fresh,
> Thy head be washed; bathe thou in water.
> Pay heed to the little one who holds fast thy hand,
> Let thy spouse delight in thy bosom!
> For this is the task of (mankind)! (*ANET*, p. 90)

Works that deal with innocent suffering and death in a more explicitly speculative and questioning way emerged both in Egypt and in Mesopotamia. The following lines come from an Egyptian work entitled *A Dispute Over Suicide* (ca. 2000 B.C.E.). In this text the speaker weighs the pros and cons of suicide as a means of escaping the turmoil of the time:

> Death is in my sight today
>   Like the odor of myrrh
>   Like sitting under an awning on a breezy day . . .

Death is in my sight today
   Like the longing of a man to see his house (again),
After he has spent many years held in captivity.
(ANET, p. 407)

Thus we see that the kinds of texts we associate with wisdom think-ing in these ancient cultures tended to take one of two directions. One direction was the more pragmatic and optimistic one represented by the first Egyptian work quoted above, *The Instruction of The Vizier Ptah-Hotep.* The biblical books of Proverbs and the Wisdom of Ben Sira reflect this approach.

Another direction, more speculative and questioning, does not take such a straightforward approach. It tends to emphasize the skeptical and tentative mode of inquiry. The Egyptian work *A Dispute Over Sui-cide* is of this type. The books of Job and Ecclesiastes are the Old Tes-tament's examples of this wing of the wisdom movement in the ancient Near East.

Allied to the royal establishment or often even an extension of it was the administrative apparatus of the local temple, which usually included its own group of scribes. These were responsible not only for the admin-istrative documents that kept track of the temple's often vast land hold-ings and commercial interests. They also provided the ritual and mythic texts necessary for the smooth functioning of an invariably lavish cult.

UNANSWERED QUESTIONS

At least two questions remain about the origins of wisdom in the ancient world. A first question regards the wisdom of the "voiceless," those outside the ruling establishment. The evidence about early wis-dom and these scribal schools comes to us from sources selected and shaped by the scribes themselves. These scribes represent a small elite minority of the total population, and their output offers only a limited sample of the wisdom and the "wise" individuals of the larger society. Their role in service of the ruling establishment determined the kind of material they left for us and the form it took. Thus, we must also be attentive to the echoes of the "voiceless," whose social status prevented them from being heard.

We might ask, for example, about the role of women in the produc-tion and preservation of this ancient wisdom. Because of the over-whelmingly patriarchal character of ancient societies, women seem to have had little if any place in the process. Yet we know that the mother was the one primarily involved in child rearing. As such, she must have played an important role in the internalization and transmission of moral values and therefore in education. Biblical tradition preserves a few hints of this in texts such as Proverbs 10:1 (see also Prov 31:1-9):

> A wise child makes a glad father,
>> but a foolish child is a mother's grief.

What about the more formal educational context, the scribal school? Was there any place for women in these institutions, either as pupils or as teachers? Recent studies have uncovered only a few references to women as professional scribes. But if we broaden the sense of "wise" beyond that of the professional bureaucrat, we do find women engaged in activities usually associated with "wisdom" in the ancient world— women as poets, as scholars, as healers. Enheduanna, daughter of the famous Akkadian ruler Sargon (2371-2316 B.C.E.), provides a good example. She was the high priestess of the moon-god Nanna, and tradition tells how she wrote and compiled a collection of Sumerian hymns to temples. Her writings and editing give evidence of her remarkable gifts as a thinker and a theologian.

Further research may clarify the role of women and others outside the centers of power. This would add depth and color to our present picture of the history and development of ancient Near Eastern wisdom.

A second question about wisdom in the ancient world requires further study. Critical scholarship, centered in Europe and the West, has tended to ignore the Bible's own tradition that wisdom comes from the East. Job was "the greatest of all the people from the East" (Job 1:3), and "wise men from the East came to Jerusalem" seeking the newborn "king of the Jews," according to Matthew's Gospel (2:1-2). Shortly after the rise of organized urban life and the invention of writing in Egypt and Mesopotamia, the Indus River Valley region of the northwest Indian subcontinent witnessed a similar development. By 2300 B.C.E. the Harappa culture and its two great cities at Mohenjodaro and Harappa give evidence of both a written script and a flourishing trade with the peoples of the Persian Gulf and Mesopotamia.

Such commercial contacts between South Asia and West Asia must also have included mutual exchange and contacts in the cultural sphere. We know, for example, that the ancient Indians and Babylonians both made use of a calendar based on a cycle of sixty years. Algebra and its first application to astronomy and geometry originated in India, as did also the so-called arabic numerals (including zero) and decimal notation. No wonder the peoples of Palestine had such veneration for the wisdom of "the East." How much did this influence and exchange include each culture's "wisdom," even from the earliest days?

Questions such as this require further research. But now we must turn our attention to the particular form and direction that this "wisdom" took in ancient Israel.

REVIEW QUESTIONS

1. As communities in ancient times reflected on their experience, what represents the results of their reflection with regard to the life and good order of society and the people as a whole? With regard to individuals and daily life in the home and family?

2. How did "scribal schools" develop in the ancient Near East? What purposes did they serve for the ruling establishment of the city-states?

3. Would you consider the description of Solomon's great achievements in 1 Kings 3-10 as an example of the kind of "propaganda" his scribal school might have produced?

4. Describe the two directions wisdom thinking tended to take both in Israel and in the wider ancient Near East.

5. Discuss the two questions about the origins of wisdom in the ancient world that require more research. Can you think of other questions that could be explored?

3

The Origins of Israel and Its Wisdom

THE ORIGINS OF ISRAEL

Archaeologists tell us that the central highlands or hill country of Palestine give evidence of a sudden growth of population during the thirteenth century B.C.E. Hundreds of new settlements appeared throughout this long backbone of mountains and hills that stretch from Galilee in the north to the Negev, or wilderness, in the south. These small unwalled villages contained clusters of dwellings that served as the homes for several extended families. Who were these new settlers and where did they come from? It seems that the majority of them consisted of peasant farmers and sheepherders fleeing from the political and social turmoil in the valleys and plains below. Large walled urban centers controlled and exploited the people and produce of the surrounding countryside in these fertile valleys and plains. These urban centers formed a network of small city-states that dominated the economic and political life in this southern part of Canaan, as the region was called in pre-Israelite days. The new settlers in the central hill area were intent on escaping subservience to these city-state rulers. They migrated from the level lowlands to the central highlands, hoping to build a new life free from domination.

These refugee peasants and sheepherders soon realized the advantages of cooperation and collaboration. They joined together to clear and develop the agricultural potential of this hill country and to resist encroachment on their precarious freedom by the city-state rulers. It is among these newly liberated peoples that we locate the origins of Israel.

A key moment in the creation of Israel came with the arrival of a small group of refugees from Egypt. These refugees told stories about a god named Yahweh, whom they credited with their miraculous escape from slavery and forced labor under Pharaoh. The struggling peasant farmers and sheepherders adopted the Egyptian refugees' story as their own and began to worship Yahweh as their patron deity. Their common allegiance to Yahweh, who stands by the poor and frees the oppressed,

15

became a powerful force for unifying these diverse groups. The Pentateuch and the so-called historical books of Joshua and Judges collect the stories and traditions of these early days and the diverse groups that first formed Israel, or "the Tribes of Yahweh." These stories and traditions were woven into a "common story" that cemented the unity of the tribes and provided a sense of identity. They gradually forged a common ethos and culture. Central to this ethos and culture were worship of the one god, Yahweh, loyalty to their covenant with him, and resistance to any form of political or economic domination, whether by foreign rulers or from among their own number.

FAMILY AND CLAN WISDOM

The Pentateuch and the Former Prophets (or Deuteronomistic History, the seven-book complex from Deuteronomy through 2 Kings) include the larger story of the people as a whole. At the heart of that story lies the Exodus experience. Thus, the people's consciousness of their origins as objects of Yahweh's liberating intervention colors all of their subsequent history and marks their identity.

Parts of the Bible such as the Pentateuch and Former Prophets provide guidance and motivation for the community as a whole. By contrast, the "wisdom writings" address mainly the individual and deal with the challenges and demands of daily life. These wisdom books put us more directly in touch with that "wisdom spirituality" we described in an earlier chapter. And we find in these wisdom books that same consciousness of a unique identity. The originality and revolutionary character of their economic and political arrangements inform these wisdom texts as well.

Take, for example, the book of Job. Wisdom writers in both Egypt and Mesopotamia dealt with similar questions—the suffering of the innocent and the justice of the gods. But the book of Job stands apart from these other texts. It lays the blame for much human suffering on the greed and exploitation of the poor by the rich and powerful. Its protagonist learns that his "innocence" cannot be simply a negative quality, an absence of malice or sin. It must include the positive as well, the struggle to establish and maintain justice. Instructional material such as some parts of Proverbs urge compassion and concern for the poor. And Psalm 112, one of the so-called wisdom psalms, is quite clear in what it expects from the wise person "who fears the LORD":

> It is well with those who deal generously and lend,
>   who conduct their affairs with justice.
>
> . . . .
>
> They have distributed freely, they have given to the
>   poor;
>   their righteousness endures forever. (vv. 5, 9)

Israel's wisdom literature thus echoes that same consciousness of this people's origins and ethos.

THE CONTEXTS FOR WISDOM IN ISRAEL

Israel appears on the scene almost two thousand years after what is traditionally referred to as "the dawn of history" (ca. 3000 B.C.E.). We have traced the development of "wisdom" in the ancient world during the two millennia of history that preceded Israel and have seen the family/clan as one "place" for wisdom. In Israel also, the family/clan served as a context for the development and transmission of a "popular" wisdom. The book of Proverbs contains many echoes of that primary process of education and socialization of the new generation in which both mother and father were involved:

> Listen, children, to a father's instruction,
>   and be attentive that you may gain insight;
> for I give you good precepts:
>   do not forsake my teaching.
> When I was a son with my father,
>   tender, and my mother's favorite,
> he taught me, and said to me,
> "Let your heart hold fast my words;
>   keep my commandments, and live.
> Get wisdom; get insight: do not
>   forget, nor turn away
> from the words of my mouth." (Prov 4:1-5)

The town council or village elders formed another context. These "elders" or leaders in the local community were expected to exercise a kind of "wisdom" in rendering judgments and in mediating disputes. We see this, for example, in Deuteronomy 25:7-8:

> But if a man has no desire to marry his brother's widow . . . . Then the elders of his town shall summon him and speak to him.

It also seems that certain individuals achieved a reputation for wisdom and were sought out for their advice and counsel. The second book of Samuel preserves two striking examples of such people, both of them women. 2 Samuel 20 tells the story of a wise woman in Abel, and 2 Samuel 14 recounts how a "wise woman" of Tekoa assisted Joab, the commander of David's army:

> Now Joab son of Zeruiah perceived that the king's mind was on Absalom. Joab sent to Tekoa and brought from there a wise woman. He said to her, "Pretend to be a mourner; put on mourn-

ing garments, do not anoint yourself with oil. . . . Go to the king and speak to him as follows." And Joab put the words into her mouth. (2 Sam 14:1-3)

SCRIBES AND THE SCRIBAL SCHOOL

But perhaps the most important context for the development of wisdom and a wisdom "tradition" in Israel was the "scribal school," a vital part of any royal court in ancient times. Thus, when Israel made the fateful step across the line from the decentralized organization of the tribal confederacy to the increasingly centralized and authoritarian state under David, the need arose for a more complex administrative apparatus.

David undoubtedly inherited a group of scribes and bureaucrats from the ruling establishment of the newly conquered city-state of Jerusalem. 2 Samuel 20 lists some of the chief officers of David's administration:

> Now Joab was in command of all the army of Israel; Benaiah son of Jehoiada was in command of the Cherethites and the Pelethites; Adoram was in charge of the forced labor; Jehoshaphat son of Ahilud was the recorder; Sheva was the secretary; Zadok and Abiathar were priests. (vv. 23-25)

According to the biblical record (1 Kgs 3-11), David's son Solomon consolidated this move toward statehood. Solomon's building projects, his extensive trade network, and the division of the kingdom into tax districts must have required a considerable corps of educated and literate civil servants or "scribes." Some have raised doubts about the historical accuracy of these accounts. Questions remain about how quickly Israel actually achieved a social and economic infrastructure capable of generating a genuine literary tradition.

Certainly such a literary tradition and culture did eventually emerge. For one thing, the Israelites were able to build on the indigenous Canaanite literary heritage already centuries old. The rich store of mythic and epic poetry discovered at Ugarit, the ancient port city on the north Syrian coast, bears witness to the vitality and antiquity of this cultural tradition, to which Israel was heir. Early on this circle of court scribes and bureaucrats founded under David and Solomon produced one of Israel's first self-conscious works of religious literature, the Yahwist epic, which forms part of the Pentateuch.

Other examples of works produced by this literary tradition would include one of world's first examples of genuine history writing, the so-called Throne Succession Narrative (2 Sam 9-20; 1 Kgs 1-2). It recounts how Solomon, even though not the eldest son and obvious heir of David, managed to succeed David on the throne. Some of the first psalm compositions would have come from among the scribes attached to Solomon's temple.

Within this "scribal school" flourished the cultivation of "wisdom" with its stress on careful and patient observance of nature, of human society, and of the world. This wisdom attitude or approach attempted to discern some kind of order within and among these various spheres of human experience, or even to impose order on these spheres of experience. The purpose of this search for order and the attempt to impose an order through linguistic and conceptual tools were not simply to satisfy curiosity or seek knowledge for its own sake. The purpose was primarily pragmatic. Once order has been discerned, those who are wise can comport themselves accordingly, ordering their lives and making decisions in ways best adapted to achieve well-being and success.

Key to this quest for order was the consciousness of the power of language, both spoken and written. Skill with language enabled one to make sense out of one's experience, to make connections and comparisons, and especially to persuade others of the truth and accuracy of one's point of view. Literacy, or the ability to read and write, as well as rhetoric—the ability to express oneself clearly and forcefully, to argue and convince—remained high on the agenda of these scribes.

Thus, the activities of this scribal school encompassed at least three areas. The most important and time-consuming task involved the day-to-day administration of the kingdom—correspondence with foreign rulers, keeping of accounts, organization of the royal archives, and so on. Second, the scribal school also played an important educative role. Not only did these scribes prepare others to take their places in the state bureaucracy. They also trained future leaders and administrators for roles as governors of provinces, ambassadors to foreign courts, or as advisors to the king.

Literary output represented a third area for the scribes. This included instructional material for use in the training of future scribes and court officials. Some parts of the book of Proverbs may have originally served this purpose, such as the collection of sayings in chapters 25-29. The collection begins with the statement, "These are other proverbs of Solomon that the officials of King Hezekiah of Judah copied" (Prov 25:1; King Hezekiah reigned 715-685 B.C.E.). Other more ambitious literary endeavors included the Yahwist epic that forms part of the Pentateuch and the Throne Succession Narrative (2 Sam 9-20; 1 Kgs 1-2) mentioned above. Both of these works betray the "social location" of their authors in the subtle bias in favor of the Davidic monarchy.

Hushai the Archite represents a striking example of the kind of training the scribal school provided. Hushai was a key advisor to David and bore the traditional title Friend of the King. 2 Samuel 16 relates how David sent him as a spy to sabotage the coup d'état of David's rebellious son Absalom. Hushai's remarkable speech before Absalom and his court convinces Absalom to embark on a course of action that would lead to disaster and defeat for Absalom and the triumphant return of David to his throne:

> Then Hushai said to Absalom, "This time the counsel that Ahithophel has given is not good." Hushai continued, "You know that your father and his men are warriors, and that they are enraged, like a bear robbed of her cubs in the field. Besides, your father is an expert in war; he will not spend the night with his troops. Even now he has hidden himself in one of the pits, or in some other place. And when some of our troops fall at the first attack, whoever hears it will say, 'There has been a slaughter among the troops who follow Absalom.' Then even the valiant warrior, whose heart is like the heart of a lion, will utterly melt with fear. . . . But my counsel is that all Israel be gathered to you, from Dan to Beersheba, like the sand by the sea for multitude, and that you go to battle in person. So we shall come upon him in whatever place he may be found, and we shall light on him as the dew falls on the ground, and he will not survive, nor will any of those with him . . . ."Absalom and all the men of Israel said, "The counsel of Hushai the Archite is better than the counsel of Ahithophel." (2 Sam 17:7-12, 14)

Hushai makes skillful use of image and metaphor ("like a bear robbed of her cubs," "like the heart of a lion," "like the sand by the sea"). His rigorous logic gives us insight into the kind of training in rhetoric a scribal school could provide in preparing officials to serve in the royal court.

THE SOCIAL LOCATION OF THE SCRIBES

The majority of the scribes worked as officials and bureaucrats in government service. It would seem that their sympathies would lie with the ruling establishment, on whom their welfare and livelihood depended. They would not have been too quick to raise a voice of protest against any injustice or abuse of power.

One must keep in mind, however, the wider context and culture of specifically *Israelite* wisdom writing, especially the present context of these writings, among the books of the biblical canon. This history and the religious culture of their people—the originating experience of the Exodus and commitment to covenant—undoubtedly had a profound impact on the outlook and mind-set of at least some.

The echoes of Israel's religious culture can be seen in a wisdom work such as Job, with its unmistakable obsession with questions of justice— God's justice first but also justice in relations between human beings.

The practical, everyday concerns of books such as Proverbs and Ben Sira focus largely on justice and fairness toward the poor and vulnerable and the health and integrity of family life. Recall the discussion above of that practical "wisdom spirituality" which spells out the demands of the covenant for daily life and concern for a just and life-giving social order. Thus, there is much that these scribes shared with both priest and prophet.

WISDOM AND REVELATION

A comment by the opponents of the prophet Jeremiah lists the three ways in which Israel understood revelation as taking place: "Then they said, 'Come, let us make plots against Jeremiah—for instruction shall not perish from the priest, nor counsel from the wise, nor the word from the prophet'" (Jer 18:18). This comment implicitly recognizes wisdom as an important component of Israel's religion and culture, on a par with prophecy and priestly *torah* (instruction on divine law later embodied in the Pentateuch). In other words, wisdom constituted one of the three principal channels of revelation, one of the three ways by which God was in communication with his people.

This statement in Jeremiah is important for grasping something of the self-understanding of the wisdom thinkers, in contrast to prophets and priests. The impact of an overwhelming encounter with the living God led the prophets to claim unmediated access to the divine word. The prophets identified their words as the very words of God himself. The priests also claimed access to God's word and God's will through the Law of Moses, which they taught and studied. This Law had been revealed by God to Moses on Mt. Sinai, and the priests presumed privileged access to the understanding and interpretation of that Law or Torah ("teaching").

The wisdom writers, however, believed that their experience of the world, and their reflection on that experience, gave them unique insight into the divine mind and the divine will. They were trained and disciplined to observe carefully the world around them and the events of everyday life. They tried to discern those hidden orders and interconnections that gave unity and a sense of meaning and purpose to that world and to those events.

The moving force and intelligence responsible for that order and that purpose which they discerned belonged to Yahweh, the Creator God. The gift of God's wisdom enabled them to observe and discern that order, to discover that divine purpose, and to express and explain the fruit of their observation and insight in finely crafted language that was both pleasing and persuasive. Thus, the scribe-sage claimed authority equal to that of the priest and the prophet as revealer of God's word and God's will.

THE SURVIVAL OF THE SCRIBAL TRADITION

The catastrophe of the Babylonian destruction of Jerusalem in 587 B.C.E. meant the end of the royal scribal school as an institution. The scribal school as such ceased, but scribes and a scribal tradition survived. Included within that tradition was the continued cultivation of wisdom, but a wisdom that took new directions as a result of the dramatic historical events. It is to this tradition, which survived and continued, that we owe some of the best examples of what we mean by "wisdom literature"—the books of Proverbs, Job, and Ecclesiastes (Qoheleth).

How did this scribal tradition survive and what were some of the contexts and occasions for the "wisdom" works attributed to them? One context in which this scribal tradition and its wisdom continued was among the court scribes carried into exile by the Babylonians. These court scribes were joined by survivors of the scribal groups associated with the Jerusalem temple.

Deuteronomic circles in the late monarchy and afterward counted among their members scribes trained in wisdom. The Deuteronomic "school" or tradition produced the Deuteronomistic History, the seven-book complex from Deuteronomy through 2 Kings. These wisdom-trained scribes among the adherents of the Deuteronomic school thus constituted a second group among whom wisdom was cultivated.

A possible institutional base for wisdom came with the restoration of a Jewish community in Judah and Jerusalem after 539 B.C.E. The Persians had replaced the Babylonians as the new imperial masters of western Asia. Cyrus, the new Persian ruler, ordered the rebuilding of Jerusalem and the establishment of the province of Judah. The new province had need of trained personnel to staff the province's administrative apparatus. No doubt the Persians recruited a good number of Jewish scribes both from among those in exile in Babylon and from the local population. Once again Jerusalem had its "scribal school," not for service to a native monarch but to foreign rulers.

The rebuilt temple also had need of scribes to administer its resources as well as to produce and copy ritual texts and other religious works. Priestly families who survived the destruction of Jerusalem and its temple in 587 B.C.E. also included some trained as scribes who would later evidence an interest in wisdom. The priest Ezra, for example, is identified as a scribe or secretary in the Persian court:

> For Ezra had set his heart to study the law of the LORD, and to do it, and to teach the statutes and ordinances in Israel.
> This is a copy of the letter that King Artaxerxes gave to the

priest Ezra, the scribe, a scholar of the text of the commandments of the LORD and his statutes for Israel. (Ezra 7:10-11)

The mention of Ezra's interest "to study the law of the LORD, and to do it" points to a new development in postexilic Israel, the gradual merging of wisdom with study and reflection on the Torah, or Law of Moses (the Pentateuch, or Five Books of Moses, in our present Bible). This will reach its full flowering in the work of the priest-scribe Ben Sira, who regarded the Torah as the very embodiment of wisdom, wisdom with a divine source, that is, wisdom as revealed by God himself. Thus, the energies of the wisdom-trained scribes would focus more and more on the study and exposition of the Torah, or Law of Moses.

REVIEW QUESTIONS

1. Describe briefly the origins of Israel. What were some of the elements of this people's ethos and culture?

2. Israel's historical traditions, the Exodus from Egypt, for example, concern mainly the people of Israel as a whole. What forms the focus of attention for the Bible's wisdom traditions? What is common to both sets of traditions?

3. Describe some of the contexts in which the wisdom tradition developed. Which was perhaps the most important context?

4. Describe briefly the wisdom attitude or approach to life. Why could one say that its purpose is primarily pragmatic?

5. What three areas did the activities of the scribal school encompass?

6. Describe the "social location" of the scribes in ancient Israel. How might this have affected their teachings?

7. What were the three principal channels of revelation in ancient Israel? What was distinctive about the wisdom tradition's understanding of revelation?

8. How did the scribal tradition continue after the end of the monarchy in 587 B.C.E.? What would become the focus of the wisdom-trained scribes' energies in the postexilic period?

4

The Historical Background for the Wisdom Writings: An Overview

ISRAEL BEFORE THE EXILE

In the previous chapter, we sketched the historical contexts for the emergence of the wisdom movement and wisdom traditions in Israel. Now we will look more closely at the historical contexts and factors that occasioned the wisdom *writings* as such—Proverbs, Job, Ecclesiastes, Ben Sira, and the Wisdom of Solomon.

The wisdom movement and wisdom traditions in Israel reflect a clear continuity with wisdom thinking throughout the ancient world, stretching back more than two thousand years to the invention of writing, first in Mesopotamia and then in Egypt around 3000 B.C.E. Israel's own history begins in the thirteenth century B.C.E. with the liberation of a number of groups from various situations of domination and oppression. These experiences were all caught up and focused in the story of the liberation of a small but important minority of what grew into "Israel" of the Tribal Confederation period, roughly 1250-1050 B.C.E. The model or paradigm story of the liberation of the people of Israel is the "Exodus" from Egypt of a small group of slaves under a leader named Moses.

Already clan and family wisdom had flourished for centuries among the various peoples who made up early Israel. This "popular wisdom" evolved over generations through parenting and the preparation of each new generation to cope with life and achieve some degree of success and satisfaction. From this point on, from the Exodus and the subsequent formation of "the tribes of Israel" in the hill country of Canaan, Israelite wisdom will bear the mark of the religious culture of these people. It was a religious culture characterized especially by their worship of Yahweh, the God who stands by the poor and frees the oppressed.

A new factor intervened with the arrival of David and Solomon and the establishment of a monarchy, around 1000 B.C.E. A new dimension of Israelite wisdom emerged that was marked specifically by its connection with writing and the concerns of court and royal temple. Scribal schools, established as a vital part of the administrative structure of palace and temple in Jerusalem, become also a forum for "wisdom thought." Contacts with international wisdom took place, and an opening up to the wisdom traditions of other peoples occurred, especially with Egypt.

Perhaps more important for us, however, was the development of an interest in creating wisdom works in written form. This interest will result during the exilic and postexilic periods in the literary works found in the Bible—Proverbs, Job, Ecclesiastes, Ben Sira, and the Wisdom of Solomon.

THE END OF THE MONARCHY:
THE DESTRUCTION OF JERUSALEM

Toward the end of the seventh and the beginning of the sixth centuries B.C.E., the major Mesopotamian power of the day, Babylon, contended with Egypt for control of the border area between them. This border area included the small kingdom of Judah. The Babylonians finally gained the upper hand, and their imperial ambitions would not tolerate the least opposition or threat to their designs. They thus reacted with devastating results to crush the pretensions to autonomy and independence of the rulers and people of Judah and Jerusalem. In 587 B.C.E. Jerusalem was destroyed, its walls pulled down, and the temple and royal palace burned to the ground. Large numbers among the leadership—the royal family and nobility, priests and temple personnel, merchants and artisans—were carried off into exile in Babylon. There they remained for the next two generations until 539 B.C.E.

THE CRISIS OF THE EXILE

The destruction of Jerusalem by the Babylonian armies in 587 B.C.E. marks a dramatic turning point in Old Testament history. For six hundred years the community of Israel had enjoyed a degree of autonomy and control over its own history and future. All that came to an end with a finality that stunned and shattered this people and threatened to send them down the path to historical oblivion.

A confusion and crisis of identity followed. At one blow, all that had appeared to be at the heart of their life as a people—the holy city of Jerusalem, its temple and rich cultic traditions, and the Davidic kingship —had been brought to a brutal end. The effort to grasp what had happened, much less to begin to pick up the pieces and rebuild, was staggering. The challenge for the Jewish people during the exile and into the postexilic period was not only to survive but also to lay the groundwork for the future without abandoning their past roots. They had literally to rebuild and re-create their identity as a people.

Efforts at this re-creation and rebuilding moved in two directions. On the one hand, there was the actual physical rebuilding with the reestablishment of a Jewish community in Judah and Jerusalem. On the other hand, this rebuilding and re-creating involved an enormous literary activity which resulted in the production of large portions of what today constitutes our Bible.

THE POSTEXILIC RESTORATION

The fall of the Babylonian empire to the Persians under Cyrus in 539 B.C.E. provided the opportunity for the reestablishment of the Jewish community in Judah and Jerusalem. It was to the advantage of the Persian central administration to have a friendly and cooperative local rule in a strategically important place such as Palestine, located at the distant western end of the empire. Thus, the Persian ruler Cyrus issued a decree encouraging groups of Jews to return to their homeland and to rebuild the city of Jerusalem and its temple to their God, Yahweh.

In March of 515 B.C.E. the new temple was dedicated, and regular conduct of the restored cult was initiated. The restoration of the temple and of a regular sacrificial ritual exercised a powerful symbolic effect for the Jewish community not only in Judah but throughout the Mediterranean world. The Jews, though many of them lived far from Judah and Jerusalem, now had a common center toward which they could turn, a symbol of hope for the future and further reestablishment.

JEWISH IDENTITY AND THE BIBLE

The composition of the various literary works that eventually formed our Bible played an even more crucial role than the rebuilding of Jerusalem and its temple in the creation of Israel's new identity as a people.

The origins of Israel in the thirteenth century B.C.E. coincided closely with the invention of the alphabetic script for writing. This greatly simplified form of writing facilitated the democratization of culture and thus provided a new dynamic for cultural change. Almost from the beginning, written documents played an important role in this new people's struggle to articulate their self-understanding and to safeguard for future generations their founding vision and hopes.

The people's struggle to survive and re-create their identity as Israel accelerated the production of written documents during and after the exile. The story of the monarchy had already been told in the "first edition" of the Deuteronomistic History (= the seven books from

Deuteronomy through 2 Kings). This "first edition" was completed sometime between the death of King Josiah in 609 and the beginning of the exile in 587 B.C.E. During the exile itself this document was revised to take into account further historical developments.

More important, however, what became this community's foundational document, its Torah, or fundamental law (our Pentateuch), reached its final form, possibly by 400 B.C.E. The production of this document acted as something of a catalyst to crystallize and put into written form other traditional materials such as sayings and oracles of various prophets. Thus, within a century or two the Pentateuch was complemented by "the prophets." What the Jews called "the prophets" encompassed the Former Prophets, or Deuteronomistic History, and the Latter Prophets, the prophetic texts themselves. "The Law and the Prophets" would soon be spoken of in a single breath as together forming the foundation for Jewish life.

Other writings also emerged during this postexilic period, including the so-called wisdom writings of the Old Testament. The "Law and the Prophets" address more directly community concerns—the articulation of the group's identity, its origins, and the specific way of life that characterized it. The wisdom writings, on the other hand, deal with family matters and individual concerns. Taken together, these wisdom writings represent a whole array not only of "survival strategies" in the midst of the confusing and challenging postexilic world. More than that, they offer a way for the "wise" individual to live a fulfilling and satisfying life of love and loyalty to Israel's covenant God, a "spirituality" for dealing with the pressures and challenges of daily life as a faithful Jew.

ECONOMIC AND SOCIAL DISORDER

Some familiarity with the social and especially economic measures imposed on the subject peoples by the successive imperial regimes can shed light on the particular challenges faced by Jews in daily life during the postexilic times.

In chapter 2, on the origins of Israel, we sketched briefly the economic and social arrangements that characterized early Israel and marked the people as a unique, even revolutionary, community in the ancient world. Scholars have used the word "communitarian" to describe the economic arrangements mandated by customary law.

Each extended family possessed a "house" or portion of land, an "inheritance," which was handed on from generation to generation and which guaranteed access to the basic resources needed for survival. That ancestral property was to remain within the family and was not supposed to be sold or mortgaged.

A system of "mutual aid" was in place to assist families in financial crisis—because of drought or crop failure, for example. This system required members of a clan or tribe to provide low interest loans or outright gifts to those families in crisis lest they be forced to sell or mortgage their "house."

During the monarchy this communitarian economy came into conflict with the demands of the Israelite and Judean kings for tribute in the form of taxes or forced labor. This imposition of a centralized monarchical government's tributary measures weakened but did not destroy the deeply rooted tributary-free communitarian order inherited from the earliest days of the tribal confederation. During the exilic and postexilic periods, both the Jews who remained in Palestine and those who fled or were deported drew on communitarian values and practices to survive as a people.

Nonetheless, the socioeconomic crisis deepened and further threatened these traditions. When the Persians assumed power they imposed a new system for the collection of taxes. Beginning with the reign of Darius (522-486 B.C.E.), the Jews were required to pay their taxes no longer as a percentage of produce from their crops but in coinage. In other words, they had first to sell the produce and then with the money from the transaction pay a fixed sum to the Persian authorities in hard currency.

Times of drought or of decline in market prices proved especially difficult for the owners of small farms and their families. Many were obliged to go into debt and mortgage their property. Some were even reduced to selling themselves and/or their children into foreign slavery to pay off their debts (see Neh 5:1-5). The book of Proverbs and the book of Job both struggle with the theological and spiritual questions generated by these developments and crisis, as we shall see in later chapters.

ALEXANDER THE GREAT AND THE GREEKS

The rule of the Persians over Judah and Jerusalem came to an end with the arrival of Alexander the Great and the Greeks in 333 B.C.E. At the same time as the armies of Alexander were sweeping across the ancient world, the aggressive militarism of the Greeks set the stage for an unparalleled expansion of Greek commercial enterprises. Greek culture, philosophy, and religion provided powerful ideological tools both for justifying and for effecting the subjugation and exploitation of the conquered nations.

The Greek rulers after Alexander continued the earlier Persian system for siphoning off the wealth of the peoples, whom they ruled by means of taxes and levies. The gap increased between the small landowners and farmers, on the one hand, and the rich aristocratic classes on the other. The elite ruling classes included both foreign officials based in

Palestine itself or elsewhere and their upper-class Jewish agents and collaborators.

Many small farmers and their families were dispossessed of their properties while the rich, aristocratic classes accumulated ever larger tracts of land for themselves and/or as agents of foreign ruling powers. The dispossessed farmers and sheepherders now worked the land as tenant farmers or day laborers.

Within this new and expanding market economy, older values and relationships based on family and kinship ties were threatened. These ties had fostered mutual aid and support among family and kinship group members. But now people of the same family or kinship group found themselves in different and opposing economic strata. Values and older ethical standards based on human loyalty and compassion gave way to more materialistic measurements of wealth and influence with the foreign ruling power and their agents. This situation and these issues form the context and questions with which the author of Ecclesiastes (Qoheleth) deals.

THE CHALLENGE OF GREEK WAYS

Finally, one of the key questions the Jews had to confront after the arrival of Alexander and the Greeks was their stance toward Greek culture. Nor was it a purely theoretical question, or matter of opinion or tastes. The Greek rulers would naturally favor those individuals and parties more open to Greek ways. Both as individuals and as a community, Jews had to make choices and take decisions that affected the shape and future of their culture and religion. Two of the wisdom writings in particular, Ben Sira and the Wisdom of Solomon, represent attempts to engage and respond to such issues.

We have sketched out the variety of contexts—historical, cultural, and socioeconomic—out of which Israel's scriptures emerged, including the wisdom writings. Within this wider picture, each work has its place and specific questions and issues with which it deals. Before we turn to each of these books individually, we will look at the literary forms employed by these wisdom writers. Many of these literary forms or patterns of speech were shared with other peoples of the ancient world, but Israel's use of them reflects this people's unique culture and faith in a liberating God.

REVIEW QUESTIONS

1. What effect did the establishment of the monarchy under David and Solomon have on the development of Israel's wisdom traditions?

2. How did the destruction of Jerusalem by the Babylonians in 587 B.C.E. mark a turning point in Old Testament history?

3. What role did the composition of the literary works that form our Bible play in the creation of Israel's new identity as a people in the postexilic period? Which was the most important of these works?

4. The "Law and the Prophets" deal mainly with community concerns. What was the focus of the wisdom writings?

5. Describe the distinctive economic and social arrangements that characterized early Israel. How did the establishment of the monarchy impact these arrangements? What further effect did Persian rule have on these arrangements?

6. How did the arrival of Alexander the Great and the Greeks affect the social and economic situation of the Jews? What effect did the new and expanding market economy have on Jewish family and kinship ties?

5

The Forms That Wisdom Takes

HEBREW POETRY

Five literary works represent our principal access to Israel's wisdom tradition: Proverbs, Job, Ecclesiastes (Qoheleth), the Wisdom of Ben Sira, and the Wisdom of Solomon. Other less polished and sophisticated means of transmitting the tradition no doubt existed: popular or folk proverbs, stories, parables, and materials utilized for instruction in schools or private tutoring. Stray bits of such material have found their way into various books of the Bible, for instance, the popular or folk proverb in 1 Samuel 24:13, "From the wicked comes forth wickedness" (see also 1 Sam 10:11-12; 1 Kgs 20:11; Ezek 16:44). But our major access remains the five so-called wisdom books, and the bulk of these books takes the form of poetry. Thus, a few remarks on the characteristics of Hebrew poetry can prove helpful.

The study of the Bible's poetry has advanced significantly in recent years. These advances are largely due to the discovery by archaeologists of numerous texts with examples of poetry from Mesopotamia, Egypt, and especially ancient Canaan. One characteristic of Hebrew poetry, however, has been explicitly recognized and studied for over two hundred years: parallelism. The parallelistic nature of Hebrew poetry was first pointed out by the Anglican bishop Robert Lowth in a series of lectures delivered at Oxford University in 1753. Among other things, Lowth noted that the lines of poetry in Hebrew are usually divided into two, and sometimes three, segments. In about half of these segmented lines of poetry, the second segment echoes or repeats the thought of the first segment. Lowth referred to this phenomenon as "synonymous parallelism":

> He does not deal with us according to our sins,
> nor repay us according to our iniquities.
> (Ps 103:10; see also Pss 6:2; 9:19)

In this example the phrase, "does he requite," repeats in different words the phrase in the first segment, "does he deal." The word "us" occurs in both segments. And "according to our crimes" in the second half echoes the phrase "according to our sins" in the first half.

Lowth and others have identified further kinds of parallelism. In "antithetic parallelism," for instance, the second segment restates the thought of the first segment through contrast. Chapter 11 of Proverbs contains a number of examples of this kind of parallelism:

> A false balance is an abomination to the LORD,
>> but an accurate weight is his delight. (Prov 11:1)

> By the blessing of the upright a city is exalted,
>> but it is overthrown by the mouth of the wicked.
>>> (Prov 11:11)

In some cases, the second segment simply develops or completes the thought of the first:

> The lazy person buries a hand in the dish,
>> and will not even bring it back to the mouth.
>>> (Prov 19:24)

> I call upon the LORD, who is worthy to be praised,
>> so I shall be saved from my enemies. (Ps 18:3)

LITERARY FORMS

Recognizing that the wisdom writings consist mostly of poetry constitutes only a first step in appreciating the variety and complexity of the forms or patterns of speech with which the wisdom writers expressed themselves. They had available to them multiple forms or ways of expression developed by the older traditions in the ancient world, those of Egypt and Mesopotamia. These include forms that only appear once or twice in the Old Testament, such as the riddle (see Judg 14:10-18) and the fable (Judg 9:8-15). More frequent is the hymn, a genre borrowed from the temple worship but used as a vehicle for wisdom material. A good example would be this hymn, which the Wisdom Woman sings in praise of herself:

> I, wisdom, live with prudence,
>> and I attain knowledge and discretion.
> The fear of the LORD is hatred of evil.
> Pride and arrogance and the way of evil
>> and perverted speech I hate.

> I have good advice and sound wisdom;
>> I have insight, I have strength.
> By me kings reign,
>> and rulers decree what is just;
> by me rulers rule,
>> and nobles, all who govern rightly.
> I love those who love me,
>> and those who seek me diligently find me.
> Riches and honor are with me,
>> enduring wealth and prosperity. (Prov 8:12-18;
>>> see also Job 28; Prov 1:20-33)

In the "confession" or autobiographical narrative the speaker gives advice or makes an observation supposedly based on his own personal experience:

> I passed by the field of one who was lazy,
>> by the vineyard of a stupid person;
> and see, it was all overgrown with thorns;
>> the ground was covered with nettles,
>> and its stone wall was broken down.
> Then I saw and considered it;
>> I looked and received instruction.
> A little sleep, a little slumber,
>> a little folding of the hands to rest,
> and poverty will come upon you like a robber,
>> and want, like an armed warrior. (Prov 24:30-
>>> 34; see also Prov 4:6-9; Qoh 1:12 - 2:26)

The onomasticon, or "name list," represents an early attempt at systematizing and ordering knowledge by listing all known members of a particular category. A good example can be found in the catalogue of precious stones included in Job 28:

> But where shall wisdom be found?
>> and where is the place of understanding?
> . . . .
> It cannot be gotten for gold,
>> and silver cannot be weighed out for its price.
> It cannot be valued in the gold of Ophir,
>> in precious onyx or sapphire.
> Gold and glass cannot equal it,
>> nor can it be exchanged for jewels of fine gold.
> No mention shall be made of coral or crystal;
>> the price of wisdom is above pearls.

> The chrysolite of Ethiopia cannot compare with it,
>   nor can it be valued in pure gold.
>   (Job 28:12, 15-19)

THE PROVERB

The most characteristic literary form found in biblical wisdom literature is the *mashal*, the "proverb." The Hebrew word *mashal*, however, includes a broader spectrum than the English word "proverb," which usually refers to the single line or sentence-saying that has gained a common currency in the culture: "Birds of a feather flock together"; "A new broom sweeps clean"; "Don't count your chickens before they're hatched." We saw above that the Bible preserves a few examples of such popular wisdom sayings or "folk proverbs" in 1 Samuel 10:11, for example, or Ezekiel 16:44:

> See, everyone who uses proverbs will use this proverb about you,
> "Like mother, like daughter."

The Hebrew word *mashal* means, literally, "a comparison" and is related to the verbal stem *mšl*, "to rule." It thus provides a "rule" or "paradigm" for understanding. It encompasses a number of literary forms, all of which attempt to gain insight into a situation by comparison or analogy. It would also include, therefore, the parable and the allegory.

In the Old Testament we find more artistic and structured "literary" proverbs. The Bible refers to them as "proverbs of (king) Solomon" and the form itself probably originated in the scribal schools of the palace and temple in Jerusalem. Thus, the phrase "proverbs of Solomon" does not mean "proverbs composed by Solomon" but "proverbs from the Solomonic school."

Such proverbs, collected by the hundreds in the books of Proverbs and Ben Sira, follow the traditional pattern of Hebrew verse. That is, they consist of a single line broken into two (sometimes three) parallel segments. In addition, such proverbs display conciseness of expression and frequently employ ellipsis and wordplay:

> The appetite of workers works for them;
>   their hunger urges them on. (Prov 16:26)

> As a door turns on its hinges,
>   so does a lazy person in bed. (Prov 26:14)

> The sated appetite spurns honey,
>   but to a ravenous appetite even the bitter
>   is sweet. (Prov 27:7)

"SAYINGS" AND "ADMONITIONS"

What we refer to in general in the Bible as "proverbs" are divided into "sayings" and "admonitions" by the form critics. "Sayings" come in two kinds. One kind of "saying" embodies the fruits of experience or it makes an observation about "the way things are." Such sayings are open-ended and invite verification and dialogue: Does this represent your experience as well? Have you observed similar people or situations? Many of the sayings in the book of Proverbs fall into this category; for example:

> Like clouds and wind without rain
>   is one who boasts of a gift never given. (Prov 25:14)

> Like cold water to a thirsty throat [lit., "soul"],
>   so is good news from a far country. (Prov 25:25)

A second kind of saying is more explicitly didactic. It aims to promote a given ideal, value, or way of acting; for example:

> Whoever is kind to the poor lends to the LORD,
>   and will be repaid in full. (Prov 19:17)

Besides the observational and didactic sayings, there also occur the positive and negative "admonitions." The positive admonition expressly commends a certain attitude, value, or course of action. It often takes the form of a command:

> Commit your work to the LORD,
>   and your plans will be established. (Prov 16:3)

The negative admonition cautions against certain actions or attitudes:

> Do not rob the poor because they are poor,
>   or crush the afflicted at the gate;
> for the LORD pleads their cause
>   and despoils of life those who despoil them.
>   (Prov 22:22-23)

CROSS-CULTURAL STUDIES OF PROVERBS

Ancient Israel did not have a monopoly on proverbial wisdom. Indeed, every language and culture possesses its own store of wise sayings and astute admonitions. Anthropologists and folklorists have done extensive studies of this "proverb-production" and have shown the role that such activity plays in educating and integrating the new generation into the values and worldview of their native culture. Especially in more traditional societies this body of proverbial sayings provides a common source of "wisdom" for discerning and decision making by communities and for "de-fusing" potential conflict situations.

Old Testament scholar Carole Fontaine, for example, has given insight into the role that traditional sayings sometimes played in ancient Israel. 1 Samuel 24, for instance, demonstrates how young David made use of a well-known proverb indirectly to challenge his superior, King Saul. David implicitly questions the justice of Saul's hostility toward him and demonstrates that he, David, is innocent of any intention to do Saul harm:

> David said to Saul, "Why do you listen to the words of those who say, 'David seeks to do you harm'? . . . See, my father, see the corner of your cloak in my hand; for by the fact that I cut off the corner of your cloak, and did not kill you, you may know for certain that there is no wrong or treason in my hands. I have not sinned against you, though you are hunting me to take my life. May the LORD judge between me and you! . . . As the ancient proverb says, 'Out of the wicked comes forth wickedness'; but my hand shall not be against you." (1 Sam 24:9, 11-13)

Saul yields not to David but to the traditional wisdom embodied in the proverbial saying. Saul admits that he has misjudged David and breaks off his pursuit of the young warrior. The use of the traditional saying helped to defuse a potentially violent situation and provided both parties with a face-saving way of avoiding a confrontation (*Traditional Sayings*, pp. 109-26).

R. B. Y. Scott is another Old Testament scholar who has done studies comparing biblical wisdom sayings with similar proverbial literature in other cultures. Scott has shown how the folk sayings of many different peoples demonstrate a remarkable similarity in literary pattern and underlying meaning. He has pointed out at least seven of these "patterns" that can be observed in the folk wisdom of peoples, ancient and modern.

The first of these patterns points to *identity, equivalence,* or *invariable association*: "This is really (or always) that"; "A friend in need is a friend indeed"; "A penny saved is a penny earned"; "You reap whatever you sow" (Gal 6:7). A second proverb pattern is *non-identity, contrast,* or *paradox*: "This is not really that"; "All that glitters is not gold"; "A soft tongue can break bones" (Prov 25:15). Other patterns include *similarity, analogy,* or *typing* ("This is like, or acts like, that"); *contrary to right order*, *futile*, or *absurd* ("What's the use of running when you are on the wrong road?"); and *characterization* of person, behavior, or situations ("He who steals an egg will steal an ox").

James G. Williams provides further insight into proverbial or aphoristic speech with his helpful description of the characteristics that this kind of speech often exhibits. First, aphoristic speech is assertive and apparently self-explanatory. It thus challenges the reader or listener by its forthrightness and almost demands a response. "Is this not true?" it implies, and thus it invites involvement and dialogue.

Second, the insight being offered is arrived at through a process. The aphorism establishes certain boundaries and, again, invites the hearers to move beyond those boundaries. For example, Jesus' response to his parents' question in Luke 2:49 itself takes the form of a question: "Why were you searching for me? Did you not know that I must be in my Father's house?" What does Jesus mean, " . . . be in my Father's house"? His question starts the mind on a journey to discover an answer.

A third characteristic of a saying or parable is the way in which it often provokes surprise and reverses expectations. This it does through paradox or exaggeration. It thus forces the listener to view the situation being described from a new perspective. The vast difference in the debts of the two servants in Jesus' parable in Matthew 18:23-35 represents a good example of how such proverbial or parabolic speech makes use of exaggeration. The servant who is absolved of a debt equivalent to ten billion dollars refuses to forgive a debt of only ten dollars. The hard-heartedness of the servant highlights the unimaginable magnitude of God's mercy, which turns on its head any human notions of indebtedness or liability.

Brevity, conciseness, and frequent plays on words also characterize aphoristic speech. Matthew Black has translated some of Jesus' sayings back into Aramaic from the Greek of the Gospels and has discovered the possible presence of wordplay. The saying in Luke 12:33 offers one example: "Make purses for yourselves that do not wear out, an unfailing treasure in heaven, where no thief comes near (*qareb*) and no moth (*ruqba*) destroys (*marqeb*)" (*Aramaic Approach*, p. 178). Note also Luke 14:5: "If one of you has a child (*běra*) or an ox (*běʿira*) that has fallen into a well (*běra*), will you not immediately pull it out on a sabbath day?" (p. 168).

Many studies have been done comparing the wisdom sayings of the Bible with similar proverbial literature, both oral and written, of other peoples and cultures. For example, the well-known Old Testament scholar, Claus Westermann, has added an appendix to his recent book *Roots of Wisdom: The Oldest Proverbs of Israel and Other Peoples*. In this appendix, he compares biblical proverbs with similar literature from modern Africa and Sumatra, as well as from ancient Egypt and Sumeria.

Finally, one should note that the sages of the Indian sub-continent have not only been aware of aphoristic or proverbial speech as a specific form of "wisdom" expression and philosophical discourse. Since ancient times they have studied and analyzed such literature and classified it according to seven different literary types: *saropadesha* (edifying discourse); *guṇapaṭhakatha* (moral stories); *upama* (parables); *sutra* (maxims); *aptavakyas* (ancestral precepts); *mantras* (sacred syllables); and *mahavakyas* (great sayings).

REVIEW QUESTIONS

1. Describe three kinds of "parallelism" used in Hebrew poetry.

2. What are some of the literary forms or patterns of speech made use of by the wisdom writers?

3. What does the Hebrew word *mashal* mean? What are some of the literary forms included under the term *mashal*?

4. Describe the "literary proverb" or "proverb of Solomon." How does it differ from the "popular proverb" or folk-saying?

5. Describe the two kinds of "sayings" and the two kinds of "admonitions." Give some examples of each from the books of Proverbs and Ben Sira.

6. Describe three "proverb patterns" pointed out by R. B. Y. Scott. Find some examples of popular English proverbs that correspond to each of these patterns.

7. Describe three of the characteristics of proverbial or aphoristic speech discussed by J. G. Williams.

6

The Liberating Potential of Proverb and Parable

THE LITERARY OR SCHOOL PROVERB:
A TOOL FOR STUDY AND ANALYSIS

Comparison between the proverbs of the Bible and proverbial literature of other peoples and cultures can prove helpful and can serve to place biblical wisdom literature in a wider context. One aspect of the biblical proverb/parable, however, sets it apart from the wisdom of other lands, its potential as a sophisticated analytical tool.

The Greeks were in the process of developing the intellectual implements of abstraction and formal logic for study and analysis, a simple example of which would be the syllogism (If A = B and B = C, then A = C). But Israel's sages had already evolved their own analytical tool for undertaking the search for knowledge and wisdom—the literary or school proverb. The proverb moves obliquely, by way of analogy. It suggests a deeper order hidden from the eyes of the naïve and untrained eye.

The parallelistic nature of the poetic proverb ideally suited the sages' search. The two parallel segments of the poetic verse often compare two items or events. The comparison can be either explicit ("like, as") or implicit, in the simple juxtaposition of the items. At first sight the items or actions seem dissimilar or unconnected. But on further reflection, similarities begin to appear. An unexpected order and larger pattern emerge as one gains a firmer grasp on one's experience and achieves an insight into the way the world works. Proverb 26:11 offers a good example:

> Like a dog that returns to its vomit
>   is the fool who reverts to his folly.

The sage observes the world of nature, and his gaze fixes on a peculiar habit of the dog, how it "returns to its vomit." He then casts his eye on the human world, and this time his eye is drawn to the puzzling practice of the fool, how he "reverts to his folly." The similarity fascinates him. Both the fool and the dog perform actions that are repulsive. Yet for some strange reason they continue to repeat those repulsive actions. In this they are alike; they share a common trait.

English translations fail to convey the artfulness and elegance of the rhymed saying in Hebrew, with its play on sound and sense:

> *kĕkeleb shāb ʿal-qēʾō*
> *kesīl shoneh bĕʾiwwaltō*

The sage has managed to expose a wider web of connections and discover intimations of an underlying order that encompasses broad areas of human experience. He has fashioned an elegant and attractive aphorism to capture the insight. He takes obvious pride in the hold he has gained on reality and the sense he has derived out of his experience.

Sages schooled in this approach to knowledge learned how to observe carefully and judge critically. They developed appreciation of the power of language to please and persuade. Their method of inquiry and analysis suggests surprising connections with the methods of today's liberation theologians.

FROM PROVERB TO PARABLE

The approach to knowledge and understanding among the wisdom writers is perhaps best seen in the expanded form of the proverb, the parable. In the way parables work one can observe the use of analogy and comparison, and the awareness of the power of language, metaphor, and story. One can appreciate how the listener or reader's own *experience* is brought into play, and how the humanizing element of humor is often at work. We will see in later chapters how the authors of wisdom books such as Job and Qoheleth make use of poetry, proverb, and parable to confront and explore profound human issues of innocent suffering and divine justice, and the meaning and purpose of life.

The proverb, or its extended form in the parable, resembles a riddle in that it teases the mind; it leads one *toward* truth or insight without stating it explicitly. The sages frequently exploited the ambiguity and multivalency of language in the play of sound and sense, challenging the reader or listener's astuteness and imagination and provoking discussion and debate.

The open-endedness of the following saying provides a good example:

> Iron sharpens iron,
> and one person sharpens the
> wits of another. (Prov 27:17)

The Hebrew reads, literally, "Iron up against iron; thus a man up against (the face of) his neighbor/friend." The sentence is suggestive, but its exact meaning eludes attempts to paraphrase or explain it. Almost every reader or listener would nuance the saying's intent in a slightly different way.

Scholars have employed the term *defamiliarization* to describe the process at work in this approach to knowledge and analysis. In other words, by means of paradox, exaggeration, or surprise, proverbs and parables force one to look at and evaluate the ordinary, the *familiar*, in new and unfamiliar ways.

The shorter form, the single-sentence proverb, predominates in the wisdom books as such. But the parable, the expanded comparison story represents an adaptation of the proverb/comparison by prophetic figures such as Samuel in his confrontation with David, and later in New Testament times, by Jesus. Thus we find a similar process, a common approach to insight and understanding, among sages and prophets. The prophets in this case "borrowed" from the sages and expanded the proverb/comparison into a parable story, in keeping with the particular interest of prophets in history and narrative. Thus they adapted the proverb form and its possibilities as an intellectual tool for analyzing and gaining insight into a situation.

PROVERB/PARABLE AS *DIALOGICAL* AND *CRITICAL*

The Indian biblical scholar George Soares-Prabhu, has focused in particular on the *dialogical* and *critical* nature of the parable. First, parables are dialogical in that they engage reader or listener in a conversation and demand a creative response on their part. Parables do not simply convey information, offer solutions, or propose lessons. Rather, by narrating a story, the parable invites the listeners to see themselves or their circumstances in a new light, to compare themselves and their own situation with the person or event in the story.

The parable that the prophet Nathan tells to David in 2 Samuel 12:1-7 represents an unusually clear example of this process at work. Nathan recounts the story of a rich man who owned many flocks and herds. Despite his great wealth, in order to feed an unexpected guest, he steals the "one little ewe-lamb" that his poor neighbor possessed. David's sense of justice and fairness is deeply offended. He condemns such an obvious and cruel abuse of power. "As the LORD lives," cries David, "the man who has done this deserves to die!" Nathan responds simply and directly, "You are the man." David is stunned; a veil is lifted from his eyes. In narrating the parable Nathan has juxtaposed the cruel abuse of power by the rich man with David's own action of stealing Uriah's wife. The similarity is obvious and David has no choice but to acknowledge the injustice and arrogance of his own actions.

One can recognize a similar process of "consciousness raising" or arrival at new awareness in the teaching of Jesus. Above we discussed the parable of the Good Samaritan. We saw how the story leads the listener back to his or her own experience of need and rescue in order to discover the answer to the lawyer's question, "Who is my neighbor?" We need only to imagine ourselves as the victim on the roadside to know what the situation demanded. The parables of Jesus are, in fact, a form of what Paulo Freire, the Brazilian educator, has called "conscientization," at least in the more general and popular meaning of the word as "awareness raising."

The "awareness" to which the biblical proverbs and parables lead us can be and frequently is a *critical* awareness. The parable subverts the world of the listeners or readers by overturning their expectations and by upsetting accepted attitudes and values. Nathan's parable reveals the destructive pride and callousness of the king; Jesus' story of the Good Samaritan exposes the hypocrisy of the priest and the levite. One can see how the wisdom writings as such perform similar functions. For example, the experience of Job calls into question accepted notions of the relationship between virtue and suffering (see Job 4:7-9, for example). Qoheleth's assertions challenge simplistic answers to hard questions (see Qoh 1:12-14; 2:14-17).

Besides its negative function of overturning expectations or upsetting accepted attitudes, the proverb/parable possesses a positive side. It can subvert and expose as unjust, unfair, or "foolish" one set of attitudes and expectations by positing another just, fair, and wise set. A key element in the strategy of the sages, then, was the offer of an alternative: a more just and life-giving vision of what human life can and should be like—in the community at large, but especially within families and among individuals.

The world as conceived in biblical wisdom knows the saving presence and rule of Israel's God:

> For human ways are under the eyes of the LORD,
>   and he examines all their paths. (Prov 5:21)

> The eyes of the LORD are in every place,
>   keeping watch on the evil and the good. (Prov
>   15:3; see also 15:11;16:1-4,9,33, and so on)

Such a world supports and fosters good, life-giving relationships within families and between friends:

> Some friends play at friendship
>   but a true friend sticks closer
>   than one's nearest kin. (Prov 18:24)

> A friend loves at all times,
> and kinsfolk are born to share adversity.
> (Prov 17:17)

Such a world encourages the right use of wealth:

> Some give freely, yet grow all the richer;
> others withhold what is due,
> and only suffer want. (Prov 11:24)

> Those who oppress the poor insult their Maker,
> but those who are kind to the needy honor him.
> (Prov 14:31)

In short, the "comparisons" (*mashal*; plural, *meshalim*) are as much for critiquing as they are for illuminating or learning. And their strategy is best understood and recognized when seen within the larger context of the canon of which they are a part and the strategy of the Bible as a whole—a strategy for liberation, a strategy for freedom from domination and oppression, a strategy for life, life with God in a just and life-giving community.

THE LIBERATING POTENTIAL OF HUMOR: THE "PLAY" OF WISDOM

In one of the most remarkable passages in biblical wisdom, the Wisdom Woman describes her origins at "the beginning of his [God's] work, the first of his acts of long ago":

> Then I was beside him, like a master worker;
> and I was daily his delight,
> rejoicing before him always,
> rejoicing in his inhabited world
> and delighting (playing) in
> the human race. (Prov 8:30-31)

This description of the Wisdom Woman delighting or "playing" among humans is consistent with the "play" inherent in the literary forms and ways of expression employed by Israel's sages. So many of the proverbs and parables take the form of an intellectual game, like a puzzle or riddle in their play with sound and sense, their obvious delight in words and ideas.

The sages deal with knowledge and truth not as with some abstract, objectified entity. They deal with them as they deal with other human beings, in a relationship of love and friendship. This way of relating to knowledge and truth, personified in the Wisdom Woman, inserts a human dimension into the search for wisdom and allows free play to humor, as in this satire on the winebibber in Proverbs 23:

> Who has woe? Who has sorrow?
>> Who has strife? Who has complaining?
> Who has wounds without cause?
>> Who has redness of eyes?
> Those who linger late over wine,
>> those who keep trying mixed wines.
> Do not look at wine when it is red,
>> when it sparkles in the cup
>> and goes down smoothly.
> At the last it bites like a serpent,
>> and stings like an adder.
> Your eyes will see strange things,
>> and your mind utter perverse things.
> You will be like one who lies down in
>>> the midst of the sea,
>> like one who lies on the top of a mast.
> "They struck me," you will say,
>> "but I was not hurt;
>> they beat me, but I did not feel it.
> When shall I awake?
>> I will seek another drink." (Prov 23:29-35)

This sense of freedom in playing with the truth inherent in the world is rooted in Israel's faith and trust in the living God who is this world's Creator and the source of its truth. That faith and trust liberated Israel from fear and anxiety about the ultimate fate of human beings. Thus, Israel's sages were able to give voice to that sense of liberation in their freedom to play with and through their wisdom.

THE WISDOM WOMAN

Who is this remarkable figure who plays in God's presence and makes merry among humans in Proverbs 8:30-31? The attention that the sages lavish on this personification of wisdom as a woman testifies to her importance in their eyes. She appears in one form or another in Proverbs 1-9; Job 28; Ben Sira 24; and the Wisdom of Solomon 9.

For one thing, this objectification of wisdom as a woman provides a clue to the strong cultural influence of Egypt. Prominent in the pedigree of the Wisdom Woman is the ancient Egyptian figure of *ma'at*, the divine personification of the "justice" and "order" in the world.

Second, the presentation of the Wisdom Woman as a beautiful bride, especially in Proverbs 1-9, reflects the pedagogical strategy of the wisdom teachers and their desire to attract and motivate the young men who made up most, if not all, of their audience. The Wisdom Woman functions as an aesthetic device meant to stress the moral beauty and personal character of God's wisdom as opposed to other kinds of so-called worldly wisdom that might allure the youth and lead them astray.

Third, this image of the Wisdom Woman provides an insight into the role of women in ancient Israel, particularly their presence in the wisdom movement. The Wisdom Woman appears throughout the wisdom writings and especially in the book of Proverbs. This may well be women's indirect way of indicating their presence and influence and of stressing the importance of women's contribution to the moral and intellectual life of Israel. Carole Fontaine comments, for example:

> Wisdom values personal experience as the starting place for doing theology and constructing a model of how the world works. . . . For those who have been mostly excluded from participation in the great traditions of covenant and prophecy, the wisdom tradition's emphasis on the world of daily life offers a basis for valuing women's experience as an authentic, revelatory way of knowing and being. ("Proverbs," pp. 146-47)

Finally, there is a twofold liberative dimension to this image of wisdom personified as a woman. First, some have suggested that the language describing the Wisdom Woman offers us a new vernacular for talking about God and our experience of God's presence in the world. It frees us from the necessity of using exclusively masculine language and images in describing God and God's activities. In some places, for example, the Wisdom Woman appears to be identified with God, and she makes statements that elsewhere only God can make, for instance, in Proverbs 8:35a: "For whoever finds *me* finds life." Thus, Kathleen O'Connor argues that the Wisdom Woman "offers biblical theology a symbol of God who breaks the boundaries of gender and nationality, who relates to humans in intimacy and mutuality, and who joins them to the earth and to one another at her banquet of life" ("Wisdom Literature," p. 195).

A second liberative dimension to this image of wisdom personified as a woman concerns its "democratizing" effect. Israelite wisdom did not remain the exclusive domain of court and temple scribes. Rather, this image enabled the wisdom writers to unify the various kinds of wisdom at every level of society. All knowledge and insight have a single source —that grand and sublime power that pervades all of creation ensuring its order and harmony. The Wisdom Woman embodies that power, and that power speaks through her voice. Thus, in every voice that teaches wisdom, her voice and her teaching are heard. This holds true whether it be the voice of king or counselor deliberating on the affairs of state in the palace, or the voices of mother and father in the home striving to imbue the growing child with the hard but simple lessons of moral character and fear of God.

The image of the Wisdom Women thus enabled the sages to affirm the presence and importance of wisdom and wise living in every dimension of daily life.

REVIEW QUESTIONS

1. Discuss how the proverb/comparison form can function as a tool for study and analysis.

2. How did the prophets expand and adapt the proverb/comparison form?

3. Explain what is meant by the "dialogical" character of a parable.

4. How can proverbs and parables lead us to a *critical* awareness?

5. How did the "alternative vision" of the sages help them in developing this critical awareness? Describe some of the components of that alternative vision.

6. What role did humor play in the sages' search for wisdom? What was the basis of their freedom to "play" with the truth?

7. How does the personification of wisdom as a woman point to the presence and influence of women in the moral and intellectual life of Israel?

8. Discuss the twofold liberative dimension of the image of wisdom personified as a woman. How does this image serve to unify the various kinds of wisdom?

7

The Book of Proverbs: An Overview

THE STRUCTURE OF PROVERBS

A first encounter with the book of Proverbs can create confusion in the mind of the modern reader. The book seems to begin over and over again, as if it were itself a mini-library containing smaller works, each with its own title, "The Proverbs of Solomon," "Words of the Wise," "The Words of Agur," and so on. Further, a number of sections simply list self-contained single-verse sayings, one after another, in what appears to be a haphazard arrangement.

A closer, more careful reading of the book, however, will dispel this initial impression of confusion. With a little patience and perseverance, one can soon discover the book's astonishing complexity and careful plan.

The Hebrew word for "proverb" (*mashal*) means, literally, "a comparison" and is related to the verbal stem *mšl*, "to rule, master." One quickly becomes aware of how this work, entitled "proverbs of Solomon" (*mishlê shĕlōmô*), represents a prodigious effort to rule or master the chaos and confusion of daily life. This attempt to impose order and meaning appears both at the micro-level of the individual proverbs and the macro-level of the book as a whole.

First, at the macro-level, the complexity of the book's structure and architecture demonstrates the wonderful ability of the author to impose a coherent and intelligent order on a rich diversity of materials and contents. The overall shape of the work communicates something of the sage's purpose—to bring order out of the chaos of daily life. The book divides neatly into ten sections, seven of which bear titles. Both numbers, seven (= titled) and ten (= titled plus untitled sections), signal purpose and planning (see table 1).

In addition to these obvious indications of structure, there appears good evidence that the author has tailored the length of these various parts of the book according to the numerical value of certain names. Like the ancient Romans, people in Israel gave the letters of their alphabet numerical values. For the Romans, the letter *V* had the number value of five; *X* represented ten; *L* was used for fifty; and so on. So also in Hebrew, the letter *aleph* (ʾ) = 1, *beth* (*b*) = 2, *gimel* (*g*) = 3, and so on.

Table 1
Outline of the Book of Proverbs

I.   Title and Introduction (1:1-7)
II.   Prologue (1:8-9:18)
III.   First Collection of "Proverbs of Solomon" (10:1-22:16)
IV.   "The Words of the Wise" (22:17-24:22)
V.   "(More) Sayings of the Wise" (24:23-34)
VI.   Second Collection of "Proverbs of Solomon" (25:1-29:37)
VII.   "The Words of Agur" (30:1-9)
VIII.   A Collection of (Mostly) Numerical Sayings (30:10-33)
IX.   "The Words of King Lemuel" (31:1-9)
X.   Poem About "the Capable Woman/Wife" (31:10-31)

The title in Proverbs 10:1 ("Proverbs of Solomon") contains the name Solomon. The numerical values of the consonants in Hebrew (*šlmh*) add up to 375. If one counts the number of single-line proverbs in this "Solomonic" collection (10:1-22:16), one finds the same sum, 375.

Again, in the title in 25:1, the name Hezekiah appears: "These are the proverbs of Solomon that the officials of King Hezekiah of Judah copied." The numerical value of the consonants in one form of this name (*yḥzkyh*) is 140. This equals, in turn, the number of lines or sayings in this "Hezekian" collection of chapters 25-29. This same correspondence between the names in the title and the number of lines occurs with 22:17-24:32 and 30:7-33. Moreover, this alignment between the numerical value of a name in the title of a section and the number of lines in that section is not limited to individual parts of the book. It appears to have been determinative for the length of the entire work as well. Proverbs 1:1 contains the three names—Solomon, David, and Israel ("The proverbs of Solomon, son of David, king of Israel")—and the numerical values of the consonants in those names in Hebrew (375 + 14 + 541) total 930. Again, this total corresponds to the number of lines in the book as a whole—930.

This striving for harmony and coherence at the macro-level of the book's overall plan and structure parallels the concern for order at the micro-level of the individual proverbs. For example, the sages repeatedly point out how wise language can establish or impose order. One who has a way with words has a distinct advantage over others and possesses a certain power, for good or for ill:

> Death and life are in the power of the tongue,
>> and those who love it will eat its fruits. (Prov
>> 18:21; see also 15:1, 4, 15)

Second, this wise language has particular force and authority when it issues from the collective voice of "the fathers" or "the mothers"; in other words, when this "wise language" expresses the wisdom and insights handed on from previous generations:

> Hear, my child, your father's instruction,
>> and do not reject your mother's teaching. (Prov 1:8)

Another example of this manifestation of order comes in the patterns of cause and effect or action–reaction that keep recurring. The sages assume, for instance, that the good prosper and the wicked inevitably meet with unhappiness:

> Treasures gained by wickedness do not profit;
>> but righteousness delivers from death. (Prov 10:2;
>> see also 11:21)

God himself is the guarantor of this manifestation of order:

> The LORD does not let the righteous go hungry,
>> but he thwarts the craving of the wicked.
>>> (Prov 10:3)

The humble effort to order one's life in view of such observations will ensure success, prosperity, and contentment.

Finally, mastery over oneself through discipline and self-control represents an example of a guarantee of "order":

> One who spares words is knowledgeable;
>> one who is cool in spirit has understanding.
>>> (Prov 17:27)

> To watch over mouth and tongue
>> is to keep out of trouble. (Prov 21:23)

The careful and complex plan of the book at the macro-level combines with the "order" asserted at the micro-level of the individual proverbs. Together they represent a remarkable attempt to grasp hold of and impose some coherence and sense on the various aspects of life and experience, both of the individual and the community.

HISTORICAL CONTEXT

The emphasis on order that pervades the book of Proverbs makes sense when one examines the historical context out of which the book comes. For the Jews it was a time of massive *disorder*. During the exilic and postexilic periods, the Jews had to struggle with uncertainty and confusion on two fronts. Internally, the people were facing a crisis of identity. The political state and the Davidic dynasty had ceased to exist. They found themselves a subject people—first to the Babylonians, then to the Persians, then to the Greeks, and finally to the Romans. To survive, they had to create for themselves a new identity and a new focus for their life as a people. A variety of groups and interests among the Jews competed for a say in the shaping of that new identity. The book of Proverbs represents one such attempt to achieve clarity and direction.

If "identity crisis" constituted a challenge within the community, the external struggle was against the unjust and exploitative economic arrangements imposed by the succession of imperial powers that dominated this people. These unjust economic arrangements provoked uncertainty and confusion. A number of passages in Proverbs describe the suffering of those who now found themselves poor and the victims of injustice:

> Wealth brings many friends,
>   but the poor are left friendless. (Prov 19:4)

> The human spirit will endure sickness;
>   but a broken spirit—who can bear? (Prov 18:14)

One hears also of the oppressive means by which the wealthy gained their riches at the expense of these unfortunate poor:

> A bribe is like a magic stone in the eyes of those who
>   give it;
>   wherever they turn they prosper. (Prov 17:8)

> Differing weights are an abomination to the LORD,
>   and false scales are not good. (Prov 20:23)

THE LIBERATING RESPONSE OF PROVERBS

In keeping with its character as a pedagogical tool and a product of postexilic Judaism, Proverbs represents a remarkable example of education for liberation. Some may interpret the emphasis on order as an attempt to exert undue control or to maintain the status quo against calls for change or reform. One should recognize, however, how this emphasis on order represents a response by the Jews to the confusion and disorder they faced. They counter that confusion and disorder by asserting instead their unique vision and hope for a more life-giving community.

On the macro-level, the very shape and architecture of the book as a whole seem to form one huge "proverb" in the comparison it poses between order and chaos. The *appearance* of confusion in the diversity and complexity of the book's contents is juxtaposed with the *reality* of meaning and harmony in the book's orderly structure. This "proverb" illumines the present experience of the people as individuals and as community. The confusion and chaos they face are only an *appearance*; the reality is in the Creator's mysterious wisdom and ordering purpose at work in the world. The book itself represents an implicit invitation to faith and trust in God's all-powerful rule.

On the micro-level of the single sayings and instructions, a liberative pedagogy is also at work. The pupil learns to discern the sources of suffering and unhappiness; individual proverbs and more lengthy discourses highlight the folly and destructiveness of unjust and oppressive ways of acting:

> The getting of treasures by a lying tongue
> is a fleeting vapor and a snare of death.
> The violence of the wicked will sweep them away,
> because they refuse to do what is just.
> (Prov 21:6-7)

The book also focuses on personal relationships and family ties. The unjust economic measures imposed by their masters undermined family unity and solidarity. Thus, proverb after proverb reinforces the pupils' appreciation of human relationships and strengthens their commitment to family networks of support and mutual help:

> Those who despise their neighbors are sinners,
> but happy are those who are kind to the poor.
> (Prov 14:21)

> Those who oppress the poor insult their Maker,
>> but those who are kind to the needy honor him.
>>> (Prov 14:31)

This "wisdom spirituality" fosters harmonious ties among family, friends, and even one's enemies:

> Do not rejoice when your enemies fall,
>> and do not let your heart be glad when they
>>> stumble,
> Or else the LORD will see it and be displeased,
>> and turn away his anger from them.
>>> (Prov 24:17-18; see also 25:21-22)

In Proverbs, loyalty to the family, particularly to one's parents, is of central importance:

> Those who do violence to their father and chase away
>> their mother
> are children who cause shame and bring reproach.
>> (Prov 19:26)

WISDOM'S OFFER OF LIFE

The bottom line for the book of Proverbs is "life." This is the message that the Wisdom Woman preaches and this is the gift she offers to those who heed her call:

> Happy is the one who listens to me,
>> watching daily at my gates,
>> waiting beside my doors.
> For whoever finds me finds life
>> and obtains favor from the LORD. (Prov 8:34-35;
>>> see also 1:33; 3:18; 10:11; 11:30; 13:12, 14;
>>> 14:27; 16:22)

Concretely "life" means riches and honor (22:4), a good name (10:7; 22:1), a long existence and many years (3:16; 28:16). This focus on "life" in Proverbs echoes the preaching of the prophets and the Pentateuch. Both Amos and Isaiah also offer "life":

> Seek good and not evil,
>> that you may live. (Amos 5:14; see also Isa 55:3)

Deuteronomy proposes the same challenge:

I call heaven and earth to witness against you today that I have set before you life and death, blessings and curses. Choose life so that you and your descendants may live, loving the LORD your God, obeying him, and holding fast to him. (Deut 30:19-20a)

In the historical context of exilic and postexilic Judaism, this emphasis on "life" makes eminent sense. Ezekiel's vision of the valley of dry bones in 37:1-14 symbolized this people's powerlessness and despair. God's question to the prophet, "Mortal, can these bones live?" is answered in one way by the book of Proverbs, and the answer is a resounding "Yes! They can and they will live." Both the book's external form, a triumph of order and meaning over apparent chaos, and its focus on "life" affirm faith and trust in God's promises:

"Therefore prophesy and say to them, Thus says the Lord GOD: I am going to open your graves, and bring you up from your graves, O my people; and I will bring you back to the land of Israel. And you shall know that I am the LORD. . . . I will put my spirit within you, and you shall live, and I will place you on your own soil; then you shall know that I, the LORD, have spoken and will act," says the LORD. (Ezek 37:12-14)

REVIEW QUESTIONS

1. Describe some of the ways in which the author of Proverbs has structured his book and imposed some order on the diversity of materials it contains.

2. What are some of the ways in which the concern for order at the macro-level (the book as a whole) is paralleled at the micro-level (the level of the individual proverbs and instructions). Give some examples.

3. How does the historical context out of which the book comes help to explain this emphasis on order?

4. How does Proverbs counter the confusion and disorder of the postexilic period at the macro-level, the level of the book as a whole?

5. How does Proverbs counter this confusion at the micro-level, the level of the individual proverb and instruction? Give some examples.

6. How does the historical context of the exilic and postexilic Judaism help to explain Proverbs' emphasis on "life"?

8

The Book of Proverbs:
The Contents

We divide the book of Proverbs into ten sections or units, based both on contents and on explicit markers such as titles ("proverbs of Solomon" in 10:1, "words of the wise" in 22:17, for example).

I. TITLE AND INTRODUCTION (1:1-7)

The first verse ("The proverbs of Solomon, son of David, king of Israel") gives the title of the collection of "instructions" in chapters 1-9; it is probably intended to serve also as the caption for the entire book. This first verse links with the series of infinitives in the following vv. 2-6. These verses define the intention of the author "to instruct . . . to teach" so that one and all "may hear and . . . understand the words of the wise and their riddles." This lengthy and elaborate introduction underscores the importance of what follows. In the final and climactic verse (v. 7) it affirms the divine source of all wisdom and insight:

> The fear of the LORD is the beginning of knowledge;
> fools despise wisdom and instruction. (1:7)

These six compact verses (1:2-7) collect together the principal vocabulary and concepts of the sages. First among them is the word "wisdom" itself, *ḥokmâ* in Hebrew, from the root *ḥākām*. It is used as a verb ("to be wise"), a substantive ("sage"), and as an adjective ("wise [person])." The Hebrew root covers a broad range. Its basic meaning is "a special skill or ability." Thus, it can describe the special skill of a magician (Gen 41:8) or a craftsman (Exod 35:35) as well as the cunning of an assassin (1 Kgs 2:6).

In the wisdom books as such, *ḥokmâ* takes on its more technical sense of the skill or ability to "steer" or "navigate" successfully in the voyage through life (the *taḥbūlôt* "skill" of v. 5; literally, "steering, shrewd guidance"). Four instances of the root *ḥākām* appear in these first seven verses (vv. 2, 5, 6, 7), and the accompanying vocabulary helps to complement and locate its meaning here in Proverbs. Each term with which it is associated adds a further nuance to the sense of *ḥākām*: "insight" (*bînâ*, v. 2), "knowledge" (*daʿat*, vv. 4, 7), "instruction" (*mûsār*, vv. 2, 3, 7), and "fear of the LORD" (*yirʾat yhwh*, v. 7).

The climactic v. 7 announces a key principle in the wisdom enterprise—the religious grounding of all intellectual pursuits:

> The fear of the LORD is the beginning of knowledge;
> fools despise wisdom and instruction.

The Hebrew word *rēʾshît*, translated "beginning" here in v. 7, can also mean "the most important part, the essence." To understand the word *rēʾshît* in this sense is to recognize the extraordinary claim that the wisdom writers are making. All true knowledge and understanding is rooted in faith. Apart from some relationship or reference to God, no wisdom can be trusted or have any claim to credibility. The comprehensiveness implied in this assertion by the wisdom writers means in effect that every aspect of human life is somehow touched by the divine; every human act becomes a way of relating to God.

The German Old Testament scholar Gerhard von Rad puts it this way:

> It was perhaps her [Israel's] greatness that she did not keep faith and knowledge apart. The experiences of the world were for her always divine experiences as well, and the experiences of God were for her experiences of the world. (*Wisdom in Israel*, p. 62)

Seen in this light, the scope and reach of the sayings and instructions that follow make better sense. They touch on almost every aspect of human experience, and rightly so. According to the sages, divine wisdom must encompass all of human life.

This God whom they encounter in the course of daily life is none other that Yahweh, the God of the Exodus and covenant. This same God led their ancestors from the slavery and suffering in Egypt into freedom. This God demands justice and compassion in their dealings with one another even in the routine and details of daily life. For this, Proverbs shows the way as it spells out its practical "wisdom spirituality" and offers its advice about the successful, satisfying, and obedient life.

The importance of this v. 7 is underlined by the repetition of a nearly identical saying toward the end of the Prologue in 9:10 ("The fear of the LORD is the beginning of wisdom, and knowledge of the Holy One is insight.") The two occurrences act as brackets to enclose and unify the instructions in this opening Prologue. The unity they provide is not only structural but also thematic. Similar statements appear in Job 28:28; Qoh 3:14; 12:13; Ben Sira 1:14; and so on.

II. THE PROLOGUE (1:8-9:18)

A number of voices make themselves heard throughout Proverbs. Parents instruct their children; the teacher guides the pupil; the sage admonishes young disciples; kings display their knowledge; the words of wise men and women from other lands and cultures contribute—for example, the mother of King Lemuel (of Massa?) in 31:1-9. But all of these voices are only echoes and variations of the one voice that dominates and pervades the entire collection—the voice of the Wisdom Woman. This personification of wisdom as a woman enabled the wisdom writers to unify the various kinds of wisdom. Through her voice, divine wisdom speaks and echoes in every human voice that utters its own concrete and specific revelation of that one wisdom, whether it be parent or teacher, foreigner or king.

In the nine chapters of the Prologue, the presence of this Wisdom Woman is particularly prominent. The very first chapter quotes her words at length (1:20-33). There she admonishes and warns of the disaster awaiting those who fail to heed her invitation:

> Because I have called and you refused,
>   have stretched out my hand and no one heeded,
> and because you have ignored my counsel
>   and would have none of my reproof,
> I also will laugh at your calamity;
>   I will mock when panic strikes you,
> when panic strikes you like a storm,
>   and your calamity comes like a whirlwind,
>   when distress and anguish come upon you.
> (Prov 1:24-27)

At the end of the Prologue she invites all who look for instruction to enter her house and nourish themselves at her table, to "lay aside immaturity, and *live*":

> "You that are simple, turn in here!"
>   To those without sense she says,
> "Come, eat of my bread
>   and drink of the wine I have mixed.
> Lay aside immaturity, and live,
>   and walk in the way of insight." (9:4-6)

Chapter 8 also contains a lengthy speech of the Wisdom Woman (vv. 4-26), again promising *life* (v. 35).

These explicit words of the Wisdom Woman at the beginning and end of the Prologue serve to frame a series of instructions obviously aimed at young men preparing to set out on their own and make their way in the world. Some scholars identify the following passages as the longer instructional poems: 1:8-19; 2:1-22; 3:1-12; 3:21-35; 4:1-9; 4:10-19; 4:20-27; 5:1-23; 6:20-35; 7:1-27.

These "instructions" in the Prologue touch on many matters, but two concerns in particular occupy the author. A first concern focuses on covenant loyalty in economic matters, especially adherence to the covenant demands regarding mutual aid. In postexilic Israel, customs and traditions concerning mutual aid and support networks among families, clans, and tribes were under severe pressure. The monetary economy first imposed by the Persians and continued under the Greeks promoted an aggressive greed and excessive individualism. Such attitudes threatened to undermine the life and identity of the Jews as a community. Thus, early on the voice of "the father" sounds a warning to his son against the temptations to greed and the acquisition of wealth through dishonesty or even violence:

> My child, if sinners entice you,
>   do not consent.
> If they say, "Come with us, let us
>   lie in wait for blood;
>   let us wantonly ambush the innocent.
>
> . . . .
> We shall find all kinds of costly things;
>   we shall fill our houses with booty.
>
> . . . .
> My child, do not walk in their way,
>   keep your foot from their paths. (1:10-11, 13, 15)

For such conduct will surely end in death (vv. 18-19).

A second concern of these "instructions" was the reinforcement of family values and warnings against those actions that threatened family stability and good order in the community. Adulterous behavior, for example, tears apart the fabric of family solidarity, so important for the maintenance of the traditional networks of support. The seductive words of the wayward woman are exposed for what they truly are—an invitation to the fool to follow her to his death:

> "Come, let us take our fill of love until morning;
>   let us delight ourselves with love.

For my husband is not at home;
    he has gone on a long journey."

.   .   .   .

With much seductive speech she persuades him;
    with her smooth talk she compels him.
Right away he follows her,
    and goes like an ox to the slaughter.

.   .   .   .

He is like a bird rushing into a snare,
    not knowing that it will cost him his life.

                              (7: 18-19, 21-23)

THE WISDOM WOMAN AND CREATION
IN PROVERBS 8

Creation plays a prominent role in the wisdom writings, principally as a point of comparison. In the stability of nature and humanity's experience of its regularity, daily and seasonally, the wisdom teachers recognized the Creator God at work. The order and harmony of the cosmos illuminated the order observable in or at least yearned for in the human experience of community and daily life, in our interaction with one another.

This creation theme finds a special place in Proverbs and represents one of the principal ways in which the book responded to the identity crisis of exilic and postexilic Israel. The challenge for the Jewish people in this period was not only to survive but also to lay the groundwork for the future. They were challenged to imitate the Creator God by creating for themselves a new identity as a people.

Chapter 8 constitutes a key text for the development of this creation theme through the image of the Wisdom Woman. In vv. 22-31 she describes her presence and role in helping to order and shape the cosmos. In vv. 27-31, for example, the Wisdom Woman declares:

When he established the heavens, I was there,
    when he drew a circle on the face of the deep,
when he made firm the skies above,
    when he established the fountains of the deep,
when he assigned to the sea its limit,
    so that the waters might not transgress his
        command,
when he marked out the foundations of the earth,
    then I was beside him like a master worker;
and I was daily his delight,
    rejoicing before him always,
rejoicing in his inhabited world
    and delighting in the human race.

This feminine imagery which dominates chapter 8 recurs all through-out the Prologue. The focus on woman in these opening nine chapters is echoed at the conclusion of Proverbs with the poem on "The Capa-ble Woman" in 31:10-31, thus providing a kind of feminine frame for the whole book.

Claudia Camp has argued that this feminine imagery in Proverbs constitutes a symbolic legitimation for the enhanced status of women in the postexilic period. With the end of the monarchy, the home emerged as a central focus for the identity and life of the Jewish community. Women's central role in the creation and maintenance of that home became a metaphor for God's role as Divine Parent creating and main-taining the dwelling place of the human community—the inhabited world.

We must be careful, however, not to appropriate uncritically this per-sonification of wisdom as a woman. The Strange Woman of the Pro-logue (see 2:16-19; 5:1-6; 7:6-27; 9:13-18), who represents folly and deadly error, serves as a contrast figure to highlight the Wisdom Woman's virtues and qualities by her wickedness. The two images are obviously stereotypes, male projections of opposing aspects of the human condition onto female figures. The Wisdom Woman represents all that is good, desirable, and profitable to men. The Strange Woman embodies everything that is harmful to men. The danger lies in allowing these images, invented by men, to perpetuate the inhuman stereotypes of women as madonna or whore. The one represents a source of the good, and the other a source of the evil of which men are beneficiaries or victims.

Nonetheless, Kathleen O'Connor argues that the figure of the Wis-dom Woman ultimately transcends narrow female stereotypes. This Wisdom Woman takes on, in the texts and in our imaginations, a life of her own:

> More than a typical potential marriage partner, she becomes a developed character in her own right, *hokmah, sophia*, inviting everyone into full human existence. She is the bridge between God and humans, and between humans and the created world. ("How to Cope," p. 63)

III. THE FIRST COLLECTION OF "PROVERBS OF SOLOMON" (10:1-22:16)

The author of Proverbs has stitched together two smaller collections, 10:1-15:33 and 16:1-22:17, to form this section. It consists of 375 sin-gle-sentence sayings employing poetic parallelism. Optimism pervades these proverbs, along with a serene confidence in God's just and fair rule of the world:

> The eyes of the LORD are in every place,
>   keeping watch on the evil and the good. (15:3)

The sayings expose the folly of vices such as pride, laziness, passion, deceit, gossip, and so on. Virtues such as generosity, faithfulness, diligence, sobriety, and family loyalty receive hearty endorsement:

> House and wealth are inherited from parents,
>   but a prudent wife is from the LORD. (19:14)

> Grandchildren are the crown of the aged,
>   and the glory of children is their parents. (17:6)

> The reward for humility and fear of the LORD
>   is riches and honor and life. (22:4)

IV. "THE WORDS OF THE WISE"
(22:17-24:22)

The words of the Wisdom Woman echo not only in the instructions of parents to their children or royal counselors in the king's palace. Her voice is heard in the advice of non-Israelite sages as well. This openness to the wisdom of other peoples and cultures appears frequently in the scriptures. In 1 Kings 10, for example, the queen of Sheba comes to hear Solomon's wisdom and "to test him with hard questions" (v. 1). The book of Proverbs also bears witness to this belief that wisdom transcends national boundaries and cultural differences. This testimony is explicit in 30:1 and 31:1, which name the foreign sages from whom these collections stem, "Agur son of Jakeh" and the mother of King Lemuel (of Massa?).

The affinities with Egyptian wisdom are particularly strong, both in the nine chapters of the Prologue and in this collection of "words of the wise" in 22:17-24:22. Scholars have long recognized the parallels between this latter section and the early-first-millennium Egyptian work known as *The Instruction of Amen-Em-Ope*. A number of commentators hold that the Israelite sage used the Egyptian work as his model and adapted some of its contents to his Israelite milieu. Compare these two passages, one from Proverbs and the other from *Amen-Em-Ope*:

> Do not wear yourself out to get rich;
>   be wise enough to desist.
> When your eyes light upon it, it is gone;
>   for suddenly it takes wings to itself,
>   flying like an eagle toward heaven. (Prov 23:4-5)

> Cast not thy heart in pursuit of riches . . .
> Place not thy heart upon externals . . .
> If riches are brought to thee by robbery,
> They will not spend the night with thee;
> At daybreak they are not seen in the house:
> Their places may be seen, but they are not.
> . . . they have made themselves wings like geese
> And are flown away to the heavens. (*ANET*, p. 422)

V. "(MORE) SAYINGS OF THE WISE"
(24:23-34)

These twelve verses form an appendix or addendum to the previous collection, as the title indicates, "These also are sayings of the wise" (v. 23a). A negative version of the golden rule appears in v. 29 (cf. Matt 5:38-45; 7:12):

> Do not say, "I will do to others
>   as they have done to me;
> I will pay them back for what
>   they have done."

VI. A SECOND COLLECTION
OF "PROVERBS OF SOLOMON" (25:1-29:37)

The number of the proverbs gathered into this collection is 140. This number appears linked to the numerical value of the Hebrew letters in one form of the name Hezekiah (*yḥzkyh*), the king of Judah in the time of Isaiah at the end of the eighth century: "These are other proverbs of Solomon that the officials of King Hezekiah of Judah copied" (25:1). Some argue that the collectors have actually combined two earlier collections, chapters 25-27 and 28-29.

Various topics are treated, but there are frequent references to the king. This plus the mention of "officials of King Hezekiah" suggest that we have here an example of a pedagogical text stemming from a scribal school connected with the royal palace in Jerusalem.

Chapters 25-27 show some evidence of more elaborate "proverb poems" in which single proverbs have been woven into a longer literary unit (for instance, 25:2-27). In other words, we have here an example, on a smaller scale, of what the book as a whole represents—the fashioning of order out of diversity and disorder.

The student was immersed in the worldview of ancient Israel by the careful study of the long list of sayings in chapters 25-29 and in the other Solomonic collection (10:1-22:16). It was a world as seen especially through the eyes of the sage. Relationships within family and clan, values, virtues and vices are clearly spelled out. Reading, reflecting, and debating on the sense and meaning of the individual verses or passages trained the mind to observe and to discern. People learned how to judge right and wrong, good and bad, what was of value and what was worthless.

VII. "THE WORDS OF AGUR
SON OF JAKEH" (30:1-9)

Both the translation and the interpretation of these verses have proved troublesome. The passage represents one of the examples of wisdom materials taken over from foreign sources. Verse 8 is echoed in the reference to one's "daily bread" or "portion for each day" in the Lord's Prayer, which Jesus taught to his disciples: "Give me neither poverty nor riches; feed me with the food that I need" (cf. Matt 6:11).

The sentiments found in this passage fit well into the worldview and practice of ancient Israel with its emphasis on mutual aid and its support of economic structures that discouraged the accumulation of excessive wealth by individuals or small groups.

VIII. A COLLECTION OF (MOSTLY)
NUMERICAL SAYINGS (30:10-33)

Sayings popularly called "numerical proverbs" cluster in the latter part of chapter 30. They consist of a title line with a number, and a list of items. The line describes the features that the items have in common, for example, the four things small but wise in Proverbs 30:

> Four things on earth are small,
>   yet they are exceedingly wise:
> the ants are a people without strength,
>   yet they provide their food in summer;
> the badgers are a people without power,
>   yet they make their homes in the rocks;
> the locusts have no king,
>   yet all of them march in rank;
> the lizard can be grasped in the hand,
>   yet it is found in king's palaces. (24-28)

The form sometimes follows a climactic pattern, "x, x + 1" ("there are three . . . there are four"; "there are six . . . there are seven"), in which the higher number represents the most important or surprising item. Examples of this genre occur elsewhere in the wisdom writings, for instance, in Job 5:19-22.

Chapters 1 and 2 of the book of Amos contain judgment oracles that make use of this same convention, for example, in Amos 2:4-5:

> Thus says the LORD:
> For three transgressions of Judah,
>   and for four, I will not revoke the punishment:
> because they have rejected the law of the LORD,
>   and have not kept his statutes,
> but they have been led astray by the same lies
>   after which their ancestors walked,
> So I will send a fire on Judah,
>   and it shall devour the strongholds of Jerusalem.

Note, however, that the prophetic writer has modified this literary form borrowed from the wisdom genres. The oracle omits the first three "transgressions" and jumps to the fourth, apparently the most heinous crime and the one that finally provokes the wrath and judgment of God on the culprits.

IX. "THE WORDS OF KING LEMUEL . . .
THAT HIS MOTHER TAUGHT HIM" (31:1-9)

The strong feminine imagery of chapters 1-9 returns in this final chapter of the book. First comes this short collection (vv. 1-9), which represents another example of non-Israelite material co-opted by the author. It credits the "queen mother" as the source, even though it names "King Lemuel" as the one responsible for the final form.

The liberation "strategy" in these verses is noteworthy. The text urges the king to "speak out for those who cannot speak":

> Speak out for those who cannot speak,
>   for the rights of all the destitute.
> Speak out, judge righteously,
>   defend the rights of the poor and needy. (vv. 8-9)

At the same time, the passage demonstrates a realism and compassion characteristic of the wise. In some situations, strong drink may be the only means available at the moment to alleviate the suffering of the poor:

> Give strong drink to one who is perishing,
>   and wine to those in bitter distress;
> let them drink and forget their poverty,
>   and remember their misery no more. (vv. 6-7)

X. A POEM DESCRIBING
"THE CAPABLE WOMAN/WIFE" (31:10-31)

The focus on women in 31:1-9 continues with this poem describing the virtues of "the capable woman/wife" (vv. 10-31). Carole Fontaine writes, "Just as Woman Wisdom began the book with promises of wealth, happiness, honor, and long life as the reward for following her prudent teachings, the Woman of Worth and her fine household represent the concrete fulfillment of those earlier promises and so make a fitting conclusion to the work" ("Proverbs," p. 152):

> A capable woman, who can find?
>   She is far more precious than jewels.
> The heart of her husband trusts in her,
>   and he will have no lack of gain.
> She does him good, and not harm,
>   all the days of her life.
>
> .   .   .   .
>
> She rises while it is still night
>   and provides food for her household
>   and tasks for her servant-girls.
>
> .   .   .   .
>
> She puts her hand to the distaff,
>   and her hands hold the spindle.
> She opens her hand to the poor,
>   and reaches out her hand to the needy.
> She is not afraid for her household when it snows,
>   for all her household are clothed in crimson.
>   (Prov 31:10-12, 15, 19-21)

The poem follows an "acrostic" pattern in which each verse begins with the next successive letter of the Hebrew alphabet. This pattern occurs frequently in Hebrew poetry and is particularly characteristic of the scribes and their interest in writing. With written texts one can actually see on paper the acrostic device at work. This acrostic pattern communicates a sense of "fullness" or "completeness," as if to say here in 31:10-31 that such a woman being described is fully capable for every task, "from A to Z."

As one might expect in male-centered scriptures, the success of this Woman of Worth is viewed from the perspective of what she provides for her husband and children. For the successful fulfillment of the roles assigned to her by society she is praised "in the city gates" (v. 31).

But this Woman of Worth represents more than simply a model for performing the everyday tasks of marital life, more than simply the woman whom the young (male) pupils reading this text might hope to marry. Her astonishing capacities and her place at the end of the book suggest that she is a symbol of wisdom, the Wisdom Woman of the Prologue, in another form. The poem thus works at two levels. First, the woman of Proverbs 31:10-31 represents the model wife. Second, she also portrays the divine wisdom whose description fills the early chapters of the book and whom the young pupils are urged to seek with all their might and make their own.

REVIEW QUESTIONS

1. Discuss the importance of Proverbs 1:7 as a key principle in the search for wisdom. What is the significance of its repetition in Proverbs 1:7 and 9:10?

2. What are some of the voices that make themselves heard throughout Proverbs? What one voice dominates and pervades the entire collection?

3. What two concerns in particular occupy the author of the "instructions" in the Prologue?

4. How does the emphasis on the creation theme represent one of the principal ways in which Proverbs responds to the identity crisis of exilic and postexilic Israel?

5. Discuss the prominence of feminine imagery in Proverbs. What might this reflect about the role of women in postexilic Judaism? Why must one exercise caution and not accept uncritically this personification of wisdom as a woman?

6. Choose one virtue—for example, generosity or marital fidelity—and list some proverbs from the Solomonic collections (chaps. 10-22, 25-29) that endorse that virtue. Why would this virtue be especially important for a Jew in the postexilic period?

7. Choose one vice—greed or adultery, for example—and list some proverbs that caution against it. Why would such an attitude or action be especially threatening to the Jewish community in the postexilic period?

8. How do the judgment oracles in Amos 1 and 2 modify the literary form of the "numerical proverbs" of Proverbs 30?

9. Explain how the poem on "the capable woman" in Proverbs 31:10-31 can be interpreted on two levels.

9

The Book of Job: An Overview

INTRODUCTION

Wisdom reflection takes its starting point from experience, and perhaps no other experience is more universal or has provoked more questions and anguished searchings than suffering. This holds true for physical suffering of disease or deprivation. It proves even more true in the case of the emotional, psychological, or spiritual suffering. These can enervate and frustrate and lead to death as quickly as any physical illness or accident.

Everyone suffers, and almost everyone raises the question Why? at one point or another. The question becomes especially acute in cases of innocent suffering, when individuals or even whole populations undergo suffering for no apparent reason.

Attempts to wrestle with the question, especially of innocent suffering, occur among the earliest of the so-called wisdom writings of the ancient world. We quoted above in chapter 2 from the Egyptian work, *A Dispute over Suicide*, written some four thousand years ago. The poetic essay from Mesopotamia, *A Man and His God*, addresses the same question:

> On the day shares were allotted to all, my
> allotted share was suffering. . . .
> My god, the day shines bright over the land,
> for me the day is black. . . .
> Tears, lament, anguish, and depression are
> lodged within me,
> Suffering overwhelms me like one who does
> (nothing but) weep. (*ANET*, p. 590)

Other ancient cultures outside the Mediterranean world also give witness to similar musings. During the sixth century B.C.E. in northern India, the young prince Siddhartha developed a philosophy and way of living and dealing with this common human experience of suffering. He came to be known by his followers as the "Buddha," or "enlightened one," and his teachings have attracted millions of followers all over Asia and elsewhere in the world.

An ancient Indian story tells of Harischandra, the king of Ayodhya, who underwent great suffering as a result of his commitment to truth. The young schoolboy Mohandas Gandhi was deeply moved by a play based on Harischandra's life. Gandhi vowed to live and embody in his own life Harischandra's steadfastness and devotion to the truth, even in the face of great difficulty and suffering.

But perhaps no other figure so clearly represents both the ideal of one who stands fast in the face of innocent suffering and the anguished questioner who asks Why? as the biblical character of Job.

The book that recounts his experiences and deals with the questions provoked by those experiences has attracted the interest and esteem of generations. The character himself, Job the steadfast, "blameless and upright, one who feared God and turned away from evil . . . was the greatest of all the people of the east" (1:1, 3). The character and the ideal of steadfastness which he represents have exercised a powerful hold on the imagination of countless writers and artists, thinkers and theologians, both the humble and the great of the human family.

JOB AND BIBLICAL WISDOM

The biblical tradition has included the book of Job in the canon of scriptures, and scholars have labeled it an example of wisdom literature, and with good reason. First, the book rightly stands within the biblical canon. The God of the Bible is the God whom Job challenged to "justify his ways to humans." Further, the interaction between Job and God presupposes a relationship of a covenanting kind.

Despite the absence of explicit covenant terminology or covenant forms, the relationship between God and Job parallels other God–human relationships throughout the scriptures. The history of such God–human relationships begins with the first human beings, Adam and Eve. It continues through Noah and Abraham, Moses and David, and on into the New Testament and the early Christian community's claim of a "new covenant." Thus, it is clear that the God to whom Job cries, the God whom Job questions and challenges, is the God of the Exodus, the one who hears the cries of the persecuted and the suffering and comes to their aid, the one who stands by the poor and rescues the oppressed.

There is a second reason for the book of Job's inclusion in the Bible. It clearly represents an example of biblical *wisdom* literature. The questions the book raises and the assertions it makes arise out of *experience*, Job's own personal experience of innocent suffering. Others in the book, like Job's friends, ground their remarks on received tradition (Bildad, in 8:8-10) or even on revelation (Eliphaz, in 4:13-16). However, as Carol Newsom points out:

> Although his arguments are sophisticated and varied, Job holds his ground for a single fundamental reason. He knows that his friends' common sense and their traditions, their rationality and their revelations are inconsistent with his own experience. For Job, to hold fast to his integrity means to insist on the validity and authority of his own experience, even when it seems to be contradicted by what all the world knows to be true. ("Job," p. 133)

There is yet a third reason why Job belongs in the Bible, and among the wisdom books. The story itself functions something like a parable, a typical *wisdom* way of proceeding. The exaggeration in the description of Job and his sufferings, almost too outrageous to be true, compels us to reevaluate our own thinking about virtue and ill fortune, their sources and significance. The parable/story form draws us in and involves us in the interplay among the characters. It almost forces us to take sides, for example, with Job and against his three friends; and even against God, whom Job accuses of oppression (10:3) and cruelty (30:21).

Job's questions become our own, and even the structure of the book, like some giant puzzle in which the pieces do not quite fit together as they should, ultimately leaves us perplexed and uncertain. Nonetheless, we rarely come away from a reading of Job without new insights and renewed admiration both for the character of Job himself and for the literary work, a monument of human creativity and spiritual depth.

THE HISTORICAL CONTEXT

The story takes place in pre-Mosaic times. But based on the language, modern scholars tend to date the actual writing of the book in the exilic (587-539 B.C.E.) or early postexilic period. Rainer Albertz has proposed a historical setting in the postexilic period, which helps us better to understand the origins of the questions and issues with which the book deals from within the life and experience of the Jewish people themselves. Seeing the book against this background, we can better grasp how the author was able to produce a masterpiece of such poetic power and spiritual depth.

The early Persian period of Jewish postexilic history represented a time of severe socioeconomic crisis. The crisis resulted from the new taxation system imposed by the Persians. As we described above in chapter 4, the Persian ruler Darius (522-486 B.C.E.) decreed that taxes should be paid in hard currency. In other words, farmers had first to sell their crops and then pay a fixed sum out of the proceeds of the transaction.

Thus, when drought occurred or the market prices dropped, the owners of small farms and their families found themselves in difficulty. Those who could not raise the needed cash to pay the tax were obliged to go into debt and mortgage their property. The potential for the exploitation of the situation by wealthy and large landowners, especially among their fellow Jews, seems to have been too great a temptation. Chapter 5 of the book of Nehemiah reports how many of the small farmers of this time were obliged finally to surrender their houses and ancestral properties:

> Now there was a great outcry of the people and of their wives against their Jewish kin. . . . "We are having to pledge our fields, our vineyards, and our houses in order to get grain during the famine." And there were those who said, "We are having to borrow money on our fields and vineyards to pay the King's tax." (Neh 5:1, 3-4)

Some were reduced even to selling their children into foreign slavery to pay off their debts to their fellow Jews, who seemed only too eager to exploit their difficulty. These wealthy money-lending Jews charged high interest rates and were more than ready to foreclose on the mortgages as soon as the opportunity presented itself (Neh 5:5).

Some of these rich and influential Jews, however, like Nehemiah and those around him, took their inspiration from the older ideals of Israel's covenant tradition and its demand for solidarity with those in difficulty. They reduced or abolished interest charges and delayed mortgage foreclosures in order to give breathing space and relief to their kinsfolk in distress:

> I and my brothers and servants are lending them money and grain. Let us stop this taking of interest. Restore to them, this very day, their fields, their vineyards, their olive orchards, and their houses, and the interest on money, grain, wine, and oil that you have been exacting from them. (Neh 5:10-11)

Doubtless some of these wealthy and pious Jews, unwilling to adhere to the cruel logic of the new Persian economic regime, put themselves in danger of financial loss. Some may even have suffered bankruptcy and economic disaster because of their piety and commitment to the covenant demands. We could imagine one such figure as a model for the protagonist of the book of Job.

In such a situation, the question of God's justice and the meaning of innocent suffering arises with all the concreteness and urgency of a real-life situation. The individual who has acted in accord with the requirements of his religious traditions and shown himself courageous in his integrity, his uprightness of life, and his devotion to God suffers disaster and loss. He and his family are thrown out into the street and humiliated and are forced to beg for bread to feed their hungry bellies and to search for clothing and shelter to protect themselves from the elements.

Such is this one's "reward" for his virtue. Yet his fellow Jew, who follows the logic of the "bottom line" and cunningly exploits the difficult circumstance of his countrymen to his own advantage, prospers and grows richer and takes a place of honor in the high councils of the community. Where is the justice of God in such circumstances, and why must our "Job" of this Persian period experience such humiliation and disaster?

This situation, in which such basic questions were so clearly framed, became the occasion for addressing these and other related issues. The author brought to bear all the riches of this community's religious heritage and wisdom to confront the questions and to create eventually the great literary and theological work that we find in our Bible today.

The author of the book may have seen himself and his role reflected in the role played by the three friends of Job. First, his purpose is to *teach*, as the three friends tried to teach and enlighten Job. The author's membership among the elite of his community had given him the advantage of education in the piety of his people, the literature and wisdom of the ancient world, and the wealth of his people's religious traditions. He is thus able to address the questions that must have been troubling his community in the confusing and difficult circumstances of this post-exilic period—the meaning of their suffering and the majesty and mystery of the God whom they worshiped.

Second, the author saw himself in the role of *pastor*, to offer solace and comfort and guidance to his people, as Job's friends sought to do for him. So many Jews of this period found themselves crushed under the weight of their foreign rulers' exploitative policies. They were in need of hope and encouragement. They had suffered loss and hardship because of their piety and loyalty to their religious traditions and its teaching about the good and virtuous life.

It was not simply financial difficulty and disaster and the resulting humiliation and loss of face. It was a spiritual crisis as well. Basic questions had arisen with regard to their "spirituality." They were forced to rethink the concrete way of living out their loyalty to the covenant with God in day-by-day contact and interaction with family members and their fellow Jews, and with those outside that community. "Job the steadfast" provides a model of faith and fidelity and serves as a beacon of hope.

THE STRUCTURE AND INTEGRITY OF THE BOOK

The most obvious structural feature of the book consists in the "frame" formed by the popular prose folktale. It tells about this heroic figure of a past already distant and ancient at the time of the book's writing. The tale recounts the experiences of this hero, apparently a contemporary of Israel's own ancestors, a resident probably of Edom, "in the east."

The prose Prologue (1:1-2:13) and Epilogue (42:7-17) begin and end the book and provide the setting within which the incomparable poems of the debates, soliloquies, and speeches find their place. On reading the book closely, one has the impression that the author started with this prose folktale, written or revised by himself or another. He then proceeded to compose and/or assemble the remaining chapters to address the challenging questions and troubling issues raised by the prose tale: Can God fashion a creature who would love him freely, with no hope of reward? Why must the innocent suffer—for example, the children of Job who are destroyed for the sake of God's wager with the satan? How can God be all-powerful and yet all-just? If he is all-powerful, is he not also responsible for evil and suffering?

The prose Prologue thus sets the stage for the poetry of the Dialogue (chaps. 3-27). Three friends of Job hear of his misfortunes and come to comfort and console him. They arrive as the Prologue ends.

After seven days and nights of silence, Job provokes the debate by his soliloquy in chapter 3. The discussion continues with each of the three friends speaking in turn, and Job responding to each. This "debate" lasts for three rounds until chapters 25-27. What should have been a fourth round in the debate begins with chapter 25, descends into confusion, and abruptly ends. Speeches in this fourth round are abbreviated or missing, and the text seemingly rearranged. Next follows in chapter 28 a poem on the inaccessibility of wisdom, presumably spoken by Job.

Job has another soliloquy in chapters 29-31 to balance the opening one in chapter 3. He recalls his happy past (chapter 29), describes his present misery (chapter 30), and utters a long and terrifying series of oaths (chapter 31). By this series of oaths he affirms his innocence and, in effect, challenges God to explain why he has inflicted this unjust treatment on Job.

The narrative takes another surprising turn when a fourth "friend" or comforter arrives on the scene, the young Elihu. He makes four long speeches (chapters 32, 33-34, 35, 36-37) and then disappears. Finally, God "answers" Job's challenge, appearing in a majestic theophany. God does not address directly any of the questions or issues raised previously in the story or debate. Instead, he holds forth in an eloquent description of his power as creator.

Twice God speaks (38:1-40:2; 40:6-41:34) and twice Job responds (40:3-5; 42:1-6). Job's second response signals a reconciliation. Job does not say that God has answered his questions. Rather, it seems that the fact of a response itself was enough ("I had heard . . . but now my eye sees you"; 42:5). The prose of the Epilogue (42:7-17) brings the book to a conclusion with Job's restoration and reward for his steadfastness.

The book appears to follow a clear narrative logic. Nonetheless, disconcerting turns and twists raise the question of the book's integrity, whether or not additions have been made in the course of the book's literary history. To begin with, two "different" Jobs confront the reader, the "patient" Job of the Prologue-Epilogue, who seems to accept the sufferings inflicted on him with a spirit of humble submission. This contrasts sharply with the Job in the poetic parts of the book (chapters 3-41), who questions and challenges God and, in the opinion of some commentators, even skirts blasphemy.

A solution to the "disruption" of chapters 25-27, the intrusion of the "wisdom" poem in chapter 28, and the source and function of the Elihu speeches in chapters 32-37 are among the difficulties commentators face when addressing the question of the book's authorship and unity. A certain consensus has emerged that an (almost) final form of the book did not include the poem on wisdom in chapter 28 and the Elihu speeches of chapters 32-37, that these constitute later additions.

Nonetheless, it is the book in its "final" form with which we must deal. Kathleen O'Connor proposes that "the enigmas created by the structural gaps among the pieces are not haphazard but deliberate":

> The structure of the Book is itself part of the message. The Book of Job is a sophisticated masterpiece, designed to entangle the reader in the ambiguities and uncertainties of Job's suffering. The more one thinks about the interrelationship of its parts, the more loose ends emerge and more possible interpretations appear. ("Job," p. 88)

This brings us back to the favorite literary form of the wisdom writers, the *mashal*, or proverb, itself a kind of puzzle. But it is a puzzle with a purpose, a pastoral purpose, to help the pious Jews of that early post-exilic period confront the confusion and anguished questions of the "dark night" some of them may have been undergoing.

The book makes accessible the wealth of their ancient wisdom and presents the example of the pious sufferer who emerges from his ordeal with renewed hope. In the person of its protagonist, the book offers pious Jews a new understanding. They are brought to appreciate the love and compassion of this mysterious One who accompanies the suffering and oppressed in their journey through the darkness and sustains their hope with his promises of life and liberation.

THE LITERARY FORM OF JOB

The book as a whole does not conform to any single literary form. The work is too original, and the author has, in effect, created a unique literary form in composing the work. Thus, scholars classify it as *sui generis*, "in its own (unique) category." The author is obviously a skilled poet, well schooled in the literature of the ancient world. He shows himself able to make use at will of a number of literary forms to deal with the issues and questions the book addresses.

First, the book makes abundant use of the literary forms or speech patterns found in the Psalms. The hymn of praise occurs, for example, in Job 5:8-13. But the author employs especially the individual lament form as a vehicle for Job to pour out his distress and to appeal for deliverance. Job's speech in chapter 7 provides a good example of the "description of distress" or *complaint* element of the lament:

> Do not human beings have a hard service on earth,
> and are not their days like the days of a laborer?
> Like a slave who longs for the shadow,
> and like laborers who look for their wages,
> so I am allotted months of emptiness,
> and nights of misery are apportioned to me.
> When I lie down I say, "When shall I rise?"
> But the night is long,
> and I am full of tossing until dawn.
> My flesh is clothed with worms and dirt;
> my skin hardens, then breaks out again.
> My days are swifter than a weaver's shuttle,
> and come to an end without hope. (7:1-6)

A modern parallel to the author of Job's adaptation of this *lament* form would be found in the Nicaraguan poet Ernesto Cardenal. He paraphrases a number of the Psalms, inserting terms and images from a modern Central American context with its economic and political oppression and suffering. The resulting poems might help the reader imagine the analogous situation of a Job in the Persian period, who voices his anguish through the powerful poetry of the biblical book. Note Cardenal's paraphrase of Psalm 5:

> Hear my words Lord
>   Hear my groans
> Hear my protest

Because you are not a God friendly to dictators
not a partisan of their politics
their propaganda does not influence you
And you are not in league with the gangster

There is no sincerity in their speeches
nor in their press releases

They speak of peace in their speeches
while they increase their production for war

They speak of peace in their Peace Conferences
and in secret they prepare themselves for war

                              Their lying radios sound all night

Their desks are filled with criminal plans
                                   and sinister documents
But you will save me from their plans

The author of Job also employs the language of *lawsuit* from the courts. Job repeatedly brings charges against God for treating him unjustly. Chapters 9 and 10 in particular abound with legal terms such as "innocence," "guilt," "appeal," "accuser," "summon," "answer," "justice," "condemn," and so forth.

Finally, from the wisdom school with its contests and debates comes the *disputation speech*. This is perhaps the most appropriate overall genre description for the dialogue or "debate" between Job and his friends in chapters 4-27. In the course of the dialogue, Job disputes not only with the friends but also with God. In chapter 9, Job addresses his friends and calls God to account as well:

> How long will you torment me,
>   and break me in pieces with words?
> These ten times you have cast reproach upon me;
>   are you not ashamed to wrong me?
> And even if it is true that I have erred,
>   my error remains with me.
> If indeed you magnify yourselves against me,
>   and make my humiliation an argument against me,
> know that God has put me in the wrong,
>   and closed his net around me.
> Even when I cry out, "Violence!"
>   I am not answered;
>   I call aloud, but there is no justice. (19:2-7)

CONCLUSION

The story of Job has been told and retold countless times down through the ages. The questions it poses and the issues it raises have formed the subject matter for countless books and articles and commentaries. Nothing can replace, however, a careful and attentive reading of the book itself, a reading undertaken with sympathy and understanding. In the following chapter we will examine more closely a few of the key passages in the text.

REVIEW QUESTIONS

1. Discuss the reasons why Job belongs in the Bible, and among the wisdom writings. How does the story itself function as a "parable"?

2. Describe the historical background for the book of Job proposed by Rainer Albertz. How does knowledge about this early Persian period help in understanding the issues and questions raised by the book?

3. How might the author of Job have seen himself as a teacher and as a pastor in his writing of the book?

4. What are some of the questions and issues raised by the prose Prologue (1:1-2:13) and Epilogue (42:7-17)?

5. Outline briefly the structure of the book of Job. What are some of the problems with the structure that have led commentators to question the book's unity?

6. What do scholars mean when they describe the literary form of the book of Job as *sui generis*?

7. What three kinds of literature (literary forms) has the author of Job drawn upon in composing the work?

10

The Book of Job: Some Key Texts

THE PROLOGUE (1:1-2:13)

The artful and imaginative narrative of the Prologue tells the story of this ancient hero who remained steadfast and loyal to God even in the face of great adversity. The Prologue provides the setting for the ensuing dialogue among Job and his three friends and it highlights some of the key issues and questions they will address. In its six scenes the action alternates between events on earth and events in the heavenly council. The conclusion comes with the arrival of the three friends, who gather to comfort Job over his losses and suffering.

Two items in particular call for comment in this Prologue, the figure of the satan, and especially the question of disinterested piety which the satan raises. First, the "satan" of the Prologue in Job is clearly not the "devil" of the New Testament times. The word in Hebrew (*śāṭān*) means "adversary, accuser." It is thus not a personal name but an office, a kind of public prosecutor or even espionage agent, whose function was to report any mischief or wrong-doing by humans. Translations often show this by giving the word with the article, "*the* satan," or by translating it "the accuser," for example.

This scene in heaven in which the satan appears presents a picture common in the literature of the time, the "divine council" or "assembly of the gods": "One day the heavenly beings came to present themselves before the LORD, and (the) Satan also came among them" (1:6; see also 2:1).

In the ancient imagination, the gods were portrayed after the model of human rulers. The chief god presided like a king over the lesser divinities. These served as his council of advisors or cabinet. This council of the gods convened to discuss important issues, receive reports, make decisions, and commission council members to undertake actions or publish decrees on its behalf. Israelite theology reduced these lesser divinities to the status of messengers for Yahweh or "angels." Old Testament prophets often presented themselves as messengers of Yahweh's divine council, commissioned to put into effect its decrees and decisions.

The satan, or "accuser," of the Prologue is a member of Yahweh's council here in Job. He holds the office similar to a modern public prosecutor or chief of government intelligence service, the CIA or KGB, for example. His job is to spy on humans and report any wrongdoing. Even aside from his official position, the character in the Prologue presents an unpleasant picture. He appears suspicious and cynical, and despite God's positive assessment of Job's loyalty and character, the satan expresses his skepticism and raises the question of motivation (1:9). It is a question that goes literally to the heart of the God–human relationship. Does Job serve God out of love, that is, aside from any self-interest and regardless of the riches and blessings he has received? If these were taken away, would Job still continue his loving service and devotion? Is a selfless, disinterested love of God even possible? In some ways it is more a question about God than a question about Job: Can God fashion a creature who will love him freely, without hope of reward?

The satan's challenge also directs our attention to the question of human freedom. From one perspective, God's assertion of Job's disinterested love is premature. Job's love can ultimately be proven only in time and by testing. Without that move from potency to act, it remains only theoretical. In that sense the wager between God and the satan and the testing of Job become necessary if Job's love is to take on some reality.

The testing takes place in two stages. First comes the destruction of all of Job's possessions, his wealth (and reputation), and finally even his ten children. Then a painful and humiliating skin disease afflicts Job's own body. So great is his suffering that he feels death is near. Three friends arrive, coming to offer solace and support to their companion. But after seven days of silent solidarity, Job ruptures both the silence and the solidarity with words that shock and provoke the three. The long rounds of discussion and debate ensue.

JOB'S OPENING SOLILOQUY (3:1-26)

Job shatters the seven-day silence with a series of seven curses. A restive Job who revolts against divine tyranny and injustice has replaced the compliant and submissive Job of the Prologue. The seven curses and the light/darkness, day/night imagery recall the seven days of creation in chapter 1 of Genesis:

> Let the day perish in which I was born,
>   and the night that said,
>   "A man-child is conceived."
> Let that day be darkness!
>   May God above not seek it,

or light shine on it.
Let gloom and deep darkness claim it.
    Let clouds settle upon it;
    let the blackness of the day terrify it.
That night—let thick darkness seize it!
    let it not rejoice among the days of the year;
    let it not come into the number of the months.
                                                    (Job 3:3-6)

In the place of God's creative and life-giving blessings come Job's curses. By his curses Job attempts to turn the world back to darkness and chaos. In his suffering he longs for death, and in his misery and frustration he tries to overturn what appears to be the harmony and life-giving order of the world. Job contends that this appearance of a just and life-giving order is a sham, and he is intent on exposing the lie. His own experience contradicts both the appearance of an orderly universe and any claim that its Maker is just and fair.

The powerful poetry of this soliloquy fits well into the historical context proposed for the book above in chapter 9. First, the poetry mirrors the experience of the whole people in their confusion and bewilderment of defeat and exile. The world they had known had come to an abrupt and brutal end. Their land, their king, their identity as a people in control of their own destiny had collapsed under the massive assault of Babylon's imperial ambitions. That world had been replaced by the pain and suffering of the exile and the struggle now to rebuild and salvage some meaning and sense out of the catastrophe.

Then the experience of the Job-figure, the pious and prosperous man of Nehemiah's time, exacerbated further some of the anomalies and perplexities of the situation. Initial attempts to find meaning and make sense out of the disaster of defeat and exile had focused on the covenant. As the prophets like Jeremiah and Ezekiel had warned, failure to observe the demands of the covenant would inevitably result in ruin. Their warning had proved accurate. The obvious response would be recommitment to the covenant and renewed fidelity to its demands. God had shown himself merciful and willing to forgive. The exile had ended, and the possibility of restoration and renewal gave new hope and encouragement to the Jews.

But the economic measures of the Persian rule put further strains on the community. Some of the wealthy and prosperous Jews saw the covenant demands of mutual aid and respect for family inheritance as obstacles to their ambitions. They demanded high interest on loans from their fellow Jews and ruthlessly foreclosed on mortgages and debts.

Others, like our Job-figure, tried earnestly to live by Moses' law. As a result they found themselves victims of the "bottom line" logic of the Persian economic regime. This experience served only to plunge them further into confusion and despair and became the occasion for raising the broad barrage of questions with which the book of Job deals.

As is commonly acknowledged, no clear and entirely satisfying answers emerge. But the sharper focusing of questions and issues and the insights that the book does offer have helped countless generations to face suffering and to find some direction and comfort and measure of meaning.

Our reading of the book has taken place against the historical background of the early Persian period. Thus, our interpretation has been determined by the concrete conditions that individual Jews and the community as a whole had to face. This helps us to see that we are not dealing with an academic treatise about abstract questions. Rather, the author is addressing a concrete community of people. By means of this narrative and the exchanges among the characters, he endeavored to help that community reshape their vision and understanding of who their God is and what it means to be in a living relationship of love and loyalty with him.

What does it mean to be human in a world of violence, injustice, selfishness, and cruelty of human beings to one another? What kind of God is this who is responsible for such a world? What are the demands and ways in which this God calls us to join in shaping a more just, peaceful, and life-giving community? How is this God calling us to build a world in which the structures and institutions that determine the way humans interact with one another promote and encourage mutual care and compassion?

Sometimes clear answers are not forthcoming. Injustice, suffering, and oppression continue despite even lifelong commitment to oppose them. Sometimes situations become even more hopeless and unbearable, and our own lives and welfare are endangered. At moments like this, the steadfastness of Job, his commitment to the truth, and his unwavering fidelity and trust in God provide direction and encouragement. Knowing something of the historical context out of which the book emerged can help us better appreciate the power of its poetry and the urgency of its prophetic protest against injustice.

THE DIALOGUE (CHAPTERS 4-27)

The lengthy dialogue or "debate" between Job and his three friends follows a simple pattern. Job alternates with each of the three in three rounds, chapters 4-14, 15-21, and 22-27. The exterior form of the speeches follows a roughly alphabetizing pattern. The twenty-two or twenty-three lines of each speech approximate the number (22) of the letters in the Hebrew alphabet. The replies of Job to his friends tend to be always a few lines longer than the statements of his friends.

The length of the dialogue allows the author to develop fully the best thought on the problem of the suffering of the just person. The friends represent the rigid and dogmatic position of the supposedly traditional wisdom that there cannot be anything such as "innocent" suffering. Actions inevitably receive their due: good will be rewarded and evil punished. If someone experiences suffering, it must be because he or she has sinned. Job suffers, therefore he must be guilty:

> Think now, who that was innocent ever perished?
>   Or where were the upright cut off?
> As I have seen, those who plough iniquity
>   and sow trouble reap the same.
> By the breath of God they perish,
>   and by the blast of his anger they
>   are consumed. (Eliphaz, in 4:7-9)

Job protests their simplistic and mechanically rigid response. He points to his own case as disproving their position. He is innocent, yet he suffers. Why?

Job gradually enlarges his argument to include other examples where the friends' assertions are contradicted. The participants enliven the discussion with personal attacks, wit, and sarcasm. Job, for example, remarks that their best wisdom would be simply to keep silence:

> As for you, you whitewash with lies;
>   all of you are worthless physicians.
> If you would only keep silent,
>   that would be your wisdom! (13:4-5)

Job not only addresses his friends. He also questions God himself and God's just government of the cosmos. Job accuses God of afflicting him cruelly and without reason. He challenges God to appear and defend himself:

> I will take my flesh in my teeth,
>   and put my life in my hand.
> See, he will kill me; I have no hope;
>   but I will defend my ways to his face.
>
> . . . .
>
> I have indeed prepared my case;
>   I know that I shall be vindicated.
>
> . . . .
>
> How many are my iniquities and my sins?
>   Make me know my transgression and my sin.
> Why do you hide your face,
>   and count me as your enemy?

> Will you frighten a windblown leaf
>> and pursue dry chaff? (13:14-15, 18, 23-25)

But God does not appear, and Job's moving appeals for some answer, some sign that God sees and cares, bear witness to a spiritual anguish as great as, if not greater than, his physical suffering:

> I loathe my life;
> I will give free utterance to my complaint;
>> I will speak in the bitterness of my soul.
> I will say to God, Do not condemn me;
>> let me know why you contend against me.
> Does it seem good to you to oppress,
>> to despise the work of your hands
>> and favor the schemes of the wicked?
>
> . . . .
>
> Your hand fashioned and made me;
>> and now you turn and destroy me.
> Remember you fashioned me like clay;
>> and will you turn me to dust again? (10:1-3, 8-9)

The debate ends inconclusively, and the confusion of chapters 25-27 may be purposeful on the author's part, a way of saying that no answer to the question can ultimately satisfy. But the author has given Job the edge in the argument and has established the fact clearly and forcefully that there *is* innocent suffering. No simple and straightforward answer is possible. But one cannot just explain it away with smug formulas and prepackaged answers.

SOLUTIONS TO SUFFERING

Readers of Job put the book down perplexed; no fully satisfying answer seems forthcoming—and especially the meaning and purpose of innocent suffering. Nonetheless, the length and density of the debate have surfaced a number of insights on the question.

At the heart of the discussion is the most obvious and accepted explanation, that suffering is *retributive*, the deserved punishment for wrong-doing. It seems only just and fair that pain and suffering ultimately return upon the head of those who act in ways harmful to themselves or others:

> Think now, who that was innocent ever perished?
>> Or where were the upright cut off?
> As I have seen, those who plow iniquity
>> and sow trouble reap the same.

> By the breath of God they perish,
>> and by the blast of his anger they are consumed.
>>> (Eliphaz in 4:7-9; see also 8:20; 22:4-5)

Job himself does not dispute this. In fact, he presumes it as the basis of his challenge to God and his claims that God is acting unjustly toward him.

Job's friends, especially Elihu, also point to the *disciplinary* function of suffering. Such a view arises from the experience within the family of parents inflicting punishment on children to shape their character and to teach them to avoid harmful ways of acting. Eliphaz, for example, advises Job: "How happy is the one whom God reproves; / therefore do not despise the discipline of the Almighty" (5:17).

Suffering can also serve a probative purpose, to *test* the genuineness of one's character and motivation. This purpose for suffering is central to the story in the Prologue and the assaying of the disinterestedness of Job's piety.

The friends attempt to comfort Job with a further argument: his suffering is only *temporary* and will soon give way once again to health and wholeness:

> See, God will not reject a blameless person,
>> nor take the hand of evildoers.
> He will yet fill your mouth with laughter,
>> and your lips with shouts of joy. (8:20-21)

The author of Psalm 73 makes use of a similar approach.

Eliphaz asserts that some suffering is *inevitable* because of human weakness and proclivity to evil: "Human beings are born to trouble, / just as sparks fly upward" (5:7). Zophar reminds Job that mortals cannot fully grasp the *mysterious* purposes of God. His ways are inevitably hidden from us: "Can you find out the deep things of God?" (11:7). God in fact never does disclose the reason for Job's suffering, and Job himself finally admits, "I have uttered what I did not understand, / things too wonderful for me which I did not know" (42:3).

Puzzlement at the seemingly *haphazard* and incidental nature of some suffering also comes to expression in the book:

> One dies in full prosperity,
>> being wholly at ease and secure.
>
> . . . .
>
> Another dies in bitterness of soul,
>> never having tasted of good.
> They lie down alike in the dust,
>> and the worms cover them. (21:23, 25-26)

Finally, the Epilogue implies an understanding of *vicarious* or redemptive suffering, by which one individual can suffer and/ or intercede on behalf of others: "My servant Job shall pray for you, for I will accept his prayer not to deal with you according to your folly" (42:8).

A mark of the genius of the book's author is the way in which he was able to weave all of these approaches into the discussion. Yet he skillfully refrains from proposing any single one as the definitive answer. The reader comes away enlightened, yet still perplexed.

JOB'S OWN CHANGE OF PERSPECTIVE

In the course of the debate, Job clearly undergoes a change of perspective. It begins with Job's soliloquy in chapter 3 itself. In the series of questions, the Why? of vv 11, 12, and 20, Job moves from a focus on his own personal experience to a wider concern about God's dealings with humanity in general: How is God's goodness demonstrated in a gift that is not really a gift—the gift of life, but a life filled with suffering and pain?

As the discussion proceeds, Job reaches out to encompass within his purview others who suffer. His questioning becomes more universal in scope until it reaches 24:2-12, a passage that liberation theologian Gustavo Gutiérrez calls "the most radical and cruel description of the wretchedness of the poor found in the Bible" (*On Job,* p. 32). Job powerfully portrays the desperate condition of the very poor who are without food, shelter, or adequate clothing, exploited by those who hire them and subject to repeated violence. Job focuses particularly on the plight of the widow and orphan, then as now, among the poorest of the poor. Job lends them a voice and speaks on their behalf. This former patrician figure, once comfortable and safe within the confines of his estate and family and reputation, stands now alone, naked and vulnerable, in solidarity with all the wretched of the earth:

> Why are times not kept by the Almighty,
>   and why do those who know him never see his
>   days?
> The wicked remove landmarks;
>   they seize flocks and pasture them.
> They drive away the donkey of the orphan;
>   they take the widow's ox for a pledge.
> They thrust the needy off the road;
>   the poor of the earth all hide themselves.
> Like wild asses in the desert
>   they go out to their toil,
> scavenging in the wasteland
>   food for their young.

> They reap in a field not their own
>   and they glean in the vineyard of the wicked.
> They lie all night naked, without clothing,
>   and have no covering in the cold.
> They are wet with the rain of the mountains,
>   and cling to the rock for want of shelter.
>
> There are those who snatch the orphan child from
>   the breast,
>   and take as a pledge the infant of the poor.
> They go about naked, without clothing;
>   though hungry, they carry the sheaves;
> between their terraces they press out oil;
>   they tread the wine presses, but suffer thirst.
> From the city the dying groan,
>   and the throat of the wounded cries for help;
>   yet God pays no attention to their prayer. (24:1-12)

The Job described in the Prologue as "blameless and upright" has now come to realize that his innocence and uprightness cannot be simply negative qualities, the absence of malice or sin. They must include the positive as well, the concern for and the commitment to free from oppression those who are poor and persecuted. Job cries out on their behalf and protests against their suffering and exploitation. As a result, the language of the book more closely resembles the language of the prophets than any of the other wisdom writings.

PARTS OF THE "PUZZLE"

The purpose and progress of the chapters that follow upon the Dialogue are not immediately evident. After the confusion of chapters 25-27 comes the surprise of chapter 28. This beautiful poem on the inaccessibility of wisdom brings a whole different perspective to the issues under debate in the preceding chapters. Humans do not have the wisdom to solve the mystery of suffering; they can only "fear" God:

> But where shall wisdom be found?
>   And where is the place of understanding?
> Mortals do not know the way to it,
>   and it is not found in the land of the living.
>
> .   .   .   .
>
> God understands the way to it,
>   and he knows its place.
>
> .   .   .   .

And he said to humankind,
"Truly, the fear of the LORD, that is wisdom;
  and to depart from evil is understanding."
                                          (28:12-13, 23, 28)

After this anonymous poem, which many consider a later addition to
the text, Job utters his lengthy soliloquy. It serves to balance his opening statement in chapter 3. He nostalgically recalls his former happy
existence (chapter 29) and movingly describes his present sufferings
(chapter 30). In a final bid to bait God into responding, Job launches
into a series of oaths in chapter 31. He runs through a whole list of sin-
ful actions and invokes fearful consequences upon himself if he is found
guilty of any such crimes. Near the end he issues his final challenge,
"Here is my signature! let the Almighty answer me!" (31:35).

But God's answer does not come immediately. Instead we have
another part of the puzzle, the speeches of Elihu in chapters 32-37.
Some say that they do not belong here but constitute another later addition, like chapter 28. Elihu appears nowhere else in the book. He deliv-
ers four speeches (chapters 32-33, 34, 35, 36-37), directed mainly at
Job. For the most part he simply elaborates on arguments already given
earlier by Job's friends, especially about the disciplinary role of suffering (33:19-33; 36:8-15; see 5:17-18).

THE YAHWEH SPEECHES

God finally answers Job in 38:1-41:34. But God's answers are not
what Job or the reader might have expected. God seems to ignore the
questions and issues raised by Job and the friends, especially about the
reason for Job's suffering. Instead, God gives voice to his own questions,
which seem to tease Job about his puniness and powerlessness in God's
presence and his lack of understanding about the way in which the
world works:

Who is this that darkens counsel by
  words without knowledge?
Gird up your loins like a man,
  I will question you and you shall declare to me.

. . . .

Have you comprehended the expanse of the earth?
  Declare, if you know all this.
Where is the way to the dwelling of light,
  and where is the place of darkness,
that you may take it to its territory
  and that you may discern the paths to its home?

> Surely you know, for you were born then,
>> and the number of your days is great! (38:2-3, 18-
> 21)

The speeches by God constitute a brilliant and eloquent coda to the
debate. Job had uttered seven curses on creation in his opening soliloquy in chapter 3. He attempted to turn the world back to darkness and
chaos. God responds with a celebration of the beauty and orderliness of
the universe. A number of passages paint vivid pictures of power, vitality, and diversity in the created world. The striking description of the
might and majesty of the horse offers a good example:

> Do you give the horse its might?
>> Do you clothe its neck with mane?
> Do you make it leap like the locust?
>> Its majestic snorting is terrible.
> It paws violently, exults mightily;
>> it goes out to meet the weapons.
> It laughs at fear, and is not dismayed;
>> it does not turn back from the sword.
>
> . . . .
>
> With fierceness and rage it swallows the ground;
>> it cannot stand still at the sound of the trumpet.
> When the trumpet sounds, it says "Aha!"
>> From a distance it smells the battle,
>> the thunder of the captains and the shouting.
>> (Job 39:19-22, 24-25)

The horse seems almost godlike in its pride and magnificence. The rich
poetic imagery that the poet employs suggests a fierce energy barely
kept in bounds by the One who brought this creature into existence.
The Creator delights in the exuberance and vigor with which he has
endowed the animal.

Although the speeches sidestep Job's questions about his suffering,
they do represent a response to him in two ways. First, to Job's implicit
challenge to God to "justify his ways to humans," they provide a clear
answer. The speeches affirm that there is order and purpose in God's
creation. But it is not possible for the human mind, with human words
and concepts, fully to understand or "explain" God and God's actions.
The speeches thus assert divine freedom and preserve the ultimate mystery that inevitably separates the transcendent Creator from mortal
creatures.

Second, God's reply to Job comes in the context of a "theophany,"
the figurative language by which the ancient imagination described an
encounter with God. This is what Job had asked for, some little sign that

God at least knew what Job was undergoing, and that God cared. At the very minimum, this is what the theophany provides, that encounter. It gives Job a new perspective on his suffering, such that he no longer requires the answers and explanations he had so earnestly sought. We offer our own version of Job's response to God:

> Therefore I have uttered what I did not understand,
> > things too wonderful for me, which I did not
> > > know.
>
> . . . .
>
> I had heard of you by the hearing of the ear,
> > but now my eye sees you;
> therefore I accept and repent,
> > a child of dust and ashes. (42:3, 5-6)

THE EPILOGUE

The last eleven verses (42:7-17) shift back to prose and to the setting of the Prologue. The common teaching of the wisdom tradition demanded that the just receive the acknowledgment and reward for their virtue. Thus, "the LORD restored the fortunes of Job" and "gave Job twice as much as he had before" (42:10).

The three friends are rebuked by God because they "have not spoken of me what is right, as my servant Job has" (42:7). God tells the three that they must offer a sacrifice (seven bulls and seven rams) in Job's presence, with Job uttering prayers on their behalf. Implied in this is the notion of vicarious atonement by which an individual can suffer and/or intercede on behalf of others. Psalm 106 alludes to this notion when it describes Moses, God's "chosen one," as offering himself on behalf of the people "to turn his [God's] wrath from destroying them" (v. 23). This insight will receive its fullest development in the Fourth Servant Song:

> Surely he has borne our infirmities
> > and carried our diseases.
>
> . . . .
>
> But he was wounded for our transgressions,
> > crushed for our iniquities;
> upon him was the punishment which made us whole,
> > and by his bruises we are healed. (Isa 53:4-5)

God trusts Job and recognizes his steadfastness and virtue even in the midst of great suffering. The prayer of such a one on behalf of others obviously has great value in God's eyes: "So Eliphaz the Temanite and Bildad the Shuhite and Zophar the Naamathite went and did what the LORD had told them; and the LORD accepted Job's prayer" (42:9).

CONCLUSION

We have focused in these two chapters on Job, whom R. A. F. MacKenzie describes as "the tormented, devout, rebellious man who has raged against the human situation and demanded that God 'justify his ways to humans'" ("Job," p. 486). We have interpreted the book as coming out of a specific historical context and as addressed to one particular group among the Jews. Obviously the exilic and postexilic periods were times of great trial and suffering for this people. Some of the literature of this time bears eloquent testimony to this fact—the book of Lamentations, the Servant Songs of the Second Isaiah, and the book of Job itself.

If one reads Job against this historical background, one can see that it does the book an injustice to privatize and overly spiritualize its message. The Jewish community faced very real challenges—economic and political oppression and social conflict. The book's "spirituality" is firmly grounded in Israel's covenant traditions and is meant, in part, to provide a response to the spiritual crises provoked by the challenges and struggles of exilic and postexilic times.

A support for this approach comes from the liberation theologian Gustavo Gutiérrez. In his powerful and moving theological reading of the text one can see that Gutiérrez has tapped into concerns and questions that parallel some of his own as a liberation theologian. He contends that central to the work is the question of *how we are to talk about God* especially in the context of the suffering poor of South America.

Gutiérrez notes that the book of Job contains two kinds of language for describing and addressing God. We have already seen the prominence of the language of prophecy in the Dialogue. Job attacks situations of injustice and deprivation and their structural causes. These unjust structures result so often in innocent suffering, like that described in chapter 24 for example.

But Gutiérrez contends that Job learns another kind of language, "the language of contemplation," especially from the Yahweh speeches. This "language of contemplation" takes into account God's plan of creation. It gives voice to the wonder that arises in the face of God's wisdom and power at work in the created world, a creative activity characterized by God's free and gratuitous love:

> The truth that he (Job) has grasped and that has lifted him to the level of contemplation is that justice alone does not have the final say about how we are to speak of God. Only when we come to realize that God's love is freely bestowed do we enter fully and definitively into the presence of the God of faith. (*On Job*, p. 87)

The free and gratuitous nature of that love is especially obvious in God's preferential love for the poor. The poor are not necessarily better or more virtuous than others. God loves them simply because they are poor and are living in an inhuman situation that is contrary to God's will.

The "language of prophecy," grounded in and arising out of the struggle on behalf of those who suffer innocently, must be joined with this "language of contemplation": "Mystical language expresses the gratuitousness of God's love; prophetic language expresses the demands this love makes" (*On Job*, p. 95).

Above in chapter 9 we mentioned how the book's author saw himself acting as both *teacher* and *pastor*. In fashioning this prophetic language of the Dialogue and the mystical language of the Yahweh speeches, we see the author in his role as pastor. He responds to the spiritual crisis of his people, firmly rooting himself in their ancient traditions of a God of justice and active involvement on behalf of the oppressed. At the same time he opens them to awe and wonder in the face of the Creator God's gratuitous love. He opens them to new horizons of hope and promise.

REVIEW QUESTIONS

1. Describe the mythological background of the "divine council" in the Prologue.

2. What does the Hebrew word *śāṭān* mean, and what is the role of the *śāṭān* ("the satan") within the divine council?

3. Discuss the key question that "the satan" raises concerning Job and his piety. How is it more a question about God than a question about Job?

4. How does the creation theme enter into Job's soliloquy in chapter 3?

5. How does the soliloquy reflect the historical background out of which the book has come?

6. Describe the structure of the dialogue or "debate" between Job and his friends in chapters 4-27.

7. Discuss the various "solutions" to the problem of suffering proposed by the book. Does any one of them provide *the* answer to the problem?

8. How does Job himself undergo a change in perspective in the course of the debate? Why does the language that Job uses so closely resemble the language of the prophets?

9. Discuss the two ways in which the speeches of Yahweh (38:1-41:34) represent a response to Job's challenge to God.

10. How is the notion of "vicarious atonement" introduced in the Epilogue (42:7-17)? Does this notion appear elsewhere in the Old Testament?

11. Describe the two kinds of language for talking about God which Gustavo Gutiérrez finds in the book of Job.

RESEARCH PROJECT

This project can form the basis for a class discussion or for an essay by the student.

Choose one of the modern adaptations of the book of Job listed below. Compare the modern work with the biblical book, addressing such questions as:

1. How faithfully does it reformulate in modern terms the questions and concerns of the biblical book?
2. How well does it capture at least some of the aspects of the response to these questions suggested by the biblical book?
3. Suppose the author of the modern work had been aware of the historical situation in which the biblical book was written. Do you think that would have made any difference in the way in which he or she adapted the Job story for a modern audience?
4. How could they have taken into account more explicitly the liberation dimensions of the biblical book?

MODERN ADAPTATIONS OF JOB

Robert Frost, *A Masque of Reason*. New York: Holt, Rinehart & Winston, 1945.

Robert Heinlein, *Job: A Comedy of Justice*. New York: Ballantine (Del Rey), 1984.

Archibald MacLeish, *J. B., a Play in Verse*. Sentry Edition. Boston: Houghton-Mifflin, 1958.

Joseph Roth, *Job, the Story of a Simple Man*. New York: Viking, 1931.

Neil Simon, *God's Favorite*. New York: Random House, 1975.

Muriel Spark, *The Only Problem*. New York: Putnam, 1984.

11

The Book of Ecclesiastes (Qoheleth):
An Overview

INTRODUCTION

Despite the brevity of this wisdom book (less than eleven pages of the NRSV), it has attracted much attention and comment down through the ages. Some readers find enchanting the stark beauty of its language and its haunting imagery; the poem on "time" in chapter 3, for example, or the description of death in chapter 12:

> . . . the silver cord is snapped, and the golden bowl is broken, and the pitcher is broken at the fountain, and the wheel is broken at the cistern, and the dust returns to the earth as it was, and the breath returns to God who gave it. (12:6-7)

Others are moved by the book's honesty and refreshing skepticism. The work sounds almost modern in its probing reflections. Still others, however, are disturbed by what they interpret as the author's pessimism and preoccupation with death.

Each of these reactions captures an aspect of this enigmatic work. To be introduced to this book is to encounter the challenging reflections of a profound thinker, a person with great intellectual and poetic gifts. Perhaps better than any other biblical writer, the author of Ecclesiastes is able to put us in touch with the mystery that is God.

The more common (Latin) name for the book, "Ecclesiastes," comes from the Septuagint Greek's translation of the Hebrew word "Qoheleth." It is not actually a name but a title. It does not mean "preacher," as some modern translations render it. It means "assembler" (of students, listeners) or "collector" (of wisdom sayings). Which of these is correct? Probably both of them. As we shall see, ambiguity and indeterminacy characterize the book's contents as well as its mode of reflection. Qoheleth *gathered* students for learning; he also *collected* sayings and reflections in this book. Further, he takes on the persona of King Solomon, who *accumulated* great wealth and wisdom while *gathering* and presiding over his subjects. Finally, Qoheleth spent his whole life trying to gather together some bits and pieces of meaning and sense out of his life and experience.

HISTORICAL SETTING

The language and the appearance of certain Persian words locate the book firmly in the postexilic period. A number of recent commentators opt for the early Hellenistic period, between 300 and 200 B.C.E., when the Ptolemies of Egypt included Palestine as a part of their empire.

These Ptolemaic kings exploited the country with ruthless efficiency. They continued the earlier Persian economic system of siphoning off the wealth of the peoples whom they ruled, especially through their taxation system, which was initiated by the Persians and continued under these Egyptian kings. As we explained above, it required payment of taxes by the small farmers not with agricultural products—percentages of the crop yields or of flocks and herds. Rather, these Hellenistic kings demanded payment each year of a fixed sum in hard currency, no matter what the amount of yield was in crops or cattle.

The introduction of this monetary or money-based economy into Palestine had a devastating effect on the life and condition of the Jewish population. In periods of drought or blight or low rainfall, many small farmers had to mortgage their property or sell it. Sometimes they even had to sell themselves and their families into slavery to obtain the necessary hard currency to pay the required taxes.

The gap increased between the small landowners and farmers, on the one hand, and the rich aristocratic class, on the other. This wealthy minority was composed of both foreign officials based in the country itself or elsewhere. It also included their upper-class Jewish agents and collaborators. Many small farmers and their families were dispossessed of their properties. At the same time, the wealthy elite accumulated ever larger tracts of land for themselves and/or as agents of foreign ruling powers, first of Persian, then of Ptolemaic kings and nobles. The dispossessed farmers and sheepherders now worked the land as tenant farmers or day laborers.

Older values and relationships based on family and kinship ties had fostered mutual aid and support among family and kinship groups. With this new and expanding monetary economy, these kinship ties and support networks began to break down. Members of the same family or kinship group were separated into different and opposing economic strata.

The values and older ethical standards based on human loyalty and compassion had given way to more materialistic values of wealth and influence with the foreign ruling power and its agents. Thus, many people could no longer understand the world and the way in which it was ordered; they could not fathom the reasons for the economic fate of individuals.

It is within this context of bewilderment and uncertainty that we would locate Qoheleth. In the face of this political and economic confusion under an oppressive rule, Qoheleth and many of his fellow Jews would have felt a sense of powerlessness and inability to change things for the better. It is under these circumstances and within these limitations that Qoheleth engages in his search to find the "wisest" way to live one's daily life.

Qoheleth responds to the economic, political, and religious crises of his people in two ways. On the one hand, he turns like a compassionate pastor toward his people, fashioning for them a spirituality of the most rigorous asceticism. On the other hand, he attacks the intellectual foundations, the so-called "wisdom," of the Hellenistic monetary economy, which was wreaking such havoc in the lives of his fellow Jews.

QOHELETH'S RESPONSE TO THE SPIRITUAL CRISIS

Qoheleth responds to the religious and spiritual crisis his people face by bringing his people to a new understanding of their God, and the mystery and hiddenness of this one whom they worshiped. Following his pastoral instincts, he offers them a way of surviving the crisis, purified and renewed.

As a wisdom teacher, he is obviously skilled in the "tools of the trade." He makes use of a dialectical style, affirming but then challenging, or qualifying traditional teachings. In chapter 2, for example, he seconds the traditional teaching of the value of wisdom over folly:

> Then I saw that wisdom excels folly as light excels
> darkness.
> The wise have eyes in their head,
> but fools walk in darkness. (2:13-14a)

But the thought of death intervenes, qualifying the worth of wisdom and denying wisdom any absolute value or advantage:

> Yet I perceived that the same fate befalls all of them. Then I said
> to myself, "What happens to the fool will happen to me also; why
> then have I been so very wise?" (2:14b-15)

Overall, the book itself forms a kind of *mashal*, or "proverb," in which positive is juxtaposed with negative. On the one hand comes the affirmation of the goodness of creation. Qoheleth again and again, at

least seven times, exhorts his readers to accept and rejoice in that goodness, when God wills to give us a share in it:

> I know that there is nothing better for them [mortals] than to be
> happy and enjoy themselves as long as they live; moreover, it is
> God's gift that all should eat and drink and take pleasure in all
> their toil. (3:12-13)

This affirmation of life's goodness is set in dialectical opposition with
the other term of the *mashal*, Qoheleth's contention that humans are
unable to seize or grasp as their own any profit from their labor. He
begins his book with the question: "What do people gain from all the
toil at which they toil under the sun?" (1:3). From all his observations
and investigations, Qoheleth's answer is—no gain, no profit: "All is
vanity and a chase after the wind":

> . . . sometimes one who has toiled with wisdom and knowledge
> and skill must leave all to be enjoyed by another who did not toil
> for it. This also is vanity and a great evil. (2:21)

Qoheleth thus affirms a sense of powerlessness and uncertainty about
achieving any lasting material gain from his efforts. He couples this with
his argument that humans are powerless as well to wrest any measure
of meaning out of life, to understand or grasp the significance of it all.

Qoheleth moves unrelentingly between these two terms of the dialectic. He asserts the goodness of God's creation and the mandate to rejoice
in it. But he affirms as well our inability to grasp and hold at will to that
goodness and that joy. Further, he asserts that we cannot know why and
when God might give or withhold them.

In his wise and skillful use of this dialectic, Qoheleth the spiritual
guide seizes this occasion of crisis in the history of his people, this
"teachable moment" as it were. He invites them to walk with him the
dark path. Thus far they had known this One only as Redeemer and
Creator. Qoheleth brings them into the presence of the One who cannot
be known, only acknowledged with awe and respect.

In the midst of their confusion and sense of powerlessness, their God
appeared silent and inaccessible. No prophet arose to bring a word from
God; no priest proved capable of producing answers from the Law.
Only now, the sage steps forward with his challenge. Sometimes you
must learn to live without explanations and allow God to be free to be
God: "God is in heaven, and you are upon earth; therefore let your
words be few" (5:2b).

Thus does J. T. Walsh describe Qoheleth's "spirituality" as "a spirituality of the most total type of asceticism. . . . It is a spirituality that
accepts the darkness, surrenders to the mystery, and finally surrenders

the dearest and deepest desire of the human heart—to make sense of life" (p. 48).

Paradoxically, the book itself represents something of a "gain," a permanent monument to the artistry, wisdom, and compassion of its author. It has proved "profitable" to countless readers and people in their search for God.

QOHELETH'S RESPONSE TO THE ECONOMIC CRISIS: THE STRATEGY OF HIS "NUMBERS GAME"

Qoheleth makes use of his skills as sage to respond as "pastor" or "spiritual guide" to the religious crisis his people faced. He also employs his ability with language and "dialectic" to sabotage some of the pre-suppositions and principles of the Hellenistic monetary economy that wreaked such havoc on his fellow Jews. As C. L. Seow notes in his Anchor Bible commentary, "While Qohelet clearly draws on timeless wisdom teachings, he also addresses people facing a new world of money and finance. Hence, he uses the vocabulary of his day to subvert the preoccupations of his contemporaries" (*Ecclesiastes,* p. 23). Qoheleth may have been reluctant to challenge openly and attack these predatory economic arrangements directly. But at least he could expose the folly of its "wisdom" and its will to power.

Many commentators have noted the "commercial character" of Qoheleth's thought and language and his obvious fascination with the mathematical, with numbers. Again and again come words denoting profit and loss, surplus and deficit, shares and wages, ownership and wealth and poverty. The word "profit," *yitrôn* in Hebrew, occurs eighteen times. In every situation, Qoheleth asks, What is to be gained? What is the profit? "What do people gain from all the toil at which they toil under the sun?" (1:3). The almost hectic commercial life that Hellenistic rule brought to Palestine forms the background for this attitude. All activity in the Ptolemaic state was oriented toward purely economic profit and productivity.

Qoheleth seems purposely to appropriate the language of commerce in order to subvert and sabotage the attitude and mind set which it pre-supposes. Such an approach to life pridefully presumes that humans can acquire some sense of security and control over their destiny by the amassing of riches. An example of his subversion of the language of commerce comes in 7:27-28. Qoheleth co-opts a bookkeeping metaphor to express his frustration and inability to find any answers to his searching questions:

> "See, this is what I learned," says Qoheleth, "adding one to one to reach the total, which my mind has sought repeatedly, but I have not found." (author's translation)

Central to the mind-set of the marketplace is the mathematical—numbers and the keeping of accounts. And numbers appear prominently in Qoheleth's work. We shall see later in this chapter how Qoheleth counted verses and constructed his text according to assorted mathematical patterns. At the same time he challenged that air of certainty and self-assurance which concreteness of quantities and numbers might imply. In 4:6, for example, he shows how mathematics, from a wisdom perspective, is an imprecise science:

> Better is a handful with quiet than two handfuls with toil and a chasing after wind.

In this case, "one" is in fact "more than" or better than "two." One finds a similar indeterminacy and lack of predictability in the author's use of numbers to structure the book. Addison Wright has shown that incomplete numerical patterns and broken chains of proportions are found throughout the book ("The Riddle of the Sphinx Revisited").

Qoheleth thus attacks the calculating wisdom of the monetary economy within which he and his fellow Jews found themselves: "See, this is what I found, says Qoheleth, adding one to one to reach the sum total, which my mind sought repeatedly, but which I could not reach" (7:27-28; author's version). In the third-century B.C.E. world of Qoheleth, with its oppression of the poor, competitive striving, and unreflective pursuit of material gain, he calls into question its "wisdom of calculation." His play with numbers and indeterminacy and the lack of predictability represent a critique of the search for success and happiness in the "bottom line," the material gain or "profit" that life supposedly could offer:

> A man may beget a hundred children, and live many years; but however many are the days of his years, if he does not enjoy life's good things, or has no burial, I say that a stillborn child is better off than he. . . . Even though he should live a thousand years twice over, yet enjoy no good—do not all go to one place? (6:3, 6)

THE STRUCTURE OF QOHELETH

Addison Wright's studies have demonstrated the unity of the book and the progression of thought. The book has a clear and uncomplicated structure in which two complementary patterns are at work. First, key words and refrains divide the book into sections. In the first half of the book Qoheleth describes his investigation of life. This first half (1:12-6:9) falls into eight sections, each section ending with "vanity of vanities" and/or "a chasing after wind." In the second half of the book (6:10-12:14), Qoheleth gives some conclusions from his investigations. This second half also divides into eight sections. Each of the first four sections ends with the verb "to find" and each of the second four concludes with "to know."

This structure, based on refrains and the repetition of key words, is confirmed and complemented by Wright's recognition of numerological patterns controlling the book's length. As with the book of Proverbs, the numerical value of the letters of key words seems determinative for the length of the book as well as for various segments within it.

The most obvious pattern builds on the key word *hebel*, "vanity," which occurs thirty-seven times. The numerical value of the consonants in *hebel* also is 37. The number of verses in each half of the book (1:1-6:9 and 6:10-12:14) totals 111, or three times 37. (Note that the "refrains" in 1:2 and 12:8 each contains three *hebels*.)

Wright has identified other mathematical patterns in addition to these. But it is enough to say that these patterns coincide with the structural indications provided by the repeated refrains. In other words, it is obvious that the author has done his work carefully and given a conscious and purposeful shape to the book both in length and organization.

QOHELETH AND WISDOM

The book concludes with an Epilogue, the six final verses, which are most likely an addition by one of Qoheleth's students or disciples (12:9-14). It asserts that the book's author was considered a "sage" or "wise man" (*ḥākām*) by his contemporaries. He "taught the people knowledge, weighing and studying and arranging many proverbs" (v. 9). There is no disputing that he makes skillful use of a number of a sage's "tools of the trade"—wisdom sayings (see 7:1-12), example stories (e.g., 9:13-16), "impossible questions" ("That which is, is far off, and deep, very deep; who can find it out?" [7:24]). He focuses on typical wisdom issues—wisdom and folly (see 1:16-18), retribution (7:15-18), the value of one thing or action over another (4:1-12). His method is wisdom's method, based on observation and experience.

Thus he stands within the wisdom movement. But he sharply critiques the often overconfident self-assurance of those who were too quick to offer pat formulas for success or give glib answers to profound human problems. Relying on his observations and experience, Qoheleth reaches his own challenging and unsettling conclusion about life and human endeavors: "All is vanity and a chasing after wind" (1:14, 17; 2:11, 17, 19, 23, 26; and so on).

Qoheleth appeals consistently and unrelentingly to *experience* as the primary source of knowledge and the criterion for judging. It leads him to conclude that too many unanswered questions remain, and the seeming arbitrariness and injustices of life find no solution. If God indeed has some purpose in allowing things to happen as they do, that purpose is hidden from us. God has put "darkness" (Hebrew ʿōlām) in the human mind; thus "they cannot find out what God has done from the beginning to the end" (3:11).

In its overall shape, the book stands alone as a literary work, *sui generis*, "in its own category," like the book of Job. The author formulates his own version of a "wisdom spirituality" that is almost frightening in the demands it makes on its readers with its assertion of the sovereignty and mystery of God and its honest acceptance of human limitation and ignorance.

One could mitigate the radicalism of Qoheleth's stance by reading the book within the larger context of the scriptural canon. But this is one work that, to a certain extent, needs to be taken on its own, to claim and "profit" fully from its wisdom. Only by giving a thorough hearing to his more extreme statements and allowing the resulting tensions to stand can one appreciate the rigorous and demanding spiritual asceticism of the book. Only in this way can one recognize the timeliness of the author's counsel to accept with joy and gratitude whatever measure of good God's gift of life brings with it:

> There is nothing better for mortals than to eat and drink, and find enjoyment in their toil. This also, I saw, is from the hand of God; for apart from him who can eat or who can have enjoyment? (2:24-25)

GOD AND CREATION IN QOHELETH

Qoheleth often speaks of God as *creator*, and it is by observing God's work in creation that Qoheleth comes to some conclusions about God. In the twelve short chapters of the book, the word for "God," ʾĕlōhîm, occurs almost forty times. Obviously God is central to Qoheleth's thought. And what God has created is *good*. Scholars have pointed out a number of parallels with the creation stories in Genesis 1-3. Some commentators have concluded that Qoheleth purposely alludes to these accounts to underscore his theme of creation and its goodness. Indeed, 3:11 asserts that God "has made everything suitable for its time," and that it is *good* for humans ". . . to be happy and enjoy themselves as long as they live; moreover, it is God's gift that all should eat and drink and take pleasure in all their toil" (3:12-13).

God's "gifts" and the fact that God "gives" are constant themes in the book. Eleven times some form of the word "give" occurs. The difficulty comes, however, when one attempts to uncover some consistency or pattern in that giving. There is none; it appears to be purely arbitrary as to who receives and who does not:

There is an evil that I have seen under the sun, and it lies heavy upon humankind: those to whom God gives wealth, possessions, and honor, so that they lack nothing of all that they desire, yet God does not enable them to enjoy these things, but a stranger enjoys them. This is vanity; it is a grievous ill. (6:1-2)

Further, God who creates or "makes" also "works" (both are possible translations of Hebrew ʿāśâ). But in line with his rigorous method, how to understand those works and their purpose remains hidden from human observation and understanding. As far as Qoheleth can see, God's working leads nowhere. From his perspective, Qoheleth can only describe it as futile and absurd. Nature follows a fixed repetitive cycle that never satisfies, that does not appear to have any purpose:

> The sun rises and the sun goes down,
>   and hurries to the place where it rises.
> The wind blows to the south,
>   and goes around to the north;
> Round and round goes the wind
>   and on its circuits the wind returns.
> All streams run to the sea,
>   but the sea is not full. (1:5-7a)

Human actions parallel those of nature. Despite constant motion and effort, there is no progress, no gain:

> What has been is what will be,
>   and what has been done is what will be done;
>   there is nothing new under the sun. (1:9)

Qoheleth thus surrenders any hope of understanding "the work of God" or of finding any meaning or purpose in what God is doing:

Then I saw all the work of God, that no one can find out what is happening under the sun. However much they may toil in seeking, they will not find it out; even though those who are wise claim to know, they cannot find it out. (8:17)

Against the background of the confused and uncertain times in which the author lived, one can understand better the picture of God that Qoheleth offers. He certainly knew Yahweh, Israel's liberator and protector. Qoheleth takes for granted the worship of Israel's God in the Jerusalem temple (see 5:1). But he gives witness to a different experience of this One in daily life. He sees no evidence in his own day nor in his own life of the "marvelous deeds" of which the Jewish scriptures speak. He sees only the uncertainty and oppression, and the inscrutable character of this One's "giving" and "working."

Qoheleth does not give up on God. He only seeks to understand God's "working" enough to be able to live day by day in both the presence, and the absence, of this One. He seeks a "spirituality" for survival in these difficult days. His experience dictates that his counsel can only be the minimum: "God has done this so that all should stand in awe (fear) before him" (3:14); for, "God is in heaven, and you upon earth; therefore let you words be few" (5:2). The writer of the Epilogue will be more explicit: "Fear God, and keep his commandments; for that is the whole duty of everyone" (12:13).

Qoheleth thus brings his people into the presence of this One who cannot be known, only acknowledged with awe and respect. And he invites them to walk with him the dark and uncertain path in these uncertain times, their faith deepened and purified.

QOHELETH, DEATH, AND "VANITY"

These two themes, "death" and "vanity," are closely linked in Qoheleth. The one leads to the other. The inexorable fact of death brings Qoheleth to conclude that "all is vanity [*hebel*], and a chasing after wind." Death cancels out all achievements and results of any human endeavor.

The word *hebel*, "vanity," occurs thirty-seven times in Qoheleth. This also equals the numerical value of its three consonants, *h* (5), *b* (2), *l* (30) (5 + 2 + 30 = 37). Its basic meaning is "vapor, breath," thus signifying something insubstantial and ephemeral—a vain, futile, even absurd thing or happening. The exasperation and frustration of the author in the face of his inability to uncover any meaning or sense in life could scarcely be expressed in stronger terms: "'Vanity of vanities,' says Qoheleth, 'Vanity of vanities! All is vanity.'" This judgment on life comes at the beginning (1:2) and at the end (12:8) of the book. It echoes again and again, along with its companion phrase, "a chasing of wind," throughout the first half of the work (1:14, 17; 2:11, 15; and so on).

One may argue with some of Qoheleth's judgments concerning the "vanity" of this or that activity or situation. But it is difficult to argue with his observation about the finality and annihilating power of death. It casts its threatening shadow over all human life. Thus, no matter how forceful and vigorous Qoheleth's exhortation to rejoice in life and the good things it provides, he is inevitably stopped in his tracks when the thought of death intervenes. It leads him to pronounce his bleak evaluation of the human situation: "All is vanity and a chasing of wind."

Again, appeal to the historical situation in which Qoheleth lived casts some light on his somber assessment of human life and possibility. The distant memory of the devastation and suffering of the exile still haunted the Jewish people. It was a collective experience of their "death" as a nation, which only the miraculous power of God's Spirit could reverse (cf. Ezek 37:1-14). Now, however, they faced once again a kind of collective death as a people with the destructive pressures—economic, cultural, and political—of the Hellenistic kings.

Their unique identity as a people was under threat from the urgency to conform to Greek customs and religion. The devastating effects of the economic exploitation by their Greek rulers sapped the lives and energy of the common people. The "shadow of death" was almost tangible in Qoheleth's day, and history did not seem to hold out much hope for rescue or release. The only alternative appeared to be a mindless surrender to the pursuit of wealth and pleasure and power that provided the sole occupation of their Hellenistic rulers.

Such was the life and experience for the Jews that Qoheleth observed and commented upon. He offers his reflections and advice as a kind of "survival spirituality" for coping with these difficult times.

REVIEW QUESTIONS

assembler
collector

1. What is the meaning of the book's Hebrew name, "Qoheleth"?

2. Describe the historical context out of which the book has come. What effect did the economic policies of the Hellenistic kings have on the lives of the Jews in Palestine?

3. Describe the response of Qoheleth to his people's spiritual crisis. How does his book function as a kind of *mashal*, or "proverb"?

4. How does Qoheleth respond to the economic pressures and difficulties his people faced? How does he attempt to subvert the "wisdom" of the Hellenistic kings?

5. Explain how two complementary patterns serve to give the book its structure. What does this reveal about the work of the author?

6. Why is the Epilogue correct in referring to Qoheleth as a "sage" or "wise man" (12:9)?

7. Discuss the role that *experience* plays in Qoheleth's thinking. To what conclusion does his reflection on his experience lead him?

8. Discuss the place of God and the theme of creation in the book. What conclusion does Qoheleth reach about God's "good gifts" and the when and why of God's "giving"?

9. What conclusion does Qoheleth reach about God's "working"? How does a knowledge of the historical context help one to understand Qoheleth's conclusion?

10. Discuss the meaning of the Hebrew word *hebel* and the role it plays in the book.

11. How does a knowledge of the historical context help one to understand Qoheleth's preoccupation with "death"?

This fourteenth-century Byzantine manuscript illumination depicts King
David flanked by two women. On David's right is "the Wisdom Woman"
(wisdom personified as a woman) and on his left, "Prophecy" (also represented in female form). (Art Resource)

King Solomon appears to teach a class in this miniature painting marking the beginning of a copy of the Book of Proverbs from the Israel Museum's collection of Hebrew manuscripts. (The Israel Museum, Jerusalem)

An artist's reconstruction of Jerusalem at the time of Solomon (10th century, B.C.E.). Solomon's temple is in the upper right corner.

Wall carving shows scribes recording the booty taken by Sennacherib, king of Assyria (704-681 B.C.E.). They used cuneiform script on a clay tablet or writing board and Aramaic on a papyrus and leather roll. (British Museum)

This remarkable bronze statue of a masked dancing woman from Alexandria in Egypt measures 20.7 centimeters in height and probably served as the lid of a monumental bronze vase. It dates from the late third century B.C.E. and demonstrates the high culture and sophistication of this city, whose Jewish community produced both the Book of Wisdom and the Greek translation of the Hebrew scriptures known as the Septuagint. (Metropolitan Museum of Art)

An imaginative reconstruction of the great library of Alexandria from a
nineteenth-century engraving. It was begun in the third century B.C.E. and
was supported by successive Ptolemaic kings. Its goal of housing copies of
all the works published in the ancient world subsequently served as a model
for similar projects in later Hellenistic and Roman times. (AKG London/The
Arts and History Picture Library)

The "Pharos" or lighthouse of Alexandria's busy harbor was of such gigantic proportions that it was considered one of the "Seven Wonders" of the ancient world. This sixteenth-century print by J.-B. Fischer of Erlach (Germany) evokes something of the legendary grandeur of this architectural monument. It was constructed in 380 B.C.E., but earthquakes between the fourth and fourteenth centuries gradually brought it to collapse and ruin.

12

The Book of Ecclesiastes (Qoheleth): Selected Passages

The lively, colorful, and thought-provoking words of this book make it a delight to read and reflect on. But such an initial impression belies the dense, complex, and multilayered text that a more careful study will uncover. This chapter will only deal with some selected passages. The interested reader will discover a multitude of commentaries, books, and articles on this popular work.

THE TITLE (1:1)
AND POEM ON TOIL (1:2-11)

The opening verse identifies the author as "son of David, king in Jerusalem" (1:1). Tradition has usually interpreted this "son of David" as Solomon, David's son and successor and the patron or source of Israel's wisdom movement. The more direct intent of the verse is to set the stage for 1:12-2:26. In these first chapters of the book, the author assumes the persona of a king like Solomon who possesses great wisdom and wealth.

But first, the "Poem on Toil" in 1:2-11 introduces key themes that will form the object of Qoheleth's inquiry in the first half (1:12-6:9) of the book. Ecclesiastes 1:2 offers Qoheleth's initial assessment of the meaning and value of human activity: "Vanity of vanities . . . vanity of vanities! All is vanity." This statement, and its alternate formulation, "All is vanity and a chasing after wind," recurs a number of times both as a theme and as a structuring device in chapters 1-6. It occurs again in 12:8 to signal the book's end.

The refrain represents Qoheleth's conclusion, that he cannot make sense of or discover any value in human activity and accomplishments. This assessment of human activity will be demonstrated by the author's repeated attempts to find any "profit" resulting from human toil:

> What do people gain from all the toil
> at which they toil under the sun? (1:3)

The term "profit" (Hebrew *yitrôn*) takes its meaning mainly from the economic sphere—the results, what is "left over" or gained from a business transaction as payment for goods or services.

Next follows a poem, a kind of *mashal*, or comparison. In it, the endless movement and repetition in nature are compared with movement and activity in human history.

> A generation goes, and a generation comes,
>   but the earth remains forever.
> The sun rises and the sun goes down
>   and hurries to the place where it rises.
> The wind blows to the south,
>   and goes around to the north;
> round and round goes the wind,
>   and on its circuits the wind returns.
> All streams run to the sea
>   but the sea is not full;
> to the place where streams flow
>   there they continue to flow. (1:4-7)

The point is clear. No matter how much movement and agitation, in fact there is no progress. There is only the purposeless activity of the sun, the wind, and the water. The comparison with human life uncovers the same phenomenon, ceaseless activity with no progress or "profit":

> A generation goes, and a generation comes,
>   but the earth remains forever.
> . . . .
> What has been is what will be,
>   and what has been done is what will be done;
>   there is nothing new under the sun. (1:4, 9)

THE "ROYAL EXPERIMENT" (1:12–2:26)

In this next section the author assumes the role of a king (Solomon?) and embarks on a "royal experiment." He tests the truth of the thesis that "there is no profit" and the resulting judgment that "all (human activity) is vanity and a chasing of wind." A king would have almost unlimited resources and authority at his disposal, especially if one assumes that Solomon, Israel's wisest and wealthiest king, is meant:

Thus King Solomon excelled all the kings of the earth in riches and in wisdom. The whole earth sought the presence of Solomon to hear his wisdom, which God had put into his mind. (1 Kgs 10:23-24)

Qoheleth 1:12-2:26 contains four interlocking units. Qoheleth 1:12-15 serves as an introduction to 2:1-11. Both units end with "vanity and a chasing after wind." They describe the author's experiment with pleasure: "I said to myself, 'Come now, I will make a test of pleasure; enjoy yourself'" (2:1). A great king like Solomon would have had the possibilities to indulge in every sort of enjoyment open to humans. But does any "profit" issue from such activity? The author does admit one important discovery, the joy inherent in "toil": "my heart found pleasure in all my toil" (2:10). But it does not last. Ultimately it leaves him empty and dissatisfied. It has no lasting worth, no gain; there is no "profit" (2:11).

A second experiment is introduced in 1:16-18 and described in 2:12-26. As some great king like Solomon, the author would be free from the obstacles that beset ordinary folk in the search for wisdom. The experiment issues in two results. First, it becomes clear that "Wisdom excels folly as light excels darkness" (2:13). In other words, there is an immediate and positive advantage to wisdom. However, death negates any possibility of a lasting advantage or "profit": "Then I said to myself, 'What happens to the fool will happen to me also; why then have I been so very wise?'" (2:15).

A REFLECTION ON HUMAN TOIL (2:18-26)

The author continues with his theme of "toil." He did admit a certain satisfaction or joy from the toil itself (2:10). But now he elaborates on his arguments against seeing any permanent value or profit in such toil. There is no way he can assure that the results of his work will be wisely utilized. They may be squandered and wasted by the one who succeeds him. Thus, nothing that he leaves behind will remain as "profit." He then addresses the very practical question of how one should live when faced with such disheartening knowledge.

In Qoheleth's response we find the first of seven similar passages in which he gives positive advice on living and enjoying it:

There is nothing better for mortals than to eat and drink, and find enjoyment in their toil. (2:24a)

He acknowledges also the source of this joy:

This also, I saw, is from the hand of God; for apart from him who can eat or who can have enjoyment? (2:24b-25)

In the wider context of Israel's life and culture, this positive attitude toward the pleasures of good food and drink should occasion no surprise. Such pleasures were recognized and accepted as part of life. To disdain them or to view Qoheleth's comments as hedonism would be considered an insult to the Creator from whom these good things come.

But Qoheleth's counsel here has an ambivalence and ambiguity about it. He recommends a whole-hearted enjoyment of the pleasures that life brings—food, drink, satisfaction in one's work. But he qualifies it with the observation on God's apparent arbitrariness in providing such gifts: "To the one who pleases him God gives wisdom and knowledge and joy." Nonetheless, to the "unlucky" (probably a more accurate translation than the NRSV's "sinner"), "he gives the work of gathering and heaping, only to give to one who pleases God" (2:26).

The wider context of the book indicates that the question of "retribution" is not being addressed here; it is not a case of rewarding the good and punishing the wicked. Rather, it is an assertion by the author of God's freedom: to whomever God decides to give, God gives. Why God would appear to be so arbitrary we cannot say. Only, when the gift comes our way, we humbly accept it in a spirit of gratitude and joy.

Commentators fall into two groups in assessing the seven passages in which Qoheleth gives positive advice on living and enjoying life. Some see these passages as constituting the true message of the book, a message of solid joy in God's creation. One author indeed speaks of it as God's "imperative of joy." To "fear God," that is, truly to honor and reverence the Creator, includes accepting whatever good thing God wills to give with a humble and joyful heart.

Other commentators, however, are not so enthusiastic about Qoheleth's advice. Roland Murphy notes, for example:

> . . . it is difficult to find more than a mood of resigned conclusion in such passages. These are not recommendations that Qoheleth finds true joy in. He can only offer them in a mysterious and incalculable world: what else can one do? So take whatever joy one can find. (*Ecclesiastes*, p. 27)

TIME AND TOIL (3:1-15)

The first eight verses of chapter 3 represent the most famous passage of Qoheleth, the enigmatic and evocative poem on "time." This poem, together with the one on old age and death in 11:7-12:8, is among the more memorable passages in the Bible and has earned a place among the classics of world literature. This poem on time (3:1-8) can and often has been used and read separately from its context. There is something about the subject matter and its treatment that allows this block of verses to stand on its own. This has prompted commentators to propose that the poem had an earlier independent existence. Qoheleth himself could have written it or taken it over from some other author or collection. Thus, the poem can be dealt with on two levels, first as an independent piece with its own integral structure and message, and second in its present context as part of 3:1-15.

Addison Wright's study of the poem as an independent piece has uncovered some important insights. In vv. 2-4, constructive and destructive actions constitute the sources, respectively, of the joys and sorrows of life. Thus, according to the poem's structure, giving birth and planting (v. 2), healing and building up (v. 3) are constructive actions. They give rise to the rejoicing and dancing of v. 4. Conversely, the destructive actions of dying and plucking up (v. 2), killing and breaking down (v. 3) give rise to the weeping and mourning of v. 4.

In the poem's second half (vv. 5-8), the love (individual level) and peace (societal level) of v. 8 represent the sources of unity, solidarity, and wholeness. These are described by the embracing of v. 5, the seeking and keeping of v. 6, and the sewing and speaking of v. 7. But the hate (individual) and war (societal) of v. 8 constitute the sources of separation, conflict, and division. These are concretized in the refusal to embrace of v. 5, the losing and throwing away of v. 6, and the tearing and keeping silence of v. 7.

Qoheleth has not exploited this sense, which the poem has when read on its own. He focuses rather on the aspect of the "right" or "appropriate" time for each action described in the poem. In this way he underscores his point about the divine determination of all events: "He [God] has made everything suitable for its time" (3:11). Thus, the moment for each happening in human life is already predetermined and fixed by God: birth, death, building up, breaking down, killing, healing, weeping, laughing, and so on. Humans have no control or ability to determine when each will occur.

The passage demonstrates Qoheleth's remarkable skill at evoking a sense of human vulnerability, helplessness, and uncertainty. If this were not unsettling enough, he takes it a step further. Not only does God have exclusive control over "the appropriate moment" for each event. In 3:11 he asserts that God has put "darkness" or "ignorance" into the human mind so that "they cannot find out what God has done from the beginning to the end." God has fixed the "appropriate time" for each event. But what that "appropriate moment" is, we humans cannot know until the event actually takes place.

The unsettling times in which Qoheleth lived help to explain his observation here. The Jews were suffering under the heel of the Hellenistic kings. The exploitative economic system and the pressures on the family and tribal solidarity system threatened to tear apart their group solidarity and to isolate individuals. Qoheleth's poetry powerfully evokes the sense of precariousness and vulnerability among his fellow

Jews. He is not one to raise false hopes or shrink from the spiritual crisis his people faced. His calm and sober counsel brings them back to the basics of everyday human life. Be thankful at least for what food and drink and satisfaction God wills to give each day (3:12-13). God is all-powerful and in control. Let God be God, and show him the reverence and respect that are his due:

> I know that whatever God does endures forever; nothing can be added to it, nor anything taken from it; God has done this, so that all should stand in awe before him. (3:14)

STRENGTH IN NUMBERS (4:1-16)

In 3:16 Qoheleth demonstrates his awareness of the injustices in his day:

> Moreover I saw under the sun that in the place of justice, wickedness was there, and in the place of righteousness, wickedness was there as well.

One can well imagine the favoritism and corruption that pervaded the judicial system under the Hellenistic kings. The administration of "justice" was skewed in favor of the Greek officials and their Jewish collaborators. The subject Jewish population had no court of appeal except to God's justice and intervention. Qoheleth affirms this belief in God's justice:

> I said in my heart, God will judge the righteous and the wicked, for he has appointed a time for every matter, and for every work. (3:17)

However, Qoheleth admits that he sees no evidence of such divine intervention or even of God's awareness of the injustice.

He takes up the theme again in 4:1, where he focuses on the victims of injustice and their suffering:

> Again I saw all the oppressions that are practiced under the sun. Look, the tears of the oppressed—with no one to comfort them! On the side of their oppressors there was power—with no one to comfort them.

The repetition of the phrase "no one to comfort them" poignantly underlines Qoheleth's sympathy with the victims' plight.

Qoheleth may acknowledge ignorance of what God's response to this situation might be. But Qoheleth himself will not sit by as an idle spectator of the suffering which he sees around him. He makes at least two moves in response to the plight of his people. The first is his "numbers game," which we discussed in the previous chapter. His play with numbers here in chapter 4 and elsewhere challenges the air of certainty and self-assurance that concreteness of quantities and numbers might imply. For those whose lives center on the marketplace, quantity or the "bottom line" constitutes the ultimate criterion. From the viewpoint of Qoheleth, however, mathematics is an imprecise science. "Two" is not always and necessarily more that "one," as we have seen (cf. 4:6).

Qoheleth makes a second move in response to the challenges his people were facing. He focuses on instances in which "two" *are* better than "one." This holds true especially when it involves people working in partnership and solidarity together. In 4:4 and 4:7-8 Qoheleth describes the sad results (or "vanity") of a competitive system in which greed and envy isolate even members of a family from one another:

> Then I saw that all toil and all skill in work come from one person's envy of another. This also is vanity and a chasing after wind. . . .
> Again I saw vanity under the sun: the case of solitary individuals, without sons or brothers; yet there is no end to all their toil, and their eyes are never satisfied with riches. "For whom am I toiling," they ask, "and depriving myself of pleasure?" This also is vanity and an unhappy business.

Such were the conditions that prevailed under the rule of the Ptolemaic kings, in which all activity was oriented toward economic profit and productivity.

These "oppressors," whom Qoheleth mentions in 4:1, had both strength (the "power" of 4:1) and numbers on their side. Indeed the Hellenistic rulers had managed to attract numerous Jewish collaborators to join with them in exploiting the majority poor in Palestine. But Qoheleth suggests that these poor, and those in solidarity with them, can stand *together*. Together they can resist and survive whatever cruelty or hardship their oppressors might impose. The series of "two are better than one" sayings in 4:9-11 culminates in v. 12, in which strength and solidarity in numbers (the "threefold cord") assures success:

> Two are better than one, because they have good reward for their toil. For if they fall, one will lift up the other; but woe to one who is alone and falls and does not have another to help. Again, if two lie together they keep warm; but how can one keep warm alone? And though one might prevail against another, two will withstand one. A threefold cord is not quickly broken.

THE "BETTER WAY" (7:1-14)

The second half of the book (6:10-11:6) divides into eight sections. The first four end in "not to find out/who can find out" and the second four conclude with "do not know/no knowledge." Verses 1-14 of chapter 7 form the first of the eight sections. The unity of the section is evidenced by the repetition in v. 1 and v. 14 of the words "good" and "day" (twice in each verse) and by the twelve occurrences of the root "good" (*ṭôb*) throughout.

This section demonstrates Qoheleth's skill and training as a sage. He gathers here a number of traditional sayings. The arrangement is not haphazard. He intends to enter into dialogue with the tradition. In 6:12 Qoheleth had posed the question, "Who knows what is good for mortals . . . ?" In 7:1-14 we find a number of attempts to answer that question by traditional wisdom. Qoheleth qualifies or critiques each of the proposed responses, giving his own unique twist to the tradition.

A close examination of two passages from this section can clarify Qoheleth's intent. Verse 1a appears to be a traditional saying expressing a value judgment. The wordplay on "name" (*shēm*) and "oil, ointment" (*shemen*) is striking: *ṭôb shēm wĕshemen ṭôb* ("A good name is better than precious ointment"). By itself the saying is clear and appears to make good sense. Roland Murphy explains:

> This proverb may have been originally directed to console a person who could not afford expensive perfume and ointments for burial but possessed a greater treasure in his reputation. (*Ecclesiastes*, p. 63)

But then in vv. 1b-4, Qoheleth introduces a number of sayings dealing with death and dying. He intends, especially in the first saying in v. 1b, to counter and undercut the positive picture presented in v. 1a. He asserts that "the day of death (is better than) the day of birth." Why? Because only with one's death is a good reputation assured. Before death, chances always occur for tarnishing or spoiling one's reputation. One can, in fact, "enjoy" a good reputation only when one is no longer able to "enjoy" anything. The ironic observations that follow in 7:2-4 underline the satirical edge of v. 1b, for example:

> It is better to go to the house of mourning
> than to go to the house of feasting;
> for this is the end of everyone,
> and the living will lay it to heart. (v. 2)

These first four verses of chapter 7 thus represent a salient example of Qoheleth's subtle gibes at the self-assurance of traditional wisdom.

Another good illustration of Qoheleth's method follows in vv. 5-7. Verses 5 and 6 make observations on the advantages of wisdom over folly:

> It is better to hear the rebuke of the wise
>> than to hear the song of fools.
> For like the crackling of thorns under a pot,
>> so is the laughter of fools.

But Qoheleth takes exception to any absolutizing of such a saying with his comment, "This also is vanity" (v. 6c). He goes on to the point out (v. 7) that even the wise can be shown up as "fools" if they become the victims of extortion or deceit (the "oppression" of v. 7a); or if they yield to temptation and accept a bribe (v. 7b):

> Surely oppression makes the wise foolish,
>> and a bribe corrupts the heart.

At the conclusion of the section in vv. 13-14, Qoheleth returns to the notion of divine determination:

> Consider the work of God:
>> who can make straight what he has
>>> made crooked? (v. 13)

Qoheleth then relativizes all human wisdom by asserting, yet again, our ignorance of future happenings and our inability to penetrate the divine plan: "Mortals may not find out anything that will come after them" (v. 14b).

YOUTH AND OLD AGE (11:7-12:7)

Along with the poem on "time" in 3:1-8, this reflection on "Youth and Old Age" is among the most familiar passages in Qoheleth. The shimmering beauty of the language and the striking images have delighted and puzzled readers and commentators down through the ages. The author appears to follow a well-ordered plan. But as with so much of the book, precise meanings and references often remain elusive.

The author contrasts youth, light, and life (11:7-10) with old age, darkness, and death (12:1-7). The poem begins with the images of light and life:

> Light is sweet, and it is pleasant for the eyes to see the sun. (11:7)

This positive note is continued with the exhortation addressed to a young man, "Rejoice . . . while you are young, and let your heart cheer you in the days of your youth" (11:9a). The bulk of the poem will focus on old age and death. Thus these opening verses with their celebration of youth and its vigor become all the more urgent and poignant:

> Follow the inclination of your heart and the desire of your eyes.
> . . . Banish anxiety from your mind, and put away pain from your body; for youth and the dawn of life are vanity. (v. 9b-10)

With 12:1, the verb "rejoice" is replaced by "remember," and the focus shifts now to darkness, old age, and death. The threefold occurrence of the conjunction "before" in vv. 1, 2, 6 signals the structure of this second part of the poem. Verses 1 and 2 set a somber mood with the mention of darkness, clouds, and rains. Verses 3-5 contain a striking description of aging. The overall atmosphere and symbolism evoke a sense of decay and collapse. But no consistent picture emerges from the mix of images and descriptions. Some have tried to read vv. 3-5 as an allegory, with old age being compared to the collapse and ruin of a house, for example. But no single interpretation has managed to find a consensus.

The imagery of the final section in vv. 6-7 is also elusive. But there is little doubt that they refer to death:

> The silver cord is snapped, and the golden bowl is broken, and the pitcher is broken at the fountain, and the wheel broken at the cistern, and the dust returns to the earth as it was, and the breath returns to God who gave it.

Uncertainty and lack of clarity surround the interpretation of much of the poem's imagery. Nonetheless, commentators are agreed that the author has succeeded admirably in evoking a mood and atmosphere. He creates an attitude in the reader toward aging and especially toward death. The poem provides a fitting conclusion to a work in which the "shadow of death" has played such a prominent role.

One question remains, however. Elsewhere in the Bible, old age is viewed in a positive light. Elders were honored and respected by the young and were sought out for advice and counsel. In this poem, old age is put in a bad light. When seen against the historical background, however, the piece makes sense. The social and economic pressures of the Ptolemaic rule precipitated the breakdown of traditional family and clan networks of support and mutual assistance. In such a situation, the elderly were among the most vulnerable, isolated and cut off from the usual sources of support. In a society dominated by competition and greed, the young would have had little time or concern for the older generation. They would have viewed the aged as a drain and a burden. Such pressures aggravated the difficulties and problems of advancing years.

The poem captures beautifully that sense of vulnerability and bewilderment which many elderly must have felt.

CONCLUSION

Qoheleth offers an important and original contribution to the "wisdom spirituality" of the Bible. He takes seriously the challenges and difficulties his people faced. Especially when we take into account the historical background of his work, we can recognize his unique legacy. His book represents a kind of "survival spirituality" to bolster the resistance of his people against the domination and exploitation of their Hellenistic rulers. He does this by exposing the folly of their "wisdom" of the marketplace and its purposeless pursuit of wealth and power. At the same time he recognizes the unique opportunity that is his. He seizes the moment to provide his people with a new syntax and vocabulary to express their experience of God's presence, but especially of God's seeming absence, in their lives and history. Every age has learned and "profited" from his wise counsels.

REVIEW QUESTIONS

1. Discuss the importance of the word "profit" (Hebrew *yitrôn*) for Qoheleth's argument. What sphere of human activity does it come from? How does the poem in 1:4-8 demonstrate Qoheleth's conclusion about "profit"?

2. Describe the "royal experiment" of 1:12-2:26. What results issue from this test of "riches" and "wisdom"?

3. Discuss Qoheleth's reflection on human "toil" in 2:18-26. What positive advice does he give as a result of his reflection?

4. Describe the two different interpretations commentators give concerning Qoheleth's advice on living and enjoying life. From your own reading of the book, which one do you think is more accurate? Why?

5. Discuss Addison Wright's interpretation of the poem on "time" in 3:1-8. What aspect of the poem has Qoheleth focused on in integrating it into his book?

6. How does knowledge about the historical context help one understand Qoheleth's reflection and advice on "time and toil" in chapter three?

7. How does Qoheleth respond to the "injustices" he alludes to in 4:1? How can an understanding of the historical background be of help for interpreting his reflections on "two are better than one"?

8. How does Qoheleth qualify the traditional saying in 7:1a ("A good name is better than precious ointment")? Why, in this case, is "the day of death (better) than the day of birth" (7:1b)?

9. How does knowledge about the historical context help to explain the negative view of old age in 12:1-7?

13

The Wisdom of Ben Sira (Ecclesiasticus):
An Overview

ITS PLACE IN THE BIBLE

The question of Ben Sira's place in the Bible is a complicated one. Mainly for historical reasons, some Bibles include the book while others do not. Martin Luther segregated Ben Sira into an appendix to the Old Testament along with other so-called "apocryphal works." Luther was influenced by the decision of the Jewish rabbis of the late first century C.E. When these Jewish rabbis defined the canon of scriptures for their community they did not include Ben Sira (and the wisdom of Solomon) as a book they considered "inspired." Nevertheless, many rabbis continued to quote from Ben Sira as an authoritative source.

Other groups of Jews, especially Greek-speaking ones, included Ben Sira in their canon of scriptures. Their collection of Jewish sacred books was translated into Greek and is known popularly as the Septuagint. This was the Bible that the early Christians adopted. Thus, Ben Sira was part of the Christian Bible until the time of Martin Luther. Roman Catholics, therefore, consider the work to be part of the inspired canon of scriptures and place it among the Old Testament wisdom writings along with Proverbs, Job, and Ecclesiastes.

Most Protestant churches follow Luther and do not accept Ben Sira as canonical, though it is valued as instructive and edifying. More important, however, is the bridge that this book and the book of Wisdom form between Old and New Testaments. Ben Witherington notes, for example, that "it definitely appears to be the late sapiential material, in particular Sirach and the Wisdom of Solomon . . . that can be said to have most deeply affected the sources and authors of the New Testament documents" ("Wisdom," p. 384). Thus, both works are worthy of close study whether one holds them as "canonical" or not.

The book is usually referred to as "the Wisdom of Ben Sira" or "Sirach" (the Greek form of the author's name). Christian churches have made much use of the book for worship and instruction down through the ages. Thus, it has also taken on the name "Ecclesiasticus," a Latin word meaning "church (book)."

THE AUTHOR

This is the only book in the Old Testament in which the author specifically identifies himself, "Jesus, son of Eleazar, son of Sirach (= Hebrew *ben Sirah*)" (50:27). He belonged to a priestly family, but he himself did not function as a priest. Rather, he was a trained "scribe," that is, a man of good education, both secular and religious, who could have followed a number of careers: bureaucrat, diplomat, counselor. From his writings, it appears that he chose employment in some form of government service for most of his life. After work and/or after retirement, he operated a private school for the sons of the wealthy and influential families in Jerusalem (see 51:23).

Most of the biblical authors manage to preserve their anonymity. We know neither their names nor much, if anything, about their personal lives and character. By contrast, we know a great deal about Ben Sira, and what we know has provoked different reactions among readers and commentators.

Some modern readers, for example, are put off by Ben Sira's obvious pride in his talents and accomplishments. Others criticize especially his attitude toward women. Such reactions fail to take into account both Ben Sira's time and his culture. As a responsible and influential member of his community and a respected teacher, Ben Sira was expected to be open and explicit about his abilities and accomplishments. For him to remain silent would have been a sign not of his humility but of his foolishness.

His comments about women must also be understood against the background of the time and culture in which he wrote (see 3:2-6; 7:19, 24-26; 9:1-9; and so forth). This is not to excuse or approve his remarks, especially the more extreme ones (see 25:13-26; 42:14a). Ben Sira reflects the typical male–oriented mind-set and outlook of the ancient world.

The passages that are derogatory toward women serve as a good reminder of the need to exercise discernment and discretion in our reading and interpretation of the scriptures. We must distinguish between the wholesome and life–giving message, on the one hand, and the potentially harmful aspects of an author's time and culture, on the other. These unwholesome aspects inevitably find a place in his or her work.

Since we know Ben Sira's name and so much about him, there is an attractive *humanness* about this author. He tells us about his career and accomplishments, and his personal beliefs and opinions. Thus he is probably the most vulnerable of the biblical writers and has attracted criticism because he is so open and candid.

Certainly Ben Sira was no "saint." At the same time there is much to appreciate in the man. His book represents a solid achievement as both a literary and a theological work. It has a consistent and coherent synthesis of wisdom teaching and sound advice in attractive and often compelling form.

In reading and studying Ben Sira's book, one can clearly recognize his deep faith in Israel's God and his dedication to his people and their scriptures. One can also appreciate his commitment to his students. His desire to help them understand and value their Jewish faith and culture provided the motivation for him to fashion this work which has instructed and inspired so many Jews and Christians down through the ages.

HISTORICAL BACKGROUND

Scholars have reached some consensus on a date and place for Ben Sira. The author lived in Jerusalem and completed his work by 180 B.C.E. He wrote in Hebrew. But around 130 B.C.E. Ben Sira's grandson translated the book into Greek for the large Greek-speaking Jewish community of Alexandria in Egypt. This Greek translation represents the form in which the book was known until recent times. In the last one hundred years, portions of Ben Sira's Hebrew text have come to light. We now possess about two-thirds of the original Hebrew version of the work.

Ben Sira lived during the Hellenistic period. He completed his work shortly after control of Palestine had shifted from the hands of the Ptolemies of Egypt to the Seleucid kings of Antioch. Above in chapter 11 we described the situation of the Jews during these years. Economic conditions were grim. Many small farmers and their families were dispossessed of their properties while the rich, aristocratic families accumulated ever larger tracts of land for themselves and/or as agents of the foreign rulers. Under these severe economic conditions, older values and relationships based on family and kinship ties began to break down. Members of the same family or kinship group would be separated into different and often antagonistic economic strata. The unity and identity of the Jewish community, held together especially by their commitment to the mutual aid and support network, was under threat.

The Greek kings at first allowed the Jews to continue their own customs and religion. But they exerted subtle pressure to adopt Greek ways —Greek names and dress, the Greek language and religion. First came the propaganda. The Greeks had conquered this region and now dominated it militarily. They had established a thriving commerce. They claimed to be more "civilized" than other people because of their philosophy, art, literature, and culture. The implication was clear: adopt Greek ways and Greek "wisdom" and you also will be successful. Material enticements were there as well. Those Jews more open to Greek ways were favored with high political offices and lucrative commercial contracts.

Thus, one of the key questions facing the Jews during these years was their stance not only toward the Greek political domination. They had to contend with attempts by the Greek rulers to impose a Greek cultural and intellectual domination as well. There were undoubted benefits for Jewish culture in contacts with this Greek or Hellenistic culture, as its Near Eastern manifestation is called. However, this Hellenistic culture held a privileged position in the society. Thus, there was clear danger that Judaism could be absorbed and its basic character distorted or lost.

The reactions of the Jews to this challenge of Greek culture ranged across the spectrum from enthusiastic embrace and acceptance of Greek ways to fierce resistance and rejection of anything Greek. Between these two extremes stood many Jews confused and not quite sure how to respond. Both Ben Sira and the book of Wisdom (see chap. 15) represent attempts to give guidance in the face of this challenge of Hellenism.

BEN SIRA'S RESPONSE

During Ben Sira's time, the Jews thus faced crises on two fronts. First, the Greek rulers had imposed a series of predatory economic measures to siphon off the wealth and resources of their subject peoples. This economic regime threatened to sabotage and undermine the traditional networks of family and kinship ties among the Jews. This support system and the mutual aid strategies dating back to their origin as a people were under seige. Connected with this first crisis was a second: the subtle attraction aimed especially at the youth to abandon their Jewish culture and religion and embrace Greek culture and ways.

Table 2
Ben Sira's Response to the Two Crises His People Faced

THREAT
The undermining of traditional family and tribal ties by the predatory economic policies of the Greeks.

RESPONSE
1. Stress on building and maintaining family ties and community solidarity by:

    a. Adapting and developing teachings from Proverbs on relation-
       ships.
    b. Urging help and compassion for the poor.
2. The grounding of all human relationships in our relationship with
   God by means of the image of the Wisdom Woman.

THREAT

The attraction of Greek ways and culture.

RESPONSE

1. The use of Greek resources and materials to express Jewish teachings.
2. The assertion of divine sovereignty to counter the Greek stress on
   human reason: "The beginning of wisdom is the fear of the
   LORD."

Ben Sira was deeply rooted in his people's traditions about a liberating God who stands by the poor and frees the oppressed. He is more
direct and explicit about these roots than any previous wisdom writer.
Despite his upper-class connections and loyalties, he demonstrates a
deep compassion for the poor and unfortunate (see, e.g., 3:30-31; 4:1-
6, 8-10). He resists the domination and exploitation of his people by the
Greek rulers. In this he follows the example of the great prophets in
their call for justice and liberation.

The genius of Ben Sira lay in his ability to discern the dangers his people faced under the oppressive heel of foreign rule. In some ways his
book represents a model for any people whose life and identity come
under threat from imperial domination and oppression. On the one
hand, his work employs strategies for countering the deterioration of
family and kinship ties under pressure from the Hellenistic economic
regime. On the other hand, he successfully demonstrates the continued
viability and relevance of his people's traditional culture and religion.
Judaism would not be absorbed by the dominant Greek culture nor its
basic character lost or distorted.

STRATEGIES FOR STRENGTHENING RELATIONSHIPS

Those who read Ben Sira for the first time are often struck by the
"relevance" of the book. I have been amazed time and again at the number of students who comment on how much they enjoy Ben Sira's work
and learn from his practical advice for daily living. The book contains
a wealth of wise counsel on family, friendship, prayer, and so forth.

Much of it is as applicable today as it was over two thousand years ago. Ben Sira's keen interest in fostering and strengthening relationships continues to find a response in contemporary readers. It represents part of his strategy to counter the damage to relationships and family support networks caused by the exploitative economic regime imposed by the Hellenistic kings.

This effort to strengthen relationships includes two moves by Ben Sira. First, he takes the earlier wisdom work, the book of Proverbs, as his model. Proverbs also aimed at building and fostering ties within families and among friends and community. In 6:5-17, Ben Sira draws together isolated sayings of Proverbs on friendship. He shapes them into a longer essay on "true and false friendship," thus developing and applying Proverbs' teaching. Note, for example, vv. 14-17:

> Faithful friends are a sturdy shelter:
>   whoever finds one finds a treasure.
> Faithful friends are beyond price;
>   no amount can balance their worth.
> Faithful friends are life saving medicine;
>   and those who fear the Lord will find them.
> Those who fear the Lord direct their friendship
>   aright,
>   for as they are, so are their neighbors also.

Besides his efforts to strengthen family and friendship ties within the community, Ben Sira modifies the teaching of Proverbs on the topic of wealth and poverty. The dominant Greek culture encouraged the accumulation of wealth. It blamed the poor for their own plight and discouraged attempts to help them.

The book of Proverbs also contains a number of sayings that demean the poor and blame them for their situation. Ben Sira eliminates such remarks and emphasizes instead compassion and respect for the poor. He insists on the obligation to support and help them. He teaches that wealth can be a relative good, but not the great good that Proverbs claims. "Be content with little or much" (29:23), he advises. "The necessities of life are water, bread, and clothing, and also a house to assure privacy" (29:21).

Ben Sira makes a second move to strengthen family relationships and support networks within the community. He grounds all human relationships in our relationship with God. In this way he fashions his own version of a "wisdom spirituality." It is through the image of the Wisdom Woman that he establishes the link. She comes from God as God's gift to humans. She takes on the concrete form of Israel's Torah, or Law.

Humans accept and make their own that gift of Law/Wisdom in living out and practicing that Law, especially those laws and customs which guide and determine our relationships with others—family, friends, foreigners, and God. We become wise by living in a wise way, which is the same as living according to and practicing the precepts of the Law. In the language of the wisdom writers, this is what it means to "fear God": to "fear God" = to live wisely = to observe the Law. Thus, Ben Sira fashions a "spirituality" that guides and permeates and gives life and meaning to every aspect of their life. Practicing the Law means participating in God's own wisdom. Practicing the Law also means building and maintaining relationships. Practicing the Law thus links us at the same time with God and with our neighbor.

There was no need to learn some "higher wisdom" from the Greeks. God had already gifted his people with the fullness of wisdom in the Law, which he had given them through Moses. This "fullness of wisdom" was nothing else than the Wisdom Woman, who had come from God and made her dwelling in Israel:

> Wisdom praises herself,
>   and tells of her glory in the midst of her people.
>
> . . . .
>
> "I came forth from the mouth of the Most High,
>   and covered the earth like a mist."
>
> . . . .
>
> Then the Creator of all things gave me a command,
>   and my creator chose the place for my tent.
> He said, "Make your dwelling in Jacob,
>   and in Israel receive your inheritance." (24:1, 3, 8)

HEBREW WISDOM AND GREEK LEARNING

Ben Sira developed and expanded Proverbs' teachings on relationships as a way of countering the erosion of family and tribal ties. But he also responded to the challenges posed by the attraction of the Greek culture and way of life. As the culture of the conquerors, it presented itself as "superior" and "more civilized" than the culture and the customs of the conquered peoples. Hellenism exercised a strong attraction on many Jews, especially the young. They recognized the many positive features of Greek culture. Greek art and literature boasted of great achievements, which all could see and recognize. Greek philosophers probed the meaning of life and promoted learning. The Greeks held the human intellect in great respect: its ability to reason, to learn and investigate, to seek "wisdom." Many Jews must have questioned whether their culture and the religion of their ancestors were adequate to cope with this new world of which they were a part.

Ben Sira himself had little doubt of the value, relevance, and truth of his people's faith and traditions. He clearly recognized the danger the

Jews faced. His response to the quandary of many of his fellow Jews took two forms. First, he argues that Jewish wisdom is equal, if not superior, to Greek learning. He even makes use of Greek resources and materials to prove his point. But he recasts them into a form that is thoroughly Jewish and compatible with earlier biblical tradition.

One widely accepted parallel involves not Greek philosophy but Greek literature. Sir 14:18 represents a clear borrowing by Ben Sira of a passage from Homer's *Iliad*:

> People come and go as leaves year by year upon trees. Those of autumn the wind sheds upon the ground, but when spring returns the forest buds forth with fresh ones. Even so is it with the generations of humankind, the new spring up as the old are passing away. (*The Iliad,* 6.146-49; cf. Skehan and Di Lella, *Wisdom of Ben Sira,* p. 260)

> Like abundant leaves on a spreading tree
>   that sheds some and puts forth others,
> so are the generations of flesh and blood;
>   one dies and another is born. (Sir 14:18)

In this way Ben Sira demonstrated to his fellow Jews that the best of foreign thought need not represent a danger to their faith. Indeed it could even be incorporated into an authentically Jewish work such as his. Jews need not abandon their own faith and traditions in order to appreciate and make use of the best of Greek learning.

A second form which Ben Sira's response to Hellenism took involved the claim by Greek philosophers concerning the autonomy of human reason—human reason as a norm unto itself. To counter this claim, Ben Sira reasserts the primacy of God: the only authentic wisdom is that which acknowledges divine sovereignty. For Ben Sira, "the fear of the Lord" constitutes the sole starting point and center of the human search for wisdom. The expression "fear of God," or its equivalent, occurs almost sixty times in the book. Further, the opening two chapters (Sir 1:1–2:18) give a detailed treatise on wisdom as "fear of God." Indeed, the book begins with the assertion:

> All wisdom is from the Lord,
>   and with him it remains forever. (1:1)

A LIBERATIVE DIMENSION

Both of these moves in Ben Sira's response to the crises faced by his people contain a liberative dimension. Both represent strategies by Ben Sira to help his people survive and resist the oppressive and exploitative pressures of Hellenistic rule. On the one hand, he counters the corrosive effect of the Greek economic policies on the family and community support networks. On the other hand, he reasserts Jewish identity, the value of its culture and traditions, and the truth of its faith claims. He resists the attempts of the Greeks to impose their culture and religion as a means of subjugating and exploiting his people.

THE BOOK AS A WHOLE

The fifty-one chapters of the book constitute a handbook for moral behavior for a pious first-century B.C.E. Jew. Ben Sira compiled it mostly from his lecture notes for the young Jewish male students in his school. He makes use of the typical literary forms of the sages, especially the *mashal,* or proverb. But unlike the book of Proverbs with its collections of single-line sayings, Ben Sira's work contains large units of ten- and twenty-two-line "discourses" or instructions. Other literary forms include the hymn of praise (see 1:1-10; 18:1-7; 39:12-35; and so on), prayers of supplication (22:27-23:6; 36:1-22), autobiographical narrative (51:13-30), lists or onomastica (as part of the hymn of praise in 39:16-35 and 42:15-43:33), and "didactic narrative" (the "Praise of the Ancestors of Old" in 44:1-50:24).

The book falls into three major divisions (1:1-23:28; 24:1-43:33; 44:1-50:24), with a foreword and conclusion with appendixes (50:25-51:30). Otherwise there does not appear to be any particular order of subject matter. Thus, some commentaries provide a descriptive list of the book's contents containing topic headings followed by chapter and verse references (see, e.g., Skehan and Di Lella, *Wisdom of Ben Sira,* pp. 4-6). Two alphabetizing poems, one at the beginning (1:11-30) and one at the end (51:13-30), form an inclusion which serves to unify the whole.

THE GRANDSON'S FOREWORD

The principal access to the book of Ben Sira until modern times has been the Greek translation of it by Ben Sira's grandson. The grandson completed his translation around 130 B.C.E. in the Egyptian port city of Alexandria. He follows the classical Greek traditions in providing this Foreword to his grandfather's work. It resembles other prologues such as the one to Luke's Gospel in Luke 1:1-4. The historical information that the grandson gives has enabled scholars to assign a date both to this Foreword and to the book itself (before 180 B.C.E.). Among other things the grandson relates:

So my grandfather Jesus, who has devoted himself especially to the Law and the Prophets and the other books of our ancestors, and had acquired considerable proficiency in them, was led to write something pertaining to instruction and wisdom, so that by becoming familiar also with his book those who love learning might make ever greater progress in living according to the Law.

FIRST MAJOR DIVISION (1:1-23:28)

The opening poem on the "Origin of Wisdom" (1:1-10) serves as an introduction to the whole book. It is followed by an alphabetizing poem (twenty-two lines, equal to the number of letters in the Hebrew alphabet) that praises the Wisdom Woman and identifies her with "fear of the Lord." The twenty-two chapters that follow contain discussions and instructions on a variety of topics, including trust in God (2:1-18), almsgiving (3:30-4:6), friendship (6:5-17; 11:29-12:18; 22:19-26). The instruction on duties toward parents (3:1-16) is a passage that is cited frequently; for example, vv. 12-16:

> My child, help your father in his old age,
>   and do not grieve him as long as he lives;
> even if his mind fails, be patient with him;
>   because you have all your faculties
>   do not despise him.
> For kindness to a father will not be forgotten,
>   and will be credited to you against your sins;
> in the day of your distress it will be remembered
>   in your favor,
>   like frost in fair weather, your sins
>   will melt away.
> Whoever forsakes a father is like a blasphemer,
>   and whoever angers a mother is cursed by the
>   Lord.

SECOND MAJOR DIVISION (24:1-43:33)

Like the opening of the first major division, this second one begins with a lengthy poem praising wisdom (24:1-33). It continues with more instructions on the giving of alms (29:8-13) and table manners (31:12-32:13), among other topics. In 39:1-11, Ben Sira provides a description of the ideal toward which he strove in his life as a scribe; for example, vv. 6-9:

> If the Lord is willing,
>   he will be filled with the spirit of understanding;
> he will pour forth words of wisdom of his own
>   and give thanks to the Lord in prayer.

The Lord will direct his counsel and knowledge,
  as he meditates on his mysteries.
He will show the wisdom of what he has learned,
  and will glory in the law of the Lord's covenant.
Many will praise his understanding;
  it will never be blotted out.
His memory will not disappear,
  and his name will live through all generations.

THE THIRD MAJOR DIVISION (44:1-50:24)

The final division of the book bears the title "Praise of the Ancestors" or "Praise of the Ancestors of Old." It represents the most unified and cohesive part of the book. In eight chapters Ben Sira reviews the history of his people through the stories of its great heroes of the past.

He begins with the ancestors, like Enoch, Noah, and Abraham. He continues through judges, kings, prophets, sages, and so on. He groups them into twelve categories and deals in some detail with almost thirty individual heroes.

There is nothing in the Bible quite like this remarkable composition, which forms the final part of Ben Sira's book. It represents the first time in the scriptures that human beings are praised, and not God. Moreover, for the first time a Jewish sage has brought together the Jewish wisdom tradition and approach with the more familiar biblical themes from Israel's history—the Exodus and the covenants, the kings and the prophets.

Ben Sira has thus created a new theological synthesis encompassing both creation and history. His work mirrors the larger project that was under way among Israel's other writers and theologians in the creation of the Bible itself. The priestly, prophetic, and wisdom traditions were being linked and blended into a larger whole which described all of history, beginning with creation, unfolding under God's gaze and with God's wise and powerful guidance.

For Ben Sira, the goal of this history had been reached in the establishment of the temple-centered community in Jerusalem, ruled by the high priest Simeon II (219-196 B.C.E.). Thus, he reserves a large portion of the final chapter of this "Praise of the Ancestors" (50:1-24) for this "leader of his brothers and pride of his people" (v. 1).

A twofold purpose appears at work in this final section of Ben Sira's book. First, his people were obviously in need of consolation and encouragement in the face of the fierce pressures of the harsh Hellenistic regime. The example of their long line of heroes would serve to bolster their confidence and strengthen their hope in God's inevitable intervention to rescue them from their distress.

A second reason for Ben Sira to compose such a unique piece lay in his intention to demonstrate the continued relevance and value of Israel's cultural and religious traditions. In this section of his work, Ben Sira follows closely the form and conventions of the Greek *encomium*, or "song of praise." But for him, this Greek *encomium* form becomes the vehicle for telling about *Jewish* history and wisdom. Thus, the literary form may be Greek, but the content comes from the Jewish traditions. For Ben Sira, the example of these heroes and the ideals they represent have more life-giving potential and relevance than anything Greek "wisdom" has to offer.

REVIEW QUESTIONS

1. What do we know about the author of the Wisdom of Ben Sira? How does this knowledge about his identity and personality affect our reading and interpretation of his work?

2. Describe the historical context for the book. What were some of the reactions of the Jews to the Greek rulers' program of hellenization?

3. Describe the two crises that the Jews faced during Ben Sira's time.

4. How does Ben Sira respond to the threat to traditional networks of family and kinship ties?

5. What are the two moves that he makes to build and foster relationships within families and among friends and community?

6. How does Ben Sira adapt and make use of the book of Proverbs and its teachings?

7. How does he make use of the image of the Wisdom Woman to ground all human relationships in our relationship with God?

8. How did Ben Sira respond to the challenge posed by the attraction of the Greek culture and way of life? What role does "the fear of the Lord" play in his response?

9. Describe briefly the structure and some of the characteristics of Ben Sira's book as a whole.

10. Describe the final section of the book, "The Praise of the Ancestors" (44:1-50:24). What two purposes appear to be at work in this section?

14

The Wisdom of Ben Sira (Ecclesiasticus):
Selected Passages

WISDOM AND FEAR OF THE LORD (1:1-10 AND 1:11-30)

At the beginning of the second century B.C.E., Hellenism posed a number of challenges to Jewish life and culture. Ben Sira's book responds to at least two of these challenges. First, the predatory economic policies of the Hellenistic kings threatened the welfare and social fabric of the Jewish community. Ben Sira responds by emphasizing the importance of relationships within the family and the wider networks of bonds or connections among people in the community. The people's relationships are linked with, indeed rooted in, their relationship with their God.

Hellenism also posed a threat to Israel's faith. Greek philosophy put the human intellect at the center of its quest for knowledge and wisdom. It exalted human reason and marginalized the importance or influence of the divine. Ben Sira responded by reasserting the ancient claim of Israel's own wisdom traditions that God alone is the source and seat of wisdom. God gives humankind a share in that wisdom through the Wisdom Woman whom he bestows especially on Israel. This Wisdom Woman assumes the form of Moses' Law or Torah; by "fearing God" and following Torah, humans become wise and act in wise ways.

The two opening poems, 1:1-10 and 1:11-30, announce and develop these key themes of the book: wisdom and "fear of the Lord." Central to the development of these themes is the Wisdom Woman, in whom and through whom the most fundamental of all relationships is established, the one between God and humans.

ISRAEL'S GOD AS THE SOURCE OF ALL WISDOM (1:1-10)

This first poem, in the form of a hymn of praise, describes the relationship between wisdom, or the Wisdom Woman, and God. It draws upon two earlier poems which speak of that same relationship, Proverbs 8:22-31 and Job 28.

The Wisdom Woman alternates with God as the subject of the poetry. This underscores her closeness to the Godhead and echoes the theme of Job 28 about the inaccessibility of wisdom to humans. God alone knows her and understands her. God's creation of her before the creation of the world emphasizes her remoteness and distance from humans:

> It is he who created her;
>> he saw her and took her measure. (1:9a)

But, as Proverbs 8:22-31 also asserts, God has provided a way to her and gives her as gift to all whom he chooses:

> He poured her out upon all his works,
> Upon all the living according to his gifts;
>> he lavished her upon those who love him.
>> (1:9b-10)

Ben Sira thus affirms that the one and only source of all wisdom is Yahweh, Israel's God:

> All wisdom is from the Lord,
>> and with him it remains forever. (1:1)

God pours out that wisdom on all of creation but especially on human beings, including Gentiles, because he is so generous in giving (v. 9b).

THE FEAR OF THE LORD (1:11-30)

The alphabetizing poem of 1:11-30 follows Ben Sira's introduction in 1:1-10. This poem contains twenty-two lines, a reference to the twenty-two letters of the Hebrew alphabet. Thus, it forms an inclusion with 51:13-30, another alphabetizing poem, which ends the book.

In the introductory poem, 1:1-10, God and the Wisdom Woman alternated as subject of the poetry to underscore their closeness. Here in vv. 11-30, the Wisdom Woman alternates with "fear of the Lord" to show the relationship, indeed the identity between the two. "Fear of the Lord," that is, human response to God's initiatives of love, is equated with wisdom. To fear the Lord is "to be wise" and to act wisely. As will become more clear, especially in chapter 24, "to fear the Lord" for Ben Sira means to observe the Law of Moses.

The two poems in the opening chapter, vv. 1-10 and vv. 11-30, thus establish the mediating role of the Wisdom Woman. She forms the link between God and humans, making possible the relationship between the two. God reaches out to humans through his gift of wisdom, which he pours out "upon all the living" and lavishes "upon those who love him" (v. 10). In being wise and "fearing the Lord" in their practice of Torah, humans in their turn embrace and respond to that gift from God. All other human relationships, guided and governed by Torah, find their source and meaning in that primal relationship between humans and God.

"THE PRAISE OF WISDOM" (24:1-33)

Chapter 24 is the best-known part of Ben Sira's book. This magnificent poem occupies a central place both physically and thematically. The ancient Greek manuscripts include a title for the chapter, "The Praise of Wisdom." In fact, the praise comes partly from wisdom herself whose own voice is heard in the alphabetizing twenty-two-line passage in vv. 3-22. Chapter 8 of Proverbs, which also focuses on the Wisdom Woman, provides both the inspiration and the model for Ben Sira's piece. Ben Sira even imitates the length of Proverbs 8; both Proverbs 8 and Sirach 24 contain thirty-five lines each.

Sirach 24 continues and develops the twin themes of the introductory hymn of praise in 1:1-10, wisdom and "fear of the Lord." The same strategy is at work as well. Ben Sira counters Greek philosophy's claim to provide understanding and meaning for one's life. He asserts that the God of Israel represents the true source of wisdom. Israel's God provides that wisdom by pouring her out on all of humankind, especially on the people of Israel. In Israel, the Wisdom Woman assumes the form of Torah, or Law. Receiving and appropriating this gift means observing Torah, another expression for which is "fearing the Lord."

Torah, most often another name for the Pentateuch, contains the stories of Israel's origins as well as collections of that people's laws and customs. The laws and customs provide the framework and the means by which the faithful Jew relates to God and to other human beings. Grounding and strengthening these relationships represent one of the principal purposes of Ben Sira's work.

Chapter 24 begins by describing the Wisdom Woman's origins with God. She is one among "the assembly of the Most High" (v. 2). To this divine council (see Job 1-2) she addresses the twenty-two-line poem that follows (vv. 3-22). First she tells of her exalted nature, as one born from God and God's own word:

> I came forth from the mouth of the Most High,
>   and covered the earth like a mist.
> I dwelt in the highest heavens,
>   and my throne was in a pillar of cloud. (vv. 3-4)

In short, she represents a poetic way of referring to that grand and sublime power which pervades all of creation, ensuring its order and harmony. All who welcome this Wisdom Woman put themselves in touch with that fundamental order of the universe. In and through her they have access to knowledge and understanding of what this world is all about.

The poem then describes how God commanded Wisdom to take up her dwelling place on Mt. Zion, among the people of Israel:

> Then the Creator of all things gave me a command,
>   and my Creator chose the place for my tent.
> He said, "Make your dwelling place in Jacob,
>   and in Israel receive your inheritance." (v. 8)

There she flourishes and bears fruit, a fruit that is life-giving, which satisfies the most basic of human hungers, to know the why and where-fore of the world and of human existence:

> Come to me, you who desire me,
>   and eat your fill of my fruits.
>   .   .   .   .
> Those who eat of me will hunger for more,
>   and those who drink of me will thirst for more.
> Whoever obeys me will not be put to shame,
>   and those who work with me
>   will not sin. (vv. 19, 21-22)

Ben Sira then takes the unprecedented step of identifying personified wisdom with Israel's Torah:

> All this is the book of the covenant of the
>   most High God,
>   the law that Moses commanded us
>   as an inheritance for the congregations
>   of Jacob. (v. 23)

In other words, he makes the astonishing claim that, if one would be wise, if one would be put in touch with the fundamental order of the universe, "fear God" and follow the Law:

> It overflows, like the Pishon, with wisdom.
>   .   .   .   .
> It runs over, like the Euphrates,
>   with understanding.

> . . . .
> It pours forth instruction like the Nile.
>
> (vv. 25a, 26a, 27a)

This most original and radical innovation of Ben Sira of identifying Wisdom and Torah implies two claims. First, true wisdom is not found in Greek humanism. It is found first and foremost in Israel, and especially in her unique way of life ordered, guided, and given meaning by the narratives and laws of the Torah.

The second claim implied in this identification of Torah and Wisdom concerns the pattern that the Torah sets down for relating to God and to other humans in day-to-day life. This Torah-guided way of living constitutes also a wise way of living. Kathleen O'Connor sums it up nicely:

> In answer to the question, "How can I be wise?," Sirach replies, "Live Torah." . . . By urging obedience to Torah, he exhorts his students to obey, worship and commune with God in all their doings, at every moment of their existence. In doing so, he expands and animates the meaning of Wisdom in Israel. Like fear of Yahweh, obedience to Torah joins one to Sophia (the Wisdom Woman) and brings one to God. ("Sirach," p. 146)

In the final part of chapter 24, Ben Sira speaks of his own role as a teacher of wisdom. He sees himself and his instruction as a source of enlightenment not only to those who come into contact with him personally. Through his book, he will instruct those "far away," that is, in the Jewish postexilic diaspora (see v. 32). Through his study, interpretation, and application of the writings of the ancient prophets, their prophetic spirit is once more alive and active in and through his own words:

> I will again pour out teaching like prophecy,
> and leave it to all future generations. (v. 33)

BEN SIRA AS PROPHET

Ben Sira's book represents a major step in the weaving together and overlapping of the three major streams of tradition and reflection—the prophetic, the priestly, and the wisdom currents. Ben Sira's work is the first wisdom writing to incorporate also Israel's historical, prophetic, and priestly traditions as matter for the sage's reflection and comment. No new prophet had arisen or been recognized for hundreds of years. What had happened to that spirit of prophecy which had once been so

alive among this people? From where was God's revealing word to
come, that word which acts so powerfully to shape history and judge
human options? Ben Sira himself lays claim to that prophetic spirit:

> I will again pour out teaching like prophecy,
> and leave it to all future generations. (v. 33)

That prophetic spirit still lives and speaks through the words of the
ancient prophets preserved in Israel's scriptures. The sage studies and
reflects upon those words. If God so wills, God will stir up that
prophetic spirit in the sage's mind and heart. Thus will he be able to
"pour out teaching like prophecy." As he studies and interprets, he
makes those words to live and speak once more to God's people in his
own day through his teaching, writing, and instruction.

A twofold strategy is at work in this claim of Ben Sira. First, he
addresses his own people, especially those guilty of injustice and
exploitation of the poor and vulnerable. Like the ancient prophets, he
lashes out at those wealthy and high-ranking Jews who are caught up in
the hectic commercial life that Hellenistic rule brought to Palestine.
They violate the rights of their fellow Jews, trample on the poor, and
ignore the demands of covenant law.

But a second strategy is at work in Ben Sira's claim to "pour out
teaching like prophecy." He had recognized the danger inherent in the
perverse claim to the autonomy of human reason in Greek philosophy
—human reason as a norm unto itself. Ben Sira's purpose, then, is to
reassert the primacy of God: the only authentic wisdom is that which
acknowledges divine sovereignty.

Ben Sira thus claims that his teaching is not the result only of his own
skill. Though skill is necessary, ultimately his unique insight comes in
the context of prayer. Hence it is a divine gift rather than a human
achievement. In 39:1-11 he describes the activity of the inspired sage,
like himself, whose "wisdom" comes as gift, and in the context of
prayer: for example, vv. 5-9:

> He sets his heart to rise early
>   to seek the Lord who made him,
>   and to petition the Most High;
> he opens his mouth in prayer
>   and asks pardon for his sins.
> If the great Lord is willing,
>   he will be filled with a spirit of understanding;
> he will pour forth words of wisdom of his own
>   and give thanks to the Lord in prayer.
> The Lord will direct his counsel and knowledge,

as he meditates on his mysteries.
He will show the wisdom of what he has learned,
    and will glory in the Law of the Lord's covenant.
Many will praise his understanding,
    it will never be blotted out.
His memory will not disappear,
    and his name will live through all generations.

Herein lies the authority for Ben Sira's teaching, his claim to be, like the prophets, one who utters speech inspired by God. This is what clearly sets his teachings apart from both Greek and earlier Jewish wisdom.

TRUE WORSHIP OF GOD
AND GOD'S PURPOSE (34:21-36:22)

This section represents one of the more obvious places in which Ben Sira assumes the voice of an inspired prophet like those of former times. Their lives and writings formed the focus of Ben Sira's study and reflection. Two passages in particular echo the themes and preaching of these ancient heroes.

In 34:21-27, Ben Sira attacks abuses in the offering of sacrifice. In the first part of the passage (vv. 21-24), he explicitly condemns deeds of robbery and injustice which give one wealth. He goes on to berate in even harsher terms those who would dare use this "tainted" wealth to make offerings to God. Verse 24 in particular employs a powerful metaphor to unmask the hypocrisy and callousness of those who would multiply sacrifices with goods gained from extorting the poor:

> If one sacrifices ill-gotten goods,
>   the offering is blemished;
>   the gifts of the lawless are not acceptable.
> The Most High is not pleased with the
>   offerings of the ungodly,
>   nor for a multitude of sacrifices does
>   he forgive sins.
> Like one who kills a son before his father's eyes
>   is the person who offers a sacrifice
>   from the property of the poor. (34:21-24)

Ben Sira further expands on the culpability of those who oppress the poor:

> The bread of the needy is the life of the poor;
>   whoever deprives them of it is a murderer.

> To take away a neighbor's living is to commit
>   murder;
>   to deprive an employee of wages
>   is to shed blood. (34:25-27)

According to covenant law, the poor have a right to their portion of the "common-wealth" of the community. Those who do not share their bread or who hold back alms from the poor are guilty not only of robbery. They are guilty of murder, since that "bread . . . is the *life* of the poor."

A second passage, 36:1-22, recalls prophetic pleas for God to deliver his people from foreign oppression. Ben Sira turns his attention from individual victims of oppression. He utters a prayer for the nation as a whole suffering under the ruthless and exploitative domination of the Hellenistic rulers. The prayer follows the traditional lament form borrowed from the Psalms. It begins with a fervent cry to God for rescue:

> Have mercy upon us, O God of all,
>   and put all the nations in fear of you.
> Lift up your hand against foreign nations
>   and let them see your might.
> As you have used us to show your holiness to them,
>   so use them to show your glory to us.
> Then they will know, as we have known
>   that there is no God but you, O Lord. (36:1-5)

In particular, he prays for God to intervene speedily in behalf of his people. He prays especially for God to humiliate the hateful pride of their oppressors:

> Hasten the day, and remember the appointed time,
>   and let people recount your mighty deeds.
> . . . .
> Crush the heads of hostile rulers
>   who say, "There is no one but ourselves."
>   (36:10, 12)

Further, he expresses hope for the complete restoration of God's people to their promised land:

> Gather all the tribes of Jacob,
>   and give them their inheritance,
>   as at the beginning. (v. 13)

The prayer arises out of Ben Sira's firm faith in the God of Israel and his prophetic hope of relief from oppression. He recalls the ancient prophecies about Israel's future deliverance, and begs:

> Bear witness to those, whom you
> created in the beginning,
> and fulfill the prophecies spoken in your name.
> Reward those who wait for you,
> and let your prophets be found trustworthy.
> (vv. 20-21)

These chapters demonstrate clearly the overlap of sage and prophet in Ben Sira. He claims no *new* prophetic message from God, but a *renewed* prophetic message. Ben Sira has studied, reflected on, and prayed with the ancient prophetic texts. He trusts in his own efforts. But above all He trusts in God's renewal of that spirit which animated and guided the prophets. Animated by that spirit, Ben Sira utters prophetic wisdom, or wise prophecy, which can teach and bring meaning and hope to the Jews of his day.

AUTOBIOGRAPHICAL POEM ON WISDOM
(51:13-30)

Ben Sira's book concludes with this autobiographical poem of twenty-three lines, reflecting the alphabetizing character of the Hebrew original. The poem describes Ben Sira's pursuit of the Wisdom Woman from his earliest years and balances the poem on wisdom at the book's beginning (1:11-30). Ben Sira is obviously imitating Proverbs here, which also concludes with an alphabetizing poem (Prov 31:10-31).

Ben Sira wrote his book for the young men who came to him for instruction. He recounts his own personal story of his pursuit of the Wisdom Woman. From the beginning of the poem his remarks reflect a tension, as he describes his own intense efforts to attain wisdom. At the same time, he affirms wisdom's character as a gratuitous gift from God. Ben Sira thus had both to pursue her and to pray to God for her:

> While I was still young, before I went on my travels,
> I sought wisdom openly in prayer.
> Before the temple I asked for her,
> and I will search for her until the end. (51:13-14)

He is frank about the effort needed from his side to acquire her:

> My soul grappled with wisdom,
> and in my conduct I was strict. (v. 19a)

But he is enthusiastic about the rewards such an endeavor brings. The wisdom of Jewish traditions and culture offers greater possibilities for both material and spiritual rewards than anything Greek learning and life-style can hope to provide:

> See with your own eyes that I have labored little
> and found for myself such serenity.
> Hear but a little of my instruction,
> and through me you will acquire
> silver and gold. (vv. 27-28)

Ben Sira offers the example of his own personal pursuit of wisdom and his testimony of the rich rewards such pursuit brings. He intends to motivate the young men who come to him for instruction to persevere in their own search. Near the center of the poem comes his invitation to "lodge in the house of instruction," that is, to join his school (v. 23).

Ben Sira follows here his strategy to counter the attraction of Greek learning and culture. The Wisdom Woman symbolizes the Torah, the wisdom and instruction that the Jews' own culture and traditions provide. He asserts that this wisdom, personified in the Wisdom Woman, is able to answer their deepest needs for meaning and satisfaction. For this he makes use of the metaphors of hunger and thirst; for example:

> Draw near to me you who are uneducated,
> and lodge in the house of instruction.
> Why do you say you are lacking in these things,
> and why do you endure such great thirst?
> I opened my mouth and said,
> Acquire wisdom for yourselves without money.
> (vv. 23-25)

Appropriately, his closing words take the form of a prayer for his students:

> May your soul rejoice in God's mercy,
> and may you never be ashamed to praise him.
> (v. 29)

CONCLUSION

Our brief introduction can only touch on some of the more significant aspects of this large and complex work of fifty-one chapters. The richness and importance of the book are obvious. It provides insight into the later directions that Jewish religion followed, the overlapping and merging of the priestly, sapiential, and prophetic traditions, for example. Ben Sira's work represents a bold and creative effort to adapt the religion and the wisdom of his ancestors to a new historical situation. At the same time, he does not abandon that which lay near its center, the hope and struggle for liberation. His work as a sage allowed the voices of the prophets once more to live and to cry for justice and right living.

REVIEW QUESTIONS

1. How does Ben Sira establish the mediating role of the Wisdom Woman in the two poems in chapter 1 (1:1-10 and 1:11-30)?

2. Explain the relationship between chapter 8 of Proverbs and Ben Sira's chapter 24.

3. How does chapter 24 continue and develop the themes and strategy of chapter 1?

4. Discuss the Wisdom Woman's description of her origin and role in her hymn of self-praise in 24:3-22.

5. What are the two claims implied in Ben Sira's identification of personified wisdom with Israel's Torah?

6. Describe Ben Sira's twofold strategy in his claim to "pour out teaching like prophecy" (24:33). Who, then, is ultimately the source of Ben Sira's teachings?

7. Discuss the "prophetic" character of 34:21-36:22. Why do we say that Ben Sira does not claim a *new* prophetic message from God but a *renewed* prophetic message?

8. What is Ben Sira's purpose for writing the autobiographical poem of 51:13-30?

RESEARCH PROJECT

This project can form the basis for a class discussion or for an essay by the student.

Alexander A. Di Lella remarks in the Anchor Bible volume on Ben Sira (p. 90):

Much of what Ben Sira writes about women appears offensive to the contemporary Western reader. See the following texts . . . that deal with woman as wife, mother, daughter, adulteress, or prostitute: 3:2-3; 7:19, 24-26; 9:1-9; 19:2-4; 22:3-5; 23:22-26; 25:1, 8; 25:13-26:18; 28:15; 33:20; 36:26-31; 40:19, 23; 42:6, 9-14.

Look at these passages in Ben Sira. What would you say to someone who questioned you about Ben Sira's attitude toward women and why such texts, especially the more offensive ones, are found among our "sacred scriptures."

REFERENCES

Alexander A. Di Lella, Part 7 ("Attitude Toward Women") in "The Teaching of Ben Sira," chapter 10 of the "Introduction" to *The Wisdom of Ben Sira*, Anchor Bible, vol. 39, pp. 90-92.
————, "Wisdom of Ben Sira," *Anchor Bible Dictionary*, 6:931-45, especially p. 944.
Dianne Bergant, "Sirach." Chapter 8 of *Israel's Wisdom Literature: A Liberation Critical Reading*, pp. 166-91; see especially pp. 184-85, 187-88.

15

The Book of Wisdom (Wisdom of Solomon): An Overview

INTRODUCTION

The book of Wisdom represents a powerful example of the Jewish people's struggle to resist the almost crushing cultural and economic domination of Hellenistic and Roman rule in the closing years of the first century B.C.E. and first century C.E. The author of the book brings to his work an unusual combination of skills. First, he possesses a profound grasp of Jewish learning and a knowledge of the Jewish traditions. He complements this with a remarkable grasp of Greek learning and an engagement with the questions and issues that occupied the philosophical schools of the day.

Further, he demonstrates a deep religiosity and commitment to the God of Israel. These lead him to propose a profound, almost mystical spirituality aimed at leading the believer to an intimate union with God:

> Those who trust in him will understand truth, and the faithful will abide with him in love, because grace and mercy are upon his holy ones, and he watches over his elect. (3:9)

But this sense of mystical union with God does not remain only an individual experience and preoccupation. The author also possesses an exemplary pastoral concern for his Jewish brothers and sisters. They had to contend with the domination of the Hellenistic and Roman rulers and their exploitative and discriminatory policies. Many of the author's contemporaries faced the temptation to abandon their Jewish religion and heritage. This situation moved the author to fashion a remarkable work that combines the best of Jewish and Greek learning. In this way he hoped to persuade his fellow Jews to remain true to their ancient faith in the God of revelation while making the most of what Hellenism had to offer.

HISTORICAL BACKGROUND

In 331 B.C.E. Alexander the Great built a port city on the Mediterranean coast of Egypt. He gave the city his own name, Alexandria. After his death, the Hellenistic kings who succeeded to his empire in Egypt made Alexandria their capital. It soon became not only the political capital but also the greatest cultural and educational center for the Hellenistic world.

Alexander himself had settled Jews in the newly founded city. Large groups soon joined them, and they established themselves in one section of the city, where their numbers were said to exceed several hundred thousand. A majority of scholars hold that it was in this city, sometime in the late first century B.C.E. or early first century C.E., that the author of the book of Wisdom lived and wrote.

Because of its importance as an educational and cultural center, Alexandria attracted philosophers and religious thinkers from all across the ancient world. The presence of such a critical mass of scholars resulted in an extraordinary ferment of religious and philosophical exchange. The Greek language was the principal medium of communication. The translation of the Jewish scriptures from Hebrew and Aramaic into Greek took place here, providing evidence of Jewish participation in the rich intellectual and cultural life.

The Jews were allowed to keep up their own cultural traditions and religious practices. Nonetheless, there was pressure from the dominant culture to conform, to surrender their traditions, their language, their culture, and their faith.

This pressure increased with the coming of Roman rule in 30 B.C.E. The Romans introduced stringent tax measures, which imposed a heavy economic burden on the Jewish population. The tolerance of Jewish distinctiveness by both Hellenistic and Roman rulers varied from one regime to the next. Life for a Jew in Alexandria could be difficult. The jealousy and occasional hostility of the native Egyptians and other non-Jews added to their troubles. As Kathleen O'Connor points out,

> Judaism was an unwelcome and barbarian religion, given to exotic rituals and to the worship of a nationalistic deity. Consequently, Jews were treated as pariahs in the sophisticated Alexandrian society. They were mocked, persecuted and ostracized. This maltreatment weakened Jewish confidence in the power of their own traditions even further. ("Wisdom," p. 162)

Many Jews were thus tempted to give up their Jewish identity and religion and to adopt Greek ways and culture. It was in response to social, economic, and religious crises such as these that the author of the book of Wisdom took up his pen to write.

THE AUTHOR AND HIS PURPOSE

Unlike the author of the book of Ben Sira, the writer of the book of Wisdom does not identify himself or give any biographical data. Nonetheless, many indications in the book itself point to its author as a teacher in one of the Jewish synagogues. He writes with a very personal style that conveys a mixture of intellectual excitement and religious intensity. The book thus lacks the technical precision of a professional theologian or philosopher. Rather, the author could be characterized as a religious thinker in the mold of Qoheleth and Ben Sira, but more open to and influenced by the cosmopolitan culture of Alexandria.

This openness to the richness and excitement of Alexandria's diverse religious and intellectual currents shows itself in many ways. First, the author demonstrates a thorough familiarity with the whole of Israelite history. He also knows about Egyptian religious practices, such as the veneration of the Egyptian goddess Isis and the hymns composed in her honor as the goddess of wisdom.

But more important, he shows an understanding of and sympathy for the burning questions and eager search for happiness and fulfillment with which the variety of contemporary Greek philosophical movements concerned themselves. His response to those questions and to that search arises out of his own Jewish faith and traditions. His enthusiasm and zeal to share this knowledge and commitment with his fellow Jews, especially the youth for whom he served as teacher and guide, still evoke admiration and praise.

But he does not limit his audience only to other Jews. His invitation to share his love and devotion to this powerful and generous God extends to anyone, Jew or Gentile, who shows some openness and willingness to listen. To inspire and convince he devises a strategy that combines traditional Jewish faith with Greek concepts and modes of expression. He shows respect for and makes use of Hellenistic philosophy and culture in order to set forth his version of biblical faith in the God of revelation. His achievement in fashioning this remarkable synthesis has enriched us all.

THE BOOK OF WISDOM'S LIBERATIVE DIMENSION

One can discern a liberative dimension to the book on two levels. At one level is the Jewish community as a whole, under pressure and threatened with extinction because of the hostility of non-Jews and the discouragement and defection of its members. The book represents an example of resistance to the pressures of the dominant culture.

The author writes with great skill and creativity to defend the value and integrity of his own faith and traditions. He ensures the survival of the Jewish community within the context of Hellenism by demonstrat-

ing the compatibility of Jewish religion and culture with key elements of
the dominant culture. He succeeds in this without having to compro-
mise Judaism's distinctiveness and essential characteristics.

According to the author, one thing clearly sets the Jewish approach
to wisdom apart from the other philosophies and religious movements.
He insists that wisdom is a gift from God and not the achievement of
human intelligence and reason. He counters the self-confidence of Hellenistic philosophers and their claim of the autonomy of human reason
—human reason as a norm unto itself. He replaces this presumption
that humans can comprehend and control their own destiny with his
forthright assertion that all true wisdom is a gift of God.

The only authentic wisdom is that which acknowledges divine sovereignty. Thus, the "fear of the Lord" constitutes the sole starting point
and center in the human search for wisdom. Humans do not create their
own destiny but are "saved by wisdom" (9:18). That faith and trust in
a God who loves and gives wisdom to those who desire her are liberating. They free one from fear and anxiety about the ultimate fate of
human beings. God loves human creatures and invites them to union
with himself.

This strategy of resistance on the macro-level serves to counter the
pressures and allurement of the dominant culture. It finds a complement
at the micro-level in the spirituality of wisdom that the author forges.
He clearly affirms that wisdom is the way to God. God's gift of wisdom
establishes that bond, that union between God and the seeker of wisdom. Philosophers and religious thinkers among the Greeks also proposed ways to union with God. But for the author of Wisdom,
acknowledgment of the God of Israel and loyalty to the demands of
Jewish traditions and covenant provide *the* "wise" way that leads to
God.

In embracing this wise way or, as the author expresses it, in embracing the Wisdom Woman, one enters into loving embrace and union with
God. The author sings the praises of this Wisdom Woman, drawing
upon the Egyptian hymns to Isis, the goddess of wisdom. This, he
argues, is the goal of human existence and the way that leads to life,
immortal or "undying" life, as we shall see below.

DATE, LANGUAGE, TITLE, AND CANONICITY

The urgency with which the author writes points to a date shortly
after 28 B.C.E. when Roman rule began in Egypt. The Romans initiated
a series of tax measures that imposed a heavy economic burden on the
Jewish community. The pressures and temptation to give up the struggle and abandon their Jewish heritage intensified. The author's compassion and sense of pastoral responsibility moved him to respond to this
crisis.

The author composed his work in Greek, although in the first half (chapters 1-10) he utilized the characteristic feature of Hebrew poetry that today we call parallelism (see chapter 5 above). His choice to write in Greek prevented his book from being incorporated into the Jewish canon of the scriptures. Thus, Martin Luther did not accept it among the "inspired" books. He segregated it apart with other writings like Ben Sira into an appendix to his German translation of the Bible.

Nonetheless, the book had been included in the Bible of the early Christians along with the other writings in the Septuagint, the Greek translation of the Jewish scriptures. In the Greek Bible it bears the name "The Wisdom of Solomon." But with St. Jerome's translation of the scriptures into Latin, it came to be known simply as "The Book of Wisdom."

LITERARY CHARACTERISTICS AND UNITY

Roland Murphy describes the book of Wisdom as "intensely Jewish and, at the same time, thoroughly stamped by Greek culture" (*Tree of Life*, p. 84). He comments further: "We have an interesting example of a biblical writer who took seriously the culture of his day, while elaborating his own vision of faith" (p. 85).

So much is the author concerned to demonstrate the compatibility of Jewish faith with the best of Greek culture that he adopts a popular Greek literary form, the *protreptic*, as the primary mode of expression. The *protreptic* is a kind of exhortation that aims at convincing people to follow a certain line of action.

The author also made use of a number of literary devices popular among Greek philosophers and writers. The "flashback" represents perhaps the most striking device that the author employed to give the book its unity and tight structure. A phrase or motif mentioned in the second half of the work alludes to or repeats a phrase or motif in the first half. Today, films and television often make use of similar techniques.

The repetition of the Greek word *theōreō*, "to seek," in 6:12 and 13:6 represents a good example of this "flashback" device. The repetition of the word with its sense of "seeking God" links these two passages. In 13:6 it describes idolatry, the (misguided) "seeking" for the divine among the works of the Creator. Some people are led astray by the beauty of created things and end up worshiping the works of the Creator rather than the God who created them:

> If through delight in the beauty of these things
>> people assumed them to be gods,
> let them know how much better than these is their
>> Lord,
> for the author of beauty created them.

. . . .

> For from the greatness and beauty of created things
> comes a corresponding perception of their Creator.
> Yet these people are little to be blamed,
> for perhaps they go astray
> while *seeking* God and desiring to find him.
>   (13:3, 5-6)

In 6:12 the author affirms that the Wisdom Woman readily makes herself known to those who "seek" her. Union with her leads to union with the one true God:

> Wisdom is radiant and unfading,
> and she is readily discerned by those who love her,
> and is found by those who *seek* her. (6:12)

Scholars have noted at least forty-five similar examples of the "flashback" technique in the book, affirming both the book's unity and the astounding literary artistry of the author.

Another device found frequently in the book is the *inclusion*, the repetition of the same key word or expression at the beginning and end of a section to mark off the separate units of the work's structure. A good example occurs in the repetition of the word "righteousness" in vv. 1 and 15 of chapter 1:

> Love *righteousness*, you rulers of the earth,
> think of the Lord in goodness and
> seek him with sincerity of heart. (1:1)

> . . . for *righteousness* is immortal. (1:15)

The author of Wisdom shares with St. Paul a fondness for the literary technique of the *diatribe*. This method of argumentation creates imaginary opponents and then engages in a debate with them. St. Paul uses it to great effect in his epistles, for example, in 1 Corinthians 9:

> Do I say this on human authority? Does not the law also say the same? For it is written in the law of Moses, "You shall not muzzle an ox while it is treading out the grain." Is it for oxen that God is concerned? Or does he not speak entirely for our sake? It was indeed written for our sake, for whoever plows should plow in hope and whoever threshes should thresh in hope of a share in the crop. If we have sown spiritual good among you, is it too much if we reap your material benefits? If others share this rightful claim on you, do not we still more?

Nevertheless, we have not made use of this right, but we endure anything rather than put an obstacle in the way of the gospel of Christ. (1 Cor 9:8-12)

Similarly, the author of Wisdom addresses an imaginary audience in chapter 6:

> To you then, O monarchs, my words are directed,
> so that you may learn wisdom and not transgress.
> For they will be made holy who observe holy
>   things in holiness,
> and those who have been taught them will
>   find a defense.
> Therefore set your desire on my words;
> Long for them and you will be instructed. (6:9-11)

Although the mode of expression follows Greek literary forms and techniques, the subject matter is thoroughly biblical. In chapters 8 and 9, for example, the author focuses on the figure of Solomon praying to God for wisdom (compare 1 Kgs 3:5-15). In chapters 6-9, the Wisdom Woman from Proverbs 7-9 plays a central role. The Exodus from Egypt forms the basis of an elaborate "meditation" in chapters 11-19.

THE STRUCTURE OF THE BOOK OF WISDOM

Addison Wright has uncovered the careful symmetry of the author's work, beginning with the division into two halves with 251 poetic verses in each half. Further subdivisions of the text are marked out by *inclusions*, such as the repetition of the word "righteousness" in Wisdom 1:1 and 15, as we have seen above.

In the discussion of key passages in our next chapter (chapter 16), we follow James Reese's proposal for a four-part interlocking structure. We shall elaborate the important theme of the *immortality* of the righteous and the role of the Wisdom Woman, both of which are central to the author's message and its explanation.

REVIEW QUESTIONS

1. Describe briefly "the unusual combination of skills" that the author of the book of Wisdom brings to his work.

2. Describe the historical background of the book. What were some of the difficulties and pressures that the Jews living in Alexandria faced?

3. Discuss the purpose that the author had in mind in writing his book. What is his attitude toward Greek learning and culture? Is his work directed only at fellow Jews?

4. How does the author attempt to resist the pressures of the dominant Hellenistic culture to ensure the survival of his community as a whole?

5. What clearly sets the Jewish approach to wisdom apart from other philosophies and movements?

6. What is the way to union with God according to the author of the book of Wisdom?

7. Discuss the date and language of the work. How did Martin Luther deal with it in his German translation of the Bible? Why?

8. What popular Greek literary form did the author adopt as his primary mode of expression?

9. Describe the "flashback" technique used by the author to give his work its unity and tight structure. Can you think of any popular films that also make use of this technique?

10. Describe the literary form of the *diatribe*. Find an example, other than those cited in this chapter, in the book of Wisdom and in the letters of St. Paul where this device is used.

16

The Book of Wisdom (Wisdom of Solomon):
Selected Passages

INTRODUCTION

James M. Reese divides the book of Wisdom into four major blocks of text. Part I (1:1-6:11 + 6:17-21), the "Book of Eschatology," describes the final goal of the righteous and their persecutors, "the ungodly." Part II (6:12-16 + 6:22-10:21) focuses on the Wisdom Woman and her place in God's plan for the world. Part III (11:15- 16:1) exposes the folly of idolatry and the harm that it has done to human beings. Part IV (11:1-14 + 16:2-19:22) contains a meditation or reflection on the exodus story.

The author makes use of various literary devices such as the "flashback" to tie these four parts into a unified work. But the deeper unity results from the author's ardent desire to help his community, especially the youth, to remain faithful to Israel's traditional belief in the God who stands with the suffering and liberates the oppressed.

The author co-opts some of the best and most attractive elements of the dominant culture and makes use of them as vehicles for expressing Israel's traditional faith. In this way he undercuts and subverts that culture's power to lure Jewish youth into apostasy and rejection of the traditions of their ancestors. He shows them how they can be both loyal and faithful Jews and good Hellenists as well.

In the process he widens and deepens the expressive power of Judaism, providing it with new language and concepts for understanding and living their ancient faith, "new songs" with which to praise and proclaim their all-powerful Lord.

PART I (1:1-6:11 + 6:17-21)

This first part of the book Reese entitles, "The Book of Eschatology." The author employs the diatribe form to portray the final end of both the righteous and the wicked. In typical wisdom fashion he draws a sharp contrast between two opposing groups. The author begins by addressing the righteous as "rulers" (see also "kings" and "judges" in 6:1 and "monarchs" in 6:9). He thus affirms the dignity that God bestowed on all human beings at creation. God commanded the first couple to "have dominion over the fish of the sea, the birds of the air, and over every living thing which moves upon the earth" (Gen 1:28). The author bolsters the pride and sense of self-worth in his people who were often the object of ridicule and persecution:

> Love righteousness, you rulers of the earth,
> think of the Lord in goodness
> and seek him with sincerity of heart;
> because he is found by those who do not put him to
>   the test,
> and manifests himself to those who
>   do not distrust him. (1:1-2)

These righteous are contrasted with "the ungodly," who are destined not for life but for death:

> But the ungodly by their works and deeds
>   summoned death;
> considering him a friend, they pined away
> and made a covenant with him [death],
> because they are fit to belong to his company. (1:16)

The sharp dichotomy between the righteous and the ungodly is typical of wisdom expression and well suits the strategy of the author. The faithful Jews who pursue righteousness and remain committed to the religion of their ancestors despite the difficulties they faced are destined for immortality:

> But the righteous live forever,
> and their reward is with the Lord;
> the Most High takes care of them.
> Therefore they will receive a glorious crown
> and a beautiful diadem from the hand of the Lord,
> because with his right hand he will cover them,
> and with his arm he will shield them. (5:15-16)

The "ungodly"—that is, those who persecute God's people, be they Hellenists or renegade Jews—have covenanted with death and face the awesome prospect of God's judgment and wrath:

> The Lord will laugh them to scorn.
> After this they will become dishonored corpses,
> and an outrage among the dead forever;
> because he will dash them speechless to the ground,
> and shake them from the foundations;
> they will be left utterly dry and barren,
> and they will suffer anguish,
> and the memory of them will perish. (4:18-19)

In his bid to bolster the sagging spirits of his fellow Jews, the author clearly sets before them what lies at stake and what consequences their choice implies. Loyalty and adherence to the traditions of their ancient faith ensure life, immortal life. Apostasy will bring only unhappiness and disaster. The author's purpose is to provide a source of encouragement and hope to a weary and disheartened Jewish community in Alexandria. As Kathleen O'Connor puts it, the author assures his people: "No matter how it appears, God does not abandon a suffering people nor tolerate injustice toward the downtrodden and afflicted. The just will be vindicated because God is just" ("Wisdom," pp. 169-70).

The author further sharpens the contrast between the wicked and the righteous. He describes in almost exaggerated terms the foolishness of the "ungodly" and asserts that, "They reasoned unsoundly" (2:1). This "unsound reasoning" blinds them to the true destiny of human beings: union with God and immortality. Instead, these ungodly ones conclude that human life ends in tragedy and death. Such "unsound" thinking leads to wicked actions. Whatever is weak they consider as useless. Thus they choose injustice, and even sheer violence, as a viable option:

> Let us oppress the righteous poor man;
> let us not spare the widow
> or regard the gray hairs of the aged.
> But let our might be our law of right,
> for what is weak proves itself to be useless.
> Let us lie in wait for the righteous man,
> because he is inconvenient to us
>   and opposes our actions.
>
> . . . .
>
> Let us test him with insult and torture,
> so that we may find out how gentle he is,
> and make trial of his forbearance.
> Let us condemn him to a shameful death,
> for, according to what he says,
>   he will be protected. (2:10-12, 19-20)

Wicked

The author describes in vivid terms the disastrous results of their "unsound reasoning":

> But the ungodly will be punished
>   as their reasoning deserves,
> those who disregarded the righteous
> and rebelled against the Lord;
> for those who despise wisdom
>   and instruction are miserable.
> Their hope is vain, their labors are unprofitable,
> and their works are useless. (3:10-11)

THE HOPE OF IMMORTALITY (3:4)

Already in the opening chapter the author makes the astounding claim that "righteousness is immortal" (1:15). He assures his readers that, even if their loyalty to God and God's covenant results in death, their union in love with their God will continue beyond the grave. "Righteousness" for the author of Wisdom is another way of describing the relationship between God and the believer. The author claims that this loving union cannot be broken by death. He does not address the question as to how such a thing is possible. He simply makes the statement based on his own profound experience of love and union with God.

That relationship between God and the loyal believer is rooted in God's gracious gift of wisdom. As long as the believer does not surrender that gift, it remains. Thus, even those righteous formerly considered "lifeless"—the childless, the eunuch, the one who dies young—these also are now recognized as destined for immortality:

> For blessed is the barren woman who is undefiled,
> who has not entered into a sinful union;
> she will have fruit when God examines souls.
> Blessed also is the eunuch whose hands have
>   done no lawless deed,
> and who has not devised wicked things against the
>   Lord;
> for special favor will be shone him
>   for his faithfulness,
> and a place of great delight
>   in the temple of the Lord. (3:13-15)

Persecution and martyrdom are no longer considered obstacles to life and union with God. A message like this could not help but console and strengthen the resolve of a community under threat.

PART II: THE WISDOM WOMAN
(6:12-16 + 6:22-10:21)

The immortality promised to the righteous in Part I is grounded in their right relationship with God. This right relationship consists in a loving union with God made possible by God's gift of wisdom. That wisdom, personified as the Wisdom Woman, forms the subject of Part II.

The author's strategy operates on two levels. On one level he directs his message to the community, subverting the attraction of the worship of Isis, the Egyptian goddess of wisdom. At another level he proposes a spirituality aimed at the individual and leading to union with God. He bases this spirituality on his own experience of finding God through wisdom.

In the first of four sections in Part II, the author introduces the Wisdom Woman (6:12-16, 22-25); for example, in 6:12-14:

> Wisdom is radiant and unfading,
> and she is easily discerned by those who love her,
> and is found by those who seek her.
> She hastens to make herself known to those
> who desire her.
> One who rises early to seek her will
> have no difficulty,
> for she will be found sitting at the gate.

In the second section of Part II (7:22-8:18), the author celebrates the praises of the Wisdom Woman. He makes use of the style and even the vocabulary of popular Hellenistic hymns to Isis, the Egyptian goddess of wisdom:

> For wisdom is more mobile than any motion;
> because of her pureness she pervades
> and penetrates all things.
> For she is a breath of the power of God,
> and a pure emanation of the glory of the Almighty;
> therefore nothing defiled gains entrance into her.
> For she is a reflection of eternal light,
> a spotless mirror of the working of God,
> and an image of his goodness. (7:24-26)

The author co-opts this religious vernacular about the goddess Isis and employs it as a medium for Jewish faith expression. Again he subverts the attractiveness of the Hellenistic religious culture by demonstrating the compatibility between the best of Hellenism and traditional Jewish beliefs. Jews need not search for union with the divine and answers to the profound questions of human existence among the competing philosophies and religions of Alexandria's sophisticated culture. That union with God and those answers about life's meaning and goal are available within their own ancestral traditions. The author updates and recasts these traditions in the more familiar and contemporary idiom drawn from Hellenism.

The writer then moves his argument in favor of Jewish wisdom from the community level to the personal level. He gives witness to his own "wisdom spirituality." He describes it with compelling enthusiasm, making use of language that almost glows with luminous and passionate intensity:

> I loved her and sought her from my youth;
> I desired to take her for my bride,
> and became enamored of her beauty.
> She glorifies her noble birth by living with God,
> and the Lord of all loves her.
> For she is an initiate in the knowledge of God,
> and an associate in his works.
> If riches are a desirable possession in life,
> what is richer than wisdom,
>   the active cause of all things?
>
> . . . .
>
> Therefore I determined to take her to live with me,
> knowing that she would give me good counsel
> and encouragement in cares and grief.
>
> . . . .
>
> Because of her I shall have immortality,
> and leave an everlasting remembrance
>   to those who come after me. (8:1-5, 9, 13)

The author demonstrates the viability of Jewish revealed religion, that it is in no way inferior to the other philosophies and religions competing in the cosmopolitan culture of Alexandria. He thus provides a basis for pride and self-worth to a people despised and harassed because of their distinctiveness and resistance to the dominant culture.

Again on the personal level he witnesses to an experience of union with God through wisdom. He describes this "wisdom spirituality," indeed this "wisdom mysticism," intended to offer assurance and hope to the individual who follows his lead. In this way he inspires confidence and encourages perseverance in the struggle to live as a faithful Jew in the midst of an often unfriendly, even hostile environment.

This wisdom mysticism finds further development in the third part of this section in the eloquent "Prayer for Wisdom" of 9:1-18. Here the author assumes the identity of King Solomon, who prayed for wisdom during his dream in the shrine at Gibeon in 1 Kings 3:3-9:

> Give your servant therefore an understanding mind [lit., "wise heart"] to govern your people, able to discern between good and evil; for who can govern this your great people? (1 Kgs 3:9)

The author introduces the prayer with an acknowledgment of wisdom's gratuitous nature. It cannot be earned or acquired by an individual acting alone. It comes only as God's gift:

> But I perceived that I would not possess wisdom
>   unless God gave her to me—
> and it was a mark of insight to know
>   whose gift she was—
> so I appealed to the Lord and implored him.
>   (Wis 8:21)

He then addresses God with his request for this gift of wisdom:

> O God of my ancestors and Lord of mercy,
> who have made all things by your word,
> and by your wisdom have formed humankind
> to have dominion over the creatures you have made,
> and rule the world in holiness and righteousness,
> and pronounce judgment in uprightness of soul,
> give me the wisdom that sits by your throne,
> and do not reject me from among your servants.
>   (9:1-4)

The closeness between God and the Wisdom Woman, who "sits by your (God's) throne," repeats throughout the prayer; for example, in 9:9-10:

> With you is wisdom, she who knows your works
> and was present when you made the world.
>
> . . . .
>
> Send her forth from the heavens,
> and from the throne of your glory send her,
> that she may labor at my side,
> and that I may learn what is pleasing to you.

The author thus implies that union with the Wisdom Woman is the means by which he attains union with God himself. To be with the Wisdom Woman means to be with God.

Beginning even at creation, the Wisdom Woman dwelt with and

assisted God ("By your wisdom you formed humankind" [9:1]). That presence and partnership with God at *creation* continue and manifest themselves in human history through God's *saving acts* on behalf of his people: "People were taught what pleases you, and were saved by wisdom" (9:18).

Thus, in the fourth and final section of Part II, the author describes this salvific activity of the Wisdom Woman throughout Israel's history. He demonstrates how she blessed and saved believers who put their trust in her. Verses 13-14, for example, summarize the experience of the patriarch Joseph in Egypt. He was betrayed by his brothers but rose to prominence in Pharaoh's court (see Gen 37-45):

> When a righteous man was sold,
>   wisdom did not desert him,
> but delivered him from sin.
> She descended with him into the dungeon,
> and when he was in prison she did not leave him,
> until she brought him the scepter of a kingdom,
> and authority over all his masters.
> Those who accused him she showed to be false,
> and she gave him everlasting honor. (10:13-14)

PART III (11:15-16:1)
AND PART IV (11:1-14 + 16:2-19:22)

These two parts of the second half of the book consist of a meditation or reflection on the Exodus story (11:1-14 + 16:2-19:22) and a polemic against idolatry (11:15-16:1). Commentators generally acknowledge that this latter portion of the book of Wisdom is not as accessible or as satisfying as chapters 1-10. For one thing, these chapters do not exhibit the careful development and precise, finished expression of chapters 1-10. The difficult syntax and unclear pronoun references give the impression of an unfinished effort, as if the author added it on just before publication.

A second source of difficulty for the modern reader comes from the pedantry of the author's style. He clearly aims to impress his students and others, both Jew and Gentile, who were well educated in the subtleties of Greek rhetoric and familiar with the contemporary philosophical and religious debates. Only those with some knowledge of the sophisticated intellectual culture of Alexandria at this time could fully appreciate the complex style and literary allusions of the author.

THE POLEMIC AGAINST IDOLATRY

The discourse on the folly of idolatry in chapters 13-15 represents the most openly apologetic part of the book. The author describes four kinds of idol worship, climaxing in his description and condemnation of animal worship. This last, animal worship, provides a key reference for locating Egypt as the place of the book's composition and audience.

Wisdom 13:1-9 describes a first form of idolatry, nature worship. This consists in the veneration of the natural elements (fire, wind, water, for example) and the heavenly bodies such as the sun, the moon, or the stars;

> For all people who were ignorant of God were
>   foolish by nature;
> and they were unable from the good things that
>   are seen to know the one who exists,
> nor did they recognize the artisan while paying heed
>   to his works;
> but they supposed that either fire or wind or swift air,
> or the circle of the stars, or turbulent water,
> or the luminaries of heaven were the gods that rule
>   the world. (13:1-2)

People who engaged in this form of idolatry failed to perceive the Creator's hand in the greatness and beauty of created things.

A second and third form of idolatry ascribe divine status to wooden images (13:10-14:11) and clay statues (15:7-13) fashioned by human hands. In 13:13-14, 17-18, for example, he exposes the folly of offering prayers to a lifeless piece of wood:

> But a cast off piece (of wood) from among them,
>   useful for nothing,
> a stick crooked and full of knots,
> he takes and carves with care in his leisure,
> and shapes it with skill gained in idleness;
> he forms it in the likeness of a human being,
> or makes it like some worthless animal.
>
> .   .   .   .
>
> When he prays about possessions and his marriage
>   and children,
> he is not ashamed to address a lifeless thing.
> For health he appeals to a thing that is weak;
> for life he appeals to a thing that is dead;
> for aid he entreats a thing that is utterly
>   inexperienced;
> for a prosperous journey, a thing that cannot
>   take a step.

The author reserves his harshest words in 15:14-19 for the Egyptians who discriminate against and persecute his people. They worshiped not only material images but animals, especially such repulsive creatures as snakes:

> But more foolish, and more miserable than an infant,
> are all the enemies who oppressed your people.
> For they thought that all their heathen idols were
>   gods,
> though they have neither the use of their eyes to see
>   with,
> nor nostrils with which to draw breath.
> . . . .
> Moreover, they worship even the most hateful
>   animals,
> which are worse than all others when judged
>   by their lack of intelligence;
> and even as animals they are not so beautiful in
>   appearance that one would desire them,
> but they have escaped the praise of God and his
>   blessing. (15:14-15, 18-19)

In this critique of animal worship the author argues that such activity debases both the worshiper and the object being worshiped. Idolatrous religious practices demonstrate how "wrong reasoning" leads to wrongheaded actions, especially the Egyptians' cruel and unjust abuse of God's chosen people (15:14).

Finally, in 16:1 he makes skillful use of irony. He points out how God had made use of these creatures to whom the Egyptians render false worship as the means of punishing their perversity. This occurred when God sent the ten plagues at the time of Moses and the Exodus (Exod 7-12):

> Therefore those people were deservedly punished
>   through such creatures,
> and were tormented by a multitude of animals.

CREATION AND SALVATION IN THE EXODUS

God's intervention by means of wisdom to rescue his people from the bondage of Egypt provides the focus for Part IV (11:1-14 + 16:2-19:22). God, who created the world through wisdom, now makes use of created things to achieve his saving purpose on behalf of his people:

> And thus the paths of those on earth were set right,
> and people were taught what pleases you,
> and were saved by wisdom. (9:18)

The author thus asserts the unity of God's activity: creation and salvation are both accomplished by means of wisdom.

The author expresses this unity in a series of contrasts. By means of created things (water, fire, animals, for example), God punishes the wicked, in this case the Egyptians who unjustly persecute and enslave his people, Israel. At the same time, God turns these same created things into the means for rescuing and saving his people:

> For creation, serving you who made it,
> exerts itself to punish the unrighteous,
> and in kindness relaxes on behalf of those who
>   trust in you. (16:24)

Thus, Israel benefits from the very things that punish Egypt.

For example, the *waters* of the Nile turn to blood to plague the people of Egypt. In the wilderness, however, *water* flows from the rock and quenches the thirst of the people of Israel:

> When they [the Israelites] were thirsty they called
>   upon you,
> and water was given them out of the flinty rock,
> and from the hard stone a remedy for their thirst.
> For through the very things by which their enemies
>   were punished,
> they themselves received benefit in their need. (11:4-5)

A more powerful and subtle logic is at work, however, in the way in which the author has fashioned his argument here. By a series of flashbacks he has linked this fourth part of the book on the Exodus story with the first part, chapters 1-5, on the final goal of the righteous and their persecutors.

We look again at the contrast involving "water" in Wisdom 11:1-14. The "ungodly" Egyptians had made use of the waters of the Nile to act unjustly and murder the infant Hebrew children (Wis 11:7; cf. Exod 1:22). God now makes use of that same element, water, to punish the Egyptians by turning the waters of the Nile into blood (Wis 11:6; cf. Exod 7:20-21).

In a sense, this represents another example of the different fates of the just and the wicked as described in chapters 1-5 of the book of Wisdom. Here in chapter 11, the persecuted Israelites are "the just" in contrast to the wicked Egyptians. The same fidelity that the Lord showed on behalf of the persecuted just one in the chapters 1-5, he now shows toward Israel in the Exodus.

Further, the author has established a close, indeed indissoluble link between God's creative and salvific acts. They represent two sides of the same coin. The waters he created at the beginning he now fashions anew into an agent by which he punishes the wicked and saves the just. Thus, in saving, God is newly creating, and in newly creating, God is saving.

In *creating* the cosmos by means of wisdom, God brought order out of the primeval chaos. In *saving* Israel in the Exodus by means of wisdom, God brings a just order out of the ethical chaos of injustice. The Exodus represents the model or paradigm for the way in which God intervenes to save the persecuted and the oppressed. He newly fashions his created world into a means for saving his people.

Such a message must have had a powerful impact on the Jewish community in Alexandria. Once again Israel was "in Egypt," persecuted and suffering at the hands of the "ungodly." Once again they find hope and courage to carry on, trusting in their God, who comes to save.

REVIEW QUESTIONS

1. Who are the "rulers of the earth" whom the author addresses in the opening verse (1:1)? Why does he make use of this term?

2. Why does the author make such a sharp dichotomy between "the righteous" and "the ungodly"? Who are these "righteous" and "ungodly" in chapters 1-5?

3. According to the author, what does "unsound reasoning" of the ungodly lead to? What ultimately results from such "unsound reasoning"?

4. What does the author of Wisdom mean by "righteousness"?

5. Explain what the author means by the statement "righteousness is immortal" in 1:15. On what does the author base this claim?

6. Discuss the author's use of the literary style and vocabulary of the Hellenistic hymns to Isis, the Egyptian goddess of wisdom. What is his purpose in praising the Wisdom Woman through such means?

7. What is the author's purpose in describing his own "wisdom spirituality" in 7:22-8:18?

8. Whose identity does the author assume in the "Prayer for Wisdom" of chapter 9?

9. Discuss the relationship of the Wisdom Woman with God and her role in God's creating and saving activity.

10. Describe the four kinds of idol worship found in chapters 13-15. Why does the author reserve his harshest criticism for those who worship animals?

11. How does the author express the unity of God's creating and saving activity in chapters 16-19?

12. Explain how the author links chapters 16-19 with chapters 1-5 by means of flashbacks.

13. With whom are "the righteous" and "the ungodly" of chapters 1-5 identified here in chapters 16-19? What does this imply about God's saving purpose? Why would this message be important to the Jewish community in Alexandria?

17

Wisdom Outside the "Wisdom Books"

INTRODUCTION

The predominantly didactic intent of the five books we have studied in detail sets them apart from the rest of the scriptures. Among the principal aims of the author in each of them is to teach and to instruct. In addition, the writers make use of the literary forms usually associated with wisdom in the ancient world. The book of Job, for example, follows the conventions of a "wisdom dispute," and the book of Proverbs consists in collections of wise sayings. Thus, these five books constitute the "wisdom literature" of the Bible as such.

Nevertheless, a number of passages outside these wisdom books employ wisdom expressions or deal with themes commonly associated with the wisdom movement. For example, in his critical analysis of the psalter, Hermann Gunkel identified a number of what he called "wisdom psalms." In addition, one finds the prophets sometimes making use of wisdom forms and themes. Finally, the rabbis who compiled the Hebrew Bible included the Song of Solomon (or "Song of Songs," "Canticle") among the wisdom books, and some scholars identify it as an example of wisdom writing. What are we to make of these texts: the Song of Solomon, the wisdom psalms, and the other wisdom passages? How are we to understand them in relation to the five wisdom books as such?

WISDOM PSALMS

Most commentators admit the presence in the Psalter of a small group of "wisdom psalms." They argue that these few psalms come from the hands of wisdom writers, since they reflect wisdom themes and terminology. Scholars have reached some consensus that at least Psalms 1, 32, 34, 37, 49, 112, and 128 represent examples of religious poetry that had its origins in wisdom circles. Other psalms also contain wisdom expressions and themes and thus demonstrate contacts with the wisdom movement, for example, Psalms 19, 73, 111, 119, 127, 133.

The criteria for identifying such wisdom psalms or at least wisdom influence on a psalm include: (1) the recognition of wisdom forms or ways of expression; and (2) the presence of wisdom themes and concerns. The most obvious formal feature is that these psalms are not addressed to God in prayer or praise but to other people, the "simple" and the unlearned. This manner of address suggests that instruction rather that worship forms the focus of these poems. They invite people to listen and learn but not necessarily to pray.

Literary characteristics associated with the wisdom tradition occur frequently, such as "better" sayings (Pss 37:16; 119:72); numerical sayings (Ps 1:6); the "blessing" formula ("How happy . . ."; see Pss 1:1; 112:1; 119:1, 2; 127:5; 128:1, 2); rhetorical questions (Ps 49:6); the address of a teacher to a "son" (Ps 37:1, 8); comparison (Pss 1:3, 4; 37:2, 20; 40:12, 14, 20; 127:4). The alphabetic acrostic structure also characterizes some of these psalms, for example, Psalms 34, 37, 111, 112, 119. In these poems the sequence of letters in the Hebrew alphabet determines the initial letter of the first word in successive lines or half-lines. This feature may reflect a school or teaching environment and the use of the alphabet as a memory device.

Besides the use of typical wisdom vocabulary and expressions, this group of psalms contains familiar wisdom themes. These include the "two ways," the way of the righteous and the way of the wicked (see Ps 1:6), and preoccupation with the problem of retribution (Pss 49, 73). The Torah, or Law of Moses, as a focus of prayerful meditation (see Pss 1, 119) and the mention of "the fear of the LORD" (Ps 34:7, 9, 11) also reflect the influence of the wisdom movement.

Psalm 112 represents a good example of the wisdom psalm genre. The use of the alphabetic acrostic device determines its structure and furnishes an important clue to the poet's interest in learning and "writing." The psalm does not open by addressing God as a prayer would. Rather, it begins with the "blessing" formula, a typical wisdom mode of expression:

> Happy are those who fear the LORD,
>   who greatly delight in his commandments.

It goes on to describe the rewards offered to the just. Thus, it functions implicitly as an admonition:

> Their descendants will be mighty in the land;
>   the generation of the upright will be blessed.
> Wealth and riches are in their houses,
>   and their righteousness endures forever. (112:2-3)

Further, the psalm contrasts the fate of "the just" and "the wicked" (v. 10) and makes mention of "the fear of the LORD" (v. 1).

ℹThe obviously didactic intent of the psalm raises the question as to why wisdom poems such as this one are found in the Psalter, a collection of songs intended for use in public worship. An answer comes if we can imagine how worship took place in the ancient shrines and temple. Undoubtedly there were moments when some instruction took place. The people were reminded of their covenant obligations and encouraged to faithful observance. A poem such as Psalm 112, sung by a choir or recited by a levite, could represent an example of such instruction. Note, for example, how it focuses on the covenant stipulations and provides motivation for faithful obedience:

> It is well with those who deal generously and lend,
>   who conduct their affairs with justice.
> . . . .
> They have distributed freely, they have
>   given to the poor;
>   their righteousness endures forever;
>   their horn is exalted in honor. (Ps 112:5, 9)

The psalm represents a good example of the spirituality that informed and undergirded the efforts of the Israelites to build and foster a just and life-giving community. Dianne Bergant comments concerning this psalm:

> The one who fears the LORD is generous, gracious, merciful, and just, all descriptive of social virtues. Just as God has showed special favor to Israel, so the one described here excels in concern for others. ("Psalms," p. 62)

Such poetry may not have the immediacy and poignancy of the preaching of the prophets against oppression and injustice. Nonetheless, psalms such as this one offered support, encouragement, and inspiration for one trying to live in accord with the covenant demands. These psalms represent firsthand contact with the words, phrases, and ideas that served to nourish the daily devotion and spiritual life of the faithful.

Once again we can turn to the work of the Nicaraguan poet Ernesto Cardenal. He has translated some of these wisdom psalms into a contemporary idiom. His versions of these psalms demonstrate well the kind of power this poetry can take on in situations of injustice and oppression.

Cardenal's translation of Psalm 19 offers a good example. The psalm implies the intimate link between creation and the Torah. It suggests parallels between the laws governing nature and the universe, on the one hand, and the Law of Moses, on the other. The order and regularity of nature mirror the just and wise order which the Torah brings to human life and society:

The Galaxies Sing the Glory of God
(Psalm 19)

The galaxies sing the glory of God
   and Arcturus 20 times larger than the sun
and Antares 487 times more brilliant than the sun
Dorado Sigma with a brightness of 300,000 suns
and Orion Alpha which is equal
      to 27,000,000 suns
Aldebaran with its diameter of 32 million miles
   Lyra Alpha 300,000 light years away
and the nebula of Boyer
     200 million light years away
all announce the work of your hand

His language is a language without words
(and not like the platitudes of politicians)
   but it is not a language that IS NOT HEARD
Galaxies send out mysterious radio signals
the cold hydrogen from interstellar spaces
is filled with visual waves and musical waves
In the intergalactic vacuums there are magnetic fields
that sing in our radio telescopes
(and perhaps there are civilizations
      transmitting messages
to our radio antennas)
There are a billion galaxies in the explorable universe
turning like carousels
    or like musical tops . . .
The sun describes a gigantic orbit
around the constellation Sagittarius
   —he is like a bridegroom who leaves his wedding bed
and travels surrounded by his planets at 45,000 miles per hour
toward the constellations of Hercules and Lyra
(and takes 150 million years to make his circle)
and does not deviate an inch from his orbit

The Law of the Lord stills the subconscious
    it is as perfect as the law of gravity
its words are like the parabola of comets
its decrees like the centrifugal spin of galaxies

its precepts are the precepts of the stars
that eternally remain fixed in their positions
                    and their speeds
                                    and their respective distances
and cross one another's route a thousand times
                                    and never collide
The judgments of the Lord are just
                    and not like propaganda
and worth more than dollars
                    and stocks and bonds
Keep me from the arrogance of money and political power
and I will be free of all crime
          and major offense
And may the words of my poems be pleasing to you
                              Lord
                                    my Liberator

THE SONG OF SOLOMON
("SONG OF SONGS" OR "CANTICLE")

The love poetry that forms the content of the Song of Solomon (or "Canticle") deals with matter quite different from the usual themes and topics of the other wisdom literature. How has it come to be considered by some as a "wisdom" book?

Both Jewish and Christian traditions have read this work as belonging among the wisdom writings. The first verse or title mentions Solomon, the traditional patron and founder of the wisdom movement: "The Song of Songs, which is Solomon's." Moreover, the Jewish rabbis who compiled the Hebrew Bible included it among the other books also associated with Solomon—Proverbs and Ecclesiastes.

A close reading of the text reveals some indications of wisdom connections. The book contains a collection of perhaps thirty poems or songs celebrating the mutual love of man and woman in verse that is rich in imagery and erotic power. The two lovers describe their experience of love and elaborate on the joys and pleasures of the sexual expression of that love without any shame or apology:

You have ravished my heart, my sister, my bride,
    you have ravished my heart with a glance of
        your eyes,
    with one jewel of your necklace.
How sweet is your love, my sister, my bride!
    how much better is your love than wine,
    and the fragrance of your oils than any spice!

> Your lips distill nectar, my bride;
>   honey and milk are under your tongue;
>   the scent of your garments is like the scent of
>   Lebanon. (Cant 4:9-11; see also 5:2-6)

We can imagine the sages who fashioned this book in its final form. They were anxious to provide teaching and instruction on the place of love and marriage in God's plan for creation. The author or authors assembled this collection of love poems, or perhaps reworked an already existing collection. The poems offer a perspective on love and marriage not found elsewhere in the scriptures. Other biblical books deal with marriage and relations between the sexes from a social point of view—the bonds among families, questions of inheritance and property, and descendants. By contrast, the poetry of the Canticle emphasizes the personal aspects of marriage. It focuses on fidelity and mutuality in love between the sexes. These concerns formed part of the wisdom teaching and figured prominently in the training of youth. See, for example, in Proverbs:

> Drink water from your own cistern,
>   flowing water from your own well.
>
> . . . .
>
> Let your fountain be blessed,
>   and rejoice in the wife of your youth,
>   a lovely deer, a graceful doe.
> May her breasts satisfy you at all times;
>   may you be intoxicated always by her love.
> Why should you be intoxicated, my son, by another
>   woman
>   and embrace the bosom of an adulteress?
>   (Prov 5:15, 18-20)

The Canticle thus offers a kind of personal spirituality of love and sexuality. Such a spirituality would give support and encourage loyalty to ideals about marriage and relations between the sexes that were viewed as important by the wisdom teachers.

A further connection exists between the Canticle and other wisdom books. We have seen how Proverbs, Ben Sira, and the book of Wisdom describe the quest for wisdom as a quest for "the beloved," the Wisdom Woman. The authors make use of language and imagery drawn from the experience of human love to describe their pursuit of the Wisdom Woman. Ben Sira, for example, tells his students, "When you get hold of her, do not let her go" (Sir 6:27). So also, the woman in the Song finds her lover and will not let him go:

> Scarcely had I passed them (the sentinels),
>   when I found him whom my soul loves.
> I held him, and would not let him go
>   until I brought him into my mother's house,
>   and into the chamber of her that conceived me.
> (Cant 3:4)

The use of the same language and imagery for human love in the Canticle and for the love and pursuit of the Wisdom Woman in these other wisdom books raises an important question. Are the sages suggesting a link, an overlap between the two—human love and the love of God? Are the love and pursuit of Wisdom, and ultimately the God who is the source of wisdom, somehow bound up with that love between man and woman?

The closing chapter of the Canticle, chapter 8, provides further insight. In this chapter, a shift occurs in the manner of expression. No longer do we hear the lovers addressing each other. The tone is more didactic and wisdom-like. Canticle 8:6-7 contains a series of four proverbs commenting on the mysterious power that God has given to love. Verse 6 in particular is suggestive:

> For love is strong as death,
>   passion fierce as the grave.
> Its flashes are flashes of fire,
>   a raging flame [lit., "a flame of Yah(weh)"].

The phrase, "a raging flame," is a superlative produced by combining the word for "flame" in Hebrew with a form of the divine name, "Yahweh" ("Yah"). Roland Murphy proposes that this phrase

> expresses a relationship between the flames of human and the flames of divine love. One cannot define this more clearly, as though Yah(weh) were the agent or origin of the flame. But the text is susceptible to broad interpretation, even to the idea that human love is in some way a participation in divine love (cf. 1 John 4:7-8). (*Anchor Bible Dictionary*, 6:154)

THE SONG OF SOLOMON ("CANTICLE") AND LIBERATION

Women who read the scriptures would probably be more alert to the liberationist potential of the Canticle. In other parts of the Bible, human sexuality, and female sexuality in particular, is subject to careful supervision and control. The freedom and mutuality of the Canticle's expression and its celebration of the joys and pleasures of love between man and woman stand in sharp contrast. In addition, the prominence of the woman in the Song sets this work apart from other biblical books. The majority of the verses are spoken by the woman. Further, nowhere else in scripture are the thoughts and yearnings, the words and imaginations of a woman given such importance as in the Song. With its acceptance into the canon of scripture the book provides a powerful legitimation of woman's voice as a source of religious insight.

Renita Weems offers some further suggestions regarding the liberative potential of the book. She indicates a number of places in the text where the lovers appear to be acting against social norms. These include, for example, restrictions or prohibitions on marriage between certain class, ethnic, or economic groups. Weems also notes the mention of the woman's dark complexion in Canticle 1:5-6:

> I am black and beautiful,
> O daughters of Jerusalem,
> like the tents of Kedar,
> like the curtains of Solomon.
> Do not gaze at me because I am dark,
> because the sun has gazed on me.

This may suggest class or racial differences between the lovers and point to social norms prohibiting contact between the two.

Nonetheless, the lovers insist again and again on their right to love each other despite such prohibitions. The poetry of the Song thus contains an implicit critique of such arbitrary boundaries. It affirms the basic human right of women and men to have a say in the choice of their marriage partner.

Further, Weems indicates how the Song functions within the canon as a critique of the scriptures themselves. It serves to counterbalance stories "where women are penalized and scandalized for their sexuality, confined to procreation without fulfilling sex, and forgotten because of their submission to repressive gender roles":

> The Song of Songs advocates a balance in female and male relationships, urging mutuality not domination, interdependence not enmity, sexual fulfilment not mere procreation, uninhibited love not bigoted emotions. ("Song of Songs," p. 160)

Although not a wisdom work in the usual sense of the word, the Canticle clearly reflects the concerns of the wisdom movement. This holds true especially if one understands wisdom teaching as resulting mainly from reflection on experience. According to the Canticle, human love represents the most powerful experience of life. Thus, there is much to learn from reflection on it.

FURTHER EVIDENCE OF CONTACTS WITH WISDOM

In recent years, scholars have noted wisdom vocabulary and themes in still other parts of the Bible in addition to the Song of Songs ("Canticle") and the "wisdom psalms." The creation story in Genesis 2 and 3, for example, mentions "the tree of the knowledge of good and evil" (Gen 2:17). Its fruit was able "to make one wise" (3:6). In addition, chapters 47-50 of Genesis focus on the ancestor figure Joseph. These chapters describe his maturation from a foolish youth to a shrewd and trusted member of Pharaoh's court in Egypt. Pharaoh praises Joseph as a "discerning and wise" counselor (Gen 41:39). Some scholars thus refer to the tale as a "didactic wisdom story." It presents Joseph as an example of one whom God has guided and gifted with wisdom.

The prophets also show contacts with wisdom. The use by the prophets and sages of similar literary forms represents the most obvious example. We have already seen in chapter 6 how the prophet Nathan indicts David for his adultery and murder by means of a parable (2 Sam 12:1-5). However, Nathan makes use of the parable not to instruct but to pronounce God's judgment and call David to repentance.

The prophet Isaiah also employs the parable form in the "parable of the vineyard" in Isaiah 5:1-7 and "the parable of the farmer" in 28:33-29. Again, in both cases, the intent of the prophet is not to instruct but to pronounce judgment and implicitly to call to repentance:

> For the vineyard of the LORD of hosts
> > is the house of Israel,
> and the people of Judah
> > are his pleasant planting;
> he expected justice,
> > but saw bloodshed;
> righteousness,
> > but heard a cry! (5:7)

Amos represents another prophetic book that makes use of literary forms usually found also in the wisdom books. In chapters 1 and 2 of Amos a series of eight oracles appears. Each of the oracles begins with the "three/four" formula. This construction is found nowhere else in the Old Testament except in the wisdom books:

> Thus says the LORD:
> For three transgressions of Edom,
> > and for four, I will not revoke the punishment;
> because he pursued his brother with the sword
> > and cast off all pity;

he maintained his anger perpetually,
    and kept his wrath forever.
So I will send a fire on Teman,
    and it shall devour the strongholds of Bozrah.
                    (Amos 1:11-12)

Compare the "numerical sayings" of Proverbs 30. Amos also uses the riddle, in 6:12, and a "better than" proverb in 6:2:

Cross over to Calneh, and see;
    from there go to Hamath the great;
    then go down to Gath of the Philistines.
Are you better than these kingdoms?
    Or is your territory greater than their territory?

How does one account for these "echoes" of wisdom in the Old Testament outside the wisdom books as such? It is not a matter of wisdom writers influencing prophets or the authors of the historical books. Nor is it the other way around, prophets influencing sages, for example. Rather, those responsible for these writings, be they prophet, sage, or history writer, possessed a fair degree of education and training. As such, they participated in a common culture and shared a world of ideas, concerns, and modes of expression. One would thus expect some themes, motifs, and literary forms to appear across the entire spectrum of Israel's literary output.

REVIEW QUESTIONS

1. What are the criteria that scholars use for identifying "wisdom influence" on a psalm? Describe some of the literary characteristics these psalms have in common with the so-called "wisdom books."

2. What are some of the familiar wisdom themes and concerns echoed in these wisdom psalms?

3. Why would such wisdom poems be included in a collection of songs used in public worship?

4. Read Psalm 1 and point out some of the features that have led scholars to include it among the "wisdom psalms."

5. What are some of the factors that point to a relationship between the Song of Solomon and the wisdom tradition?

6. What sets the Song of Solomon apart from the other biblical books in the treatment of marriage and the relationship between the sexes? Why would this aspect of the Song be of interest to the sages?

7. What is the relationship between the personification of wisdom as a woman in the "wisdom books" and the language of love in the Song? Discuss the possible importance of Canticle 8:6 with regard to the relationship between human love and the love of God.

8. Describe the prominence of woman in the Song and its importance for a liberationist reading of the book. Discuss the significance of the mention of the woman's color in Canticle 1:5-6.

9. What other evidence is there of contacts between the wisdom tradition and the other biblical books, the book of Genesis, for example?

10. What are some of the literary forms typical of the wisdom tradition that have been "borrowed" by the prophets? What is the difference between the wisdom writers' use of these forms and the purpose for which the prophets make use of them?

11. How might one account for these "echoes" of wisdom outside the wisdom books as such?

18

Old Testament Wisdom and the New Testament

INTRODUCTION

In chapters 15 and 16 we looked at the book of Wisdom. The time of that book's writing, the late first century B.C.E. or early first century C.E., overlaps with the New Testament period. In other words, the wisdom movement was alive and flourishing among the Jews during the lifetime of Jesus and the early Christian community. Thus, it comes as no surprise to see the profound impact of this movement on the authors and writings of the New Testament.

Indeed, a familiarity with the wisdom writings of the Old Testament helps one to read the New Testament with new and enlightened eyes. Wisdom's influence in the New Testament is pervasive and touches almost every aspect of these early Christian writings. Wisdom's influence can be seen as well in the person and teachings of the central figure of the New Testament, Jesus Christ.

JESUS AS A WISDOM TEACHER

Jesus of Nazareth presented himself principally as an eschatological prophet, one whose life and words challenged the pervasive injustices of the society of his day. He implicitly called into question the legitimacy of the brutal and exploitative Roman rule. His words and presence constituted a threat to those Jews who collaborated with the Roman authorities. Jesus called his contemporaries to a "change of heart" or "renewal of outlook" (*metanoia*). He claimed that in his person and proclamation the rule of God was breaking into history in a final and definitive way. He was inaugurating a new stage in the history of God's dealings with humankind.

But there is another side of Jesus, another aspect of his life and career.

In the Gospels we see Jesus also as a teacher, in fact, a wisdom teacher very much in the mold of another sage whom we have studied, Ben Sira.

These two different ways of viewing and describing the person and activity of Jesus, as a prophet and as a sage, do not contradict each other. Rather, they complement each other, giving a more rounded picture of the life and ministry of Jesus. They help to explain the impact he had on his followers. Recognizing this double aspect of his life and career, as sage and as prophet, allows us to understand the richness and diversity of the tradition he inspired.

In this section we investigate especially the wisdom side of Jesus. His person and thinking were deeply rooted in the wisdom movement, which we have been following and which stretches back to the origins of the biblical tradition. Above in chapter 6 we saw how prophets took over and expanded the basic wisdom form, the *mashal* or "comparison," into the narrative parable form. This "comparison" by means of a story suited well the strategy of the prophets. It allowed them to challenge the injustices of the present order and implicitly to call for a more fair and just counterorder.

The prophet Nathan's parable in 1 Samuel 12:1-5 exposed the ruthless pride and callousness of David in his double sin of adultery and murder. Jesus' parable of the Good Samaritan revealed the hypocrisy and narrow-mindedness of the religious leaders of his day. Implicit in both parables is a worldview at odds with the actions and institutions these prophets judged as unjust. Theirs was a worldview informed by God's righteousness and wisdom.

But the wisdom connections of Jesus go beyond simply that of a prophet adapting the literary forms of the wisdom movement. Jesus presented himself also as a sage, a wisdom teacher with perhaps the closest parallels in Ecclesiastes and Ben Sira. The similarities with Ben Sira offer the most striking parallels. In Ben Sira, the various streams of the biblical traditions were clearly beginning to overlap.

Ben Sira, for example, was the first wisdom writer who explicitly made use of Israel's historical traditions. Ben Sira also claimed to speak with prophetic authority. The same spirit that had inspired the ancient prophets now inspired his interpretation of their prophecies. Thus, his teaching, his wisdom, ultimately came from God, a revealed wisdom and renewed prophetic word.

Jesus appears to be a continuation and development of this understanding of the role and activity of the sage. Jesus also taught "with authority" (Mark 1:27; Matt 7:29; Luke 4:32). His parables and counsels walk a fine line between wisdom teaching based on observation and reflection on the one hand ("the birds of the air . . . the lilies of field" [Matt 6:26, 28]), and revealed wisdom and prophecy on the other. One can see this revelatory aspect of Jesus' teaching in Matthew 11:25-30; in v. 27, for example, Jesus says:

All things have been handed over to me by my Father; and no one knows the Son except the Father, and no one knows the Father except the Son and anyone to whom the Son chooses to reveal him.

Ben Witherington offers a number of striking parallels both in form and content between the work of Ben Sira and the Jesus tradition (*Jesus the Sage,* pp. 143-44). Compare, for example, Sirach 29:11 and Matthew 6:19:

Lay up your treasure according to the commandments of the Most High, and it will profit you more than gold. Store up almsgiving in your treasury, and it will rescue you from every disaster. (Sir 29:11)

Do not store up for yourselves treasures on earth, where moth and rust consume . . . but store up for yourselves treasures in heaven. (Matt 6:19)

See also Sirach 23:9 and Matthew 5:34:

Do not accustom your mouth to oaths, nor habitually utter the name of the Holy One. (Sir 23:9)

But I say to you, Do not swear at all, either by heaven, for it is the throne of God, or by the earth for it is his footstool. (Matt 5:34)

Thus, there appear to be striking similarities between Jesus and Ben Sira in their teaching and in their common understanding of the role and authority of the teacher.

But a closer inspection of the two reveals also some differences. First, Ben Sira's teaching does not pose any threat or challenge to the status quo. He is a respected and learned scribe. Any change in the way things are would undermine his own secure place in the social and religious hierarchies of the postexilic Jewish world.

Jesus, by contrast, was not a member of the scribal class like Ben Sira. Jesus claimed no special skill or training in the study and interpretation of the Torah. He was from a lower strata of society and had chosen a more popular audience. When he did address the wealthy and powerful, it was often to criticize their values, especially the emphasis placed on accumulating wealth:

No one can serve two masters; for a slave will either hate the one and love the other, or be devoted to the one and despise the other. You cannot serve God and wealth. (Matt 6:24//Luke 16:13; see also Luke 12:16-21)

This contrasting "social location" of the two is apparent in their attitude toward the "conventional wisdom" that confirmed the status quo.
Ben Sira's proverbs preserved and propagated traditional wisdom, while
Jesus' sayings challenged it. Jesus' wisdom presupposed an alternative
image of society, an alternative paradigm for behavior. The conventional wisdom of his day proposed purity or holiness as standards for
determining behavior:

> Now when the Pharisees and some of the scribes who had come
> from Jerusalem gathered around him, they noticed that some of
> his disciples were eating with defiled hands, that is, without wash-
> ing them. . . . So the Pharisees and scribes asked him, "Why do
> your disciples not live according to the tradition of the elders, but
> eat with defiled hands?" (Mark 7:1-2, 5)

For Jesus, it was not purity or holiness. For him, compassion represented the bottom line, the ultimate criterion in determining the way
one should live: "Be compassionate, even as God is compassionate" (see
Luke 6:36//Matt 5:48). Be compassionate like the father who welcomed
back with open arms his prodigal son (Luke 15:20). Be compassionate
like the Samaritan who showed pity to the victim of the robbers' violence on the road to Jericho (Luke 10:33).

The voice of Jesus echoes with a uniqueness and an originality that
are clearly recognizable in the traditions about him and in his teachings
preserved in the Gospels. His was a "popular wisdom," and he, a sage
"from below." He demonstrates in a striking way the liberating potential of proverb and parable, which we pointed out above in chapter 6.
The strategy of Jesus in proposing his counterorder through story and
wisdom sayings represents a strategy for liberation, a strategy for life,
life with God in a just and life-giving community.

One sees a good example of this counterorder in the many parables
of Jesus about meals and banquets and in his own practice of dining
with all types of people, high and low, saint and sinner. Jesus claims that
his openness and welcome to everyone reflect and reveal the all-
inclusive love of God, who accepts everyone and grants blessing and
well-being to all.

Kathleen O'Connor, among others, traces this banquet imagery and
this teaching about God's inclusive love and goodness back to the sages
of the Old Testament and their description of the Wisdom Woman:

> These are the characteristics of the Creator God, the Sophia-God
> of the wisdom traditions. Jesus' announcement of the rule of God
> in parables and images of the meal further elaborates the inclusive
> invitation he extends to his followers in the name of Sophia-
> God. . . .

The meal sharing of Christians, therefore, is a feast celebrating and actualizing the radical inclusiveness of Sophia-God. For the One who prepared the Banquet sent out her disciples to call from the highest places so that all could hear,
"Whoever is simple turn in here!"
To him who is without sense she says,
"Come and eat of my bread and drink of the
    wine I have mixed" (Provs 9:3-5; see
    also Sir 24:19-22). (*Wisdom Literature,* p. 190)

Another divergence between the wisdom of Ben Sira and the wisdom of Jesus emerges in regard to the identity of personified wisdom. Ben Sira sees the Torah as the full embodiment and revelation of God's own wisdom. Thus he says about Wisdom:

Come to her like one who plows and sows. . . . Put your feet into her fetters and your neck into her collar. Bend your shoulders and carry her. . . . For at last you will find the rest she gives. . . . Then her fetters will become for you a strong defense, and her collar a glorious robe. Her yoke is a golden ornament. (Sir 6:19, 24-25, 28-31)

But Jesus employs similar terminology about *himself* as the embodiment of wisdom:

Take my yoke upon you, and learn from me; for I am gentle and humble in heart, and you will find rest for your souls. For my yoke is easy, and my burden is light. (Matt 11:29-30)

The rootedness of Jesus in the wisdom of the Old Testament is clear. Thus, it is not surprising that the early followers of Jesus made use of these same texts and traditions. It is to the wisdom writings that they turned for the language and imagery with which to express their beliefs about Jesus' identity and the significance of his life and teachings. The impact of wisdom on early developments in "christology" appears prominent especially in three places in the New Testament: in the early christological hymns, in the Sayings Source or "Q" document made use of by the Gospels of Matthew and Luke, and in the Johannine writings.

EARLY CHRISTOLOGICAL HYMNS

The sages of the Old Testament assigned a "personality" to that creating, saving, revealing, and governing power of God which they perceived in the universe. They particularized and personified this power as the Wisdom Woman. We have seen how the development of this personification took diverse forms and paths in Job 28, Proverbs 1-9, Sirach 24, and Wisdom 6-9.

This personification of wisdom in the figure of the Wisdom Woman provided the language and imagery by which the early Christians could articulate the saving significance and identity of Jesus of Nazareth. Thus began the process of transferring to the historical person of Jesus the words, functions, and characteristics of this personified Wisdom. We find Jesus presented as Wisdom's envoy or messenger, or even as Wisdom herself.

A good example of this kind of reflection and identification occurs in Colossians 1:15-20. The opening verses of the passage express the close association of Christ in the work of creation:

> He is the image of the invisible God, the firstborn of all creation; for in him all things in heaven and on earth were created, things visible and invisible, whether thrones or dominations or rulers or powers—all things have been created through him and for him. He himself is before all things, and in him all things hold together. (Col 1:15-17)

This early Christian hymn obviously depends on Old Testament wisdom texts that speak of the Wisdom Woman. Compare, for example, these verses from the book of Wisdom:

> For she is a reflection of eternal light,
> a spotless mirror of the working of God,
> and an image of his goodness.
> Although she is but one, she can do all things,
> and while remaining in herself, she renews all things.
> .   .   .   .
> She reaches mightily from one end of the earth
>   to the other,
> and she orders all things well. (Wis 7:26-27; 8:1)

THE Q DOCUMENT AND MATTHEW

The "Q document," or Sayings Source, has been reconstructed by scholars from their studies of the Synoptic Gospels (Matthew, Mark, Luke). It consisted of a collection of the sayings of Jesus assembled by early Jewish Christian communities in Palestine or western Syria. In both its form and its content it reflects the influence of the Old Testament wisdom tradition. It presents Jesus as the messenger or envoy of Wisdom, a spokesperson for Wisdom even greater than wise Solomon:

The queen of the South will rise up at the judgment with this generation and condemn it, because she came from the ends of the earth to listen to the wisdom of Solomon, and see, something greater than Solomon is here! (Matt 12:42//Luke 11:31)

The author of Matthew's Gospel incorporated this Q document or Sayings Source into his Gospel, but Matthew took the relationship of Jesus and Wisdom a step further. In Matthew's Gospel, Jesus is not just a messenger or envoy of Wisdom; Jesus is the embodiment of Wisdom. Just as Wisdom came to earth in the Torah for Ben Sira (chapter 24), Matthew implies that she became present in the person of Jesus.

Ben Sira invites his readers to take up Wisdom's yoke:

> Come to her with all your soul,
>   and keep her ways with all your might.
>
> . . . .
>
> her yoke is a golden ornament,
>   and her bonds a purple cord. (Sir 6:26, 30)

But as Wisdom personified, Jesus invites the disciples to take up *his* yoke:

> Come to me, all you that are weary and are carrying heavy burdens, and I will give you rest. Take my yoke upon you, and learn from me; for I am gentle and humble in heart, and you will find rest for your souls. For my yoke is easy, and my burden is light. (Matt 11:28-30)

THE GOSPEL OF JOHN

Finally, toward the end of the New Testament period, the author of John's Gospel continues and further develops this use of Old Testament wisdom language for christological reflection. The author of John goes beyond earlier images of Jesus as envoy or messenger of Wisdom. He goes beyond speaking of Jesus as the embodiment of personified Wisdom. He adds the notion of preexistent wisdom. In John's Gospel, preexistent Wisdom has become incarnate, "taken on flesh," in Jesus: "The Word became flesh and lived among us" (John 1:14).

Even though the Gospel writer makes use of the Greek term *logos* ("word") here, the Hebrew *hokmâ* ("wisdom"; Greek, *sophia*) is clearly one of the principal elements included in this claim about the identity of Jesus. The opening of the Gospel posits the preexistence of this Word/Wisdom:

In the beginning was the Word, and the Word was with God, and the Word was God. He was in the beginning with God. All things came into being through him, and without him not one thing came into being. (John 1:1-3)

This passage echoes similar statements about the origins of personified Wisdom:

> The LORD created me at the beginning of his work,
>   the first of his acts of long ago.
> Ages ago I was set up,
>   at the first, before the beginning of the earth.
> . . . .
> When he established the heavens, I was there,
>   when he drew a circle on the face of the deep.
> . . . .
> When he marked out the foundations of the earth,
>   then I was beside him, like a master worker;
> and I was daily his delight,
>   rejoicing before him always,
> rejoicing in his inhabited world
>   and delighting in the human race.
>   (Prov 8:22-23, 27, 29-31)

John's Gospel also marks a further stage in this wisdom reflection about Jesus in the presentation of his ministry in terms of the career of the Wisdom Woman. Like the Wisdom Woman, Jesus preaches in public places. Compare Proverbs 1:20-21 and John 7:28, for example:

> Wisdom cries out in the street;
>   in the squares she raises her voice.
> At the busiest corner she cries out;
>   at the entrance of the city gates she speaks.
>   (Prov 1:20-21)

Then Jesus cried out as he was teaching in the temple: "You know me, and you know where I am from." (John 7:28)

Like the Wisdom Woman, Jesus invites people to come, eat and drink, and he makes use of the symbols of bread and wine (see Prov 9:1-6 and John 6:35). Like the Wisdom Woman, Jesus teaches and instructs people in the truths about God (see Prov 8:7; Wis 6:22) and leads them to life (see Prov 4:13; 8:32-35) and immortality (Wis 6:18-19):

Jesus said to [Martha], "I am the resurrection and the life. Those who believe in me, even though they die, will live, and everyone who lives and believes in me will never die." (John 11:25-26)

A "WISDOM" CHRISTOLOGY

Recognition of the impact of Old Testament Wisdom on the New Testament has important implications for contemporary Christian theology. It opens up new directions for the articulation of the identity and significance of Jesus Christ for the Christian believer ("christology"). These new directions retain deep roots in early Christian tradition. At the same time they offer the possibility of a christology sensitive to and aware of the hopes and aspirations of women struggling to take their rightful place in society and the community of faith.

Elizabeth Johnson sums up nicely the potential of these new insights:

What is being argued here is the possibility of a christology which is faithful to the hard-won insights of the tradition but which uses, in addition to categories of Father and Son or God and his Word the categories of Sophia-God and her child, who is Sophia incarnate. . . . The combination of Jesus Christ/Sophia leads to a healthy blend of female and male imagery that empowers everyone, and works beautifully to symbolize the one God who is neither male nor female, but creator of both, delighter in both, savior of both, and imaged by both together. ("Jesus," pp. 293-94)

REVIEW QUESTIONS

1. Describe the two different ways of viewing the person and activity of Jesus. How do they complement each other?

2. How did the narrative parable form of the *mashal,* or "comparison," suit the strategy of the prophets?

3. Discuss the similarities of Jesus to a sage like Ben Sira. How did Jesus differ from Ben Sira?

4. Describe the challenge that Jesus posed to the conventional wisdom of his day, for example, in its emphasis on wealth and success. For Jesus, what represented the most important standard or criterion for determining behavior?

5. Discuss the importance of meals and banquet imagery in the teaching and practice of Jesus. What connection does this have with the Old Testament image of the Wisdom Woman?

6. Describe the identity of personified Wisdom according to Ben Sira. Who is personified Wisdom for the New Testament writers?

7. How was the wisdom tradition able to provide language and imagery with which the early Christians could articulate the saving significance and identity of Jesus? Comment on Colossians 1:15-20 in this regard.

8. What is Jesus' relationship to personified Wisdom in the "Q" document, or Sayings Source, used by Matthew and Luke? What happens to that relationship in Matthew's Gospel?

9. What further development takes place in Jesus' relationship with personified Wisdom in the Gospel of John? How does the ministry of Jesus parallel the career of the Wisdom Woman?

10. Discuss some of the implications of this recognition of the wisdom tradition's impact on New Testament traditions for contemporary christology.

19

Conclusion:
Some Common Threads

EXPERIENCE AS A BASIS FOR WISDOM

Among the common threads that run through the various chapters, certainly *experience* as a source for knowledge and insight represents one of the most pervasive. Reflection on one's own life experience provides an important criterion for determining behavior. It also offers a basis for faith statements, both implicit and explicit, about who God is and how we are to relate to him and to one another.

The book of Job offers an obvious example. Job holds fast to his own integrity and asserts that his experience of innocent suffering contradicts the claims of his friends about his presumed guilt. "I have not sinned, and yet I suffer. Why?" Job appeals to his experience over and over again and utters his anguished cry for some way to make sense out of his suffering.

The sources of authority to which Job's friends appeal for their explanations are powerful ones: tradition (8:8-10), "common sense" (4:7; 5:27), and revelation (4:13-14), for example. Job brings forward a variety of reasonings and arguments to counter his friends' claims. But ultimately it is his own experience to which he appeals. The author of the book clearly sides with Job and shows sympathy for Job's claims. In the author's mind, there is no doubt about God's approval of Job's stand against his friends (42:7).

The book of Ecclesiastes (Qoheleth) offers another example of the centrality of experience for the wisdom writers. For Qoheleth, experience represents the primary source of knowledge and basis for judging. In a context of confusion and the breakdown of traditional family ties and relationships in his day, Qoheleth is led to conclude: "All is vanity and a chasing after wind" (1:14, 17; and so on). He finds no solution to the seeming arbitrariness and injustices in life. On the basis of his experience he takes issue with traditional wisdom. He offers his people a way to deal with the ambiguities and struggles of their situation. Thus, he fashions a "spirituality" based on the humble acknowledgment of God's radical freedom and a grateful and temperate enjoyment of whatever gifts God wills to give.

The other books we have seen also give a primary place to experience. Proverbs appeals principally to the experience of previous generations in the received wisdom and advice that it offers. Ben Sira reworks and refashions traditional wisdom. But his own fulfilling experience of following that wisdom provides a firm basis for the authority behind his teaching. The description of his own pursuit of and union with the Wisdom Woman represents his way of asserting divine authority for his advice.

The appeal of the author of the book of Wisdom is also a personal one. His profound experience of union with a loving and gracious God leads him to conclude that death itself cannot terminate such a relationship. Somehow it will, it must, survive beyond the grave. Such an assertion surely brought hope and encouragement to a suffering and persecuted people in his day.

Finally, no experience is more powerful than that of human love. The Song of Solomon gives expression to that experience in poetry praising the ways of love between man and woman.

For dominated and marginalized groups, this affirmation of experience as having validity and authority can be a powerful one. The common sense to which the majority or dominant minority appeals often proves intimidating and even overwhelming in its denial of the legitimacy of their construction of reality. A book like Job offers a biblical basis for countering such attempts at domination and marginalization. This is an aspect of the wisdom writings that feminist scholars in particular have focused on. Carol Newsom remarks about Job, for example:

> To be sure, Job and his friends are not engaged in a debate about men's and women's experience. But what is important for feminist thought is that the issue of different sources of authority is explicitly raised in this book in such a way as to authenticate the crucial role of personal experience in the critique of received tradition. ("Job," p. 133)

The indigenous peoples of the Americas or the Dalits and "tribals" (Adivasis) of the Indian subcontinent would find encouragement and hope from an approach like this as well. They struggle for the recognition of the value and legitimacy of their own cultural heritage, which the dominant cultures marginalize and threaten to overwhelm. The wisdom writings' recognition of the importance of personal experience lends powerful support in legitimating the inherited experience from their ancestors. It confirms their own experience of the beauty and life-giving qualities of their way of life.

THE CENTRALITY OF GOD

Those who read the wisdom writings often fail to recognize an important fact—how central God is in almost every page. So subtle and pervasive is God's presence that only on conscious reflection and attention to these writings does one become aware of this. God is simply taken for granted by the writers—*Israel's* God, whose relationship with his people began with the Exodus from Egypt and the covenant at Sinai. In the book of Job, for example, the dilemma under discussion at first appears to be that of the suffering but innocent Job. But on further reflection, one comes to realize that it is really *God*, and the relationship between God's power and God's justice, that lies at the heart of the book's argument.

The same holds true for Qoheleth. The word "God" (*ʾĕlōhîm*) occurs some forty times in the twelve chapters of this brief book. God appears to be a remote and almost forbidding figure in the author's mind, one with whom a person must deal with great caution and circumspection. But a close study of the text reveals that God's *freedom* represents a central concern and teaching of the book. With skill and conviction, the author exposes the "vanity" of the human quest for Godlike wisdom.

Books like Proverbs and Ben Sira deal principally with the mundane issues and details of daily life. "Religion" as such does not appear to occupy much space. Nonetheless, generous helpings of individual proverbs and longer passages do explicitly refer to God and to God's presence and activity. In fact, this constitutes one of the main arguments implicit in these texts—God *is* present and active in the midst of this "busy-ness," and the wise individual must take cognizance of this fact and act accordingly.

The book of Wisdom represents perhaps the most "spiritual," even "mystical," of the wisdom writings. One cannot help but be moved and inspired by the fervor and intensity with which the author expresses his love for and attachment to the God of his people and that God's "Wisdom." The book's place at the intersection between Old and New Testaments provides a fitting transition to the new era for Judaism and Christianity.

THE WISDOM WOMAN

Another thread that traces its way through many of the wisdom writings is the image of personified Wisdom, the Wisdom Woman, as we have called her. Job 28 represents most likely her earliest appearance.

There the emphasis is on wisdom's inaccessibility. Only God knows the way to her.

The Wisdom Woman takes on a variety of forms in subsequent books: Proverbs, Ben Sira, and the book of Wisdom. In Proverbs she is contrasted with "the strange woman" and "Lady Folly" in chapters 1-9. The book emphasizes the Wisdom Woman's offer of "life" to those who embrace her. Ben Sira identifies her with Torah, the fullest revelation of God's own wisdom to Israel. In the book of Wisdom she represents God's gift of himself to those who seek her.

One can thus see how her identity and character vary from one context to another. Roland Murphy comments:

> It is not really possible to reduce all these identities to a unity. The best one can say is that Lady Wisdom is a divine communication: God's communication, exterior of self, to human beings. (*Tree of Life*, p. 147)

In their observation of the world and their experience of everyday life, the wisdom writers recognized God's voice speaking. For them, the voice of a woman, the Wisdom Woman, was the best way they could describe who and what they heard. Through her voice God was speaking, revealing wisdom to the world.

STRATEGIES FOR SURVIVAL AND RESISTANCE

The exilic and postexilic periods represent the historical context for the writing of the wisdom books. The people of Israel, or "Jews" as they were now called, were a subject people. They were no longer in control of their own history. They formed a minority group under the domination of the successive imperial powers who ruled western Asia and the eastern Mediterranean basin. We have seen how this historical context had a decisive impact on these wisdom writings. Indeed, the struggle to survive and preserve their identity as a people motivated in part the writing of Proverbs, Ben Sira, and the book of Wisdom.

More than simply a strategy for survival, however, these writings also represent an implicit move to resist imperial rule and the pressures toward assimilation. During the period of Greek rule in particular, these pressures were fierce at times. The combined political, economic, and cultural weight of Hellenism threatened to destroy Judaism or at least substantially alter its character. Fierce military resistance by some Jews emerged in the Maccabean revolt. The wisdom works that we have studied represent a parallel religious and cultural response to the crisis.

The confusion and suffering caused by the ruthless economic exploitation of the Persian and Greek regimes form the background for Job and Qoheleth in particular. These works also emerged from the struggle to survive. In addition, they achieved new insights into the meaning of fidelity to ideals and values, and they traced new directions in the search to know and understand God.

These wisdom works and the efforts to produce them offer hope and encouragement to peoples in similar situations today. Minority groups who are marginalized and under pressure to assimilate into the dominant culture can learn from the courage and strategies portrayed in these books to persevere and to stand firm against such assimilation.

This becomes especially crucial in this age of "globalization." The engines of a global capitalist economy recall the efforts of the Greek hellenization program to control and shape the markets of the world toward a "global culture." Such a global culture does not tolerate diversity or deviation. In this context, the example and resources offered by the wisdom writings provide much scope for study and reflection.

REVIEW QUESTIONS

1. Discuss how your own personal experience can be a source for reflecting about who God is and how God is present and active in our world today. How can this kind of reflection "test" and develop or modify what previous generations have said about God?

2. Describe some of the differences in the picture of God presented by each of the wisdom books. What are some of the similarities?

3. Describe the various appearances or "identities" of the Wisdom Woman. Which one do you find most appealing? Why?

4. Do you know of strategies used by minority groups today to survive and to resist assimilation into a dominant culture that are similar to what we find portrayed in the wisdom writings? What values in particular are they intent on preserving?

5. How successful have these minority groups been in accommodating and even co-opting elements from the dominant culture (cf. the book of Wisdom)? What has the dominant culture learned from them?

Bibliography

1. INTRODUCTION

Alexander, Jon, O.P. "What Do Recent Writers Mean by Spirituality?" *Spirituality Today* 32 (1980): 247-56.

Chathanatt, John, S.J. "'Bharat' vs. 'India': The New Economic Policy and the Marginalized." *Vidyajyoti: Journal of Theological Reflection* 61 (1997): 816-30.

Collins, John J. "Introduction: Jesus and Wisdom." In *Proverbs, Ecclesiastes*, pp. 11-12. Knox Preaching Guides. Atlanta: John Knox Press, 1980.

Gandhi, Mohandas. *The Collected Works of Mahatma Gandhi*. 90 volumes. New Delhi: Government of India.

Irwin, William H. "Spirituality as an Object of Old Testament Research." *Toronto Journal of Theology* 12 (1996): 7-16.

O'Connor, Kathleen M. *The Wisdom Literature*. Message of Biblical Spirituality 5. Wilmington, Del.: Michael Glazier, 1988.

2. WISDOM IN THE ANCIENT WORLD

Ancient Near Eastern Texts Relating to the Old Testament, with Supplement. Edited by James B. Pritchard. 3rd edition. Princeton: Princeton University Press, 1969. [= *ANET*]

Blenkinsopp, Joseph. "The Sage." Chapter 1 in *Sage, Priest, Prophet: Religious and Intellectual Leadership in Ancient Israel*, pp. 9-65. Library of Ancient Israel. Louisville: Westminster John Knox Press, 1995.

Ceresko, Anthony R. "Wisdom in Israel." Chapter 23 in *Introduction to the Old Testament: A Liberation Perspective*. Maryknoll, N.Y.: Orbis Books, 1992.

Clifford, Richard J. "Introduction to Wisdom Literature." In *The New Interpreter's Bible*, 5:1-16. Nashville: Abingdon, 1997.

Fontaine, Carole R. "The Social Roles of Women in the World of Wisdom." In *A Feminist Companion to Wisdom Literature*, edited by Athalya Brenner, pp. 24-49. The Feminist Companion to the Bible 9. Sheffield: Sheffield Academic Press, 1995.

Harris, Rivkah. "The Female 'Sage' in Mesopotamian Literature (with an Appendix on Egypt)." In *The Sage in Israel and the Ancient Near East*, edited by John G. Gammie and Leo G. Perdue, pp. 3-17. Winona Lake, Ind.: Eisenbrauns, 1990.

Kramer, Samuel Noah. "The Sage in Sumerian Literature: A Composite Portrait." In *The Sage in Israel and the Ancient Near East*, pp. 31-44.

Matthews, Victor H., and Don C. Benjamin. *Old Testament Parallels: Laws and Stories from the Ancient Near East*. New York and Mahwah, N.J.: Paulist Press, 1991.

Radakrishnan, S. *Indian Philosophy*, volume 1. Delhi: Oxford University Press, 1997.

Thapar, Romila. *A History of India*. 2 volumes. London: Penguin Books, 1990.

3. THE ORIGINS OF ISRAEL AND ITS WISDOM

Blenkinsopp, Joseph. "The Sage." Chapter 1 in *Sage, Priest, Prophet*, pp. 9-65.

Ceresko, Anthony R. "The 'Conquest' of Canaan" and "Israel in the Period of the Judges." Chapters 9 and 10 in *Introduction to the Old Testament: A Liberation Perspective*, pp. 89-109.

———. "Potsherds and Pioneers: Recent Research on the Origins of Israel." *Indian Theological Studies* 34 (1997): 5-22.

Crenshaw, James L. *Education in Ancient Israel: Across the Deadening Silence*. New York: Doubleday, 1998.

Gottwald, Norman K. "Traditions About Intertribal Israel's Rise to Power in Canaan." Chapter 6 in *The Hebrew Bible: A Socio-Literary Introduction*, pp. 229-88. Philadelphia: Fortress Press, 1985.

———. *The Tribes of Yahweh: A Sociology of the Religion of Liberated Israel 1250-1050 B.C.E.* Maryknoll, N.Y.: Orbis Books, 1979. Parts 5-10.

The Sage in Israel and the Ancient Near East, edited by John G. Gammie and Leo G. Perdue. See especially the essays of R. N. Whybray ("The Sage in the Israelite Royal Court," pp. 133-39), Carol R. Fontaine ("The Sage in Family and Tribe," pp. 155-64), André Lemaire ("The Sage in School and Temple," pp. 165-81).

4. THE HISTORICAL BACKGROUND
FOR THE WISDOM WRITINGS: AN OVERVIEW

Albertz, Rainer. *A History of Israelite Religion in the Old Testament Period*. 2 volumes. Old Testament Library. Louisville: Westminster John Knox Press, 1994.

Ceresko, Anthony R. Chapters 3, 4, 7, 8, 9, 10, 12, 13, 14, 19, 21, 23, 24, 25, in *Introduction to the Old Testament: A Liberation Perspective*.

———. "Commerce and Calculation: The Strategy of the Book of Ecclesiastes (Qoheleth)." *Indian Theological Studies* 30 (1993): 205-19. Reprinted in Anthony R. Ceresko, *Psalmists and Sages: Studies in Old Testament Poetry and Religion*, pp. 222-36. Indian Theological Studies Supplements 2. Bangalore: Institute Publications, 1994.

———. "The Function of 'Order' (*ṣedeq*) and 'Creation' in the Book of Proverbs, with Some Implications for Today." *Indian Theological Studies* 32 (1995): 208-36.

———. "Gustavo Gutiérrez, *On Job*: Some Questions of Method." *Indian Theological Studies* 29 (1992): 223-33. Reprinted in Anthony R. Ceresko, *Psalmists and Sages*, pp. 195-204.

———. "The Liberative Strategy of Ben Sira: The Sage as Prophet." *Toronto Journal of Theology* 13 (1997): 169-85.

————. "Potsherds and Pioneers: Recent Research on the Origins of Israel." *Indian Theological Studies* 34 (1997): 5-22.

Gottwald, Norman K. *The Hebrew Bible*, pp. 563-71.

5. THE FORMS THAT WISDOM TAKES

Alter, Robert. *The Art of Biblical Poetry*. New York: Basic Books, 1985.

Bergant, Dianne. "Proverbs." Chapter 4 in *Israel's Wisdom Literature: A Liberation-Critical Reading*, pp. 78-107. Minneapolis: Fortress, 1997.

Berlin, Adele. *The Dynamics of Biblical Parallelism*. Bloomington and Indianapolis: Indiana University Press, 1985.

Black, Matthew. *An Aramaic Approach to the Gospels and Acts*. 3rd edition. Oxford: Clarendon Press, 1967.

Crenshaw, James E. "Wisdom." In *Old Testament Form Criticism*, edited by John H. Hayes, pp. 225-64. San Antonio: Trinity University, 1974.

Fontaine, Carole R. *Traditional Sayings in the Old Testament: A Contextual Study*. Bible and Literature Series. Sheffield: Almond Press, 1982. Pp. 109-26.

Gottwald, Norman K. *The Hebrew Bible*, pp. 563-71.

Kugel, James L. *The Idea of Biblical Poetry: Parallelism and Its History*. New Haven: Yale University Press, 1981.

Manickam, Thomas. "Proverbs in Indian Religious Culture." *Jeevadhara: A Journal of Christian Interpretation* 20, no. 116 (Kottayam 686 041 India; March 1990): 105-19.

Murphy, Roland E. "Basic Wisdom Forms." In *Wisdom Literature: Job, Proverbs, Ruth, Canticle, Ecclesiastes, and Esther*. The Forms of Old Testament Literature 13. Grand Rapids: Eerdmans, 1981. Pp. 4-6.

————. "Introduction." In *The Tree of Life: An Exploration of Biblical Wisdom Literature*, pp. 1-14. Anchor Bible Reference Library. New York: Doubleday, 1990.

Owan, Kris J. N. "African Proverbial Wisdom and Biblical Proverbial Wisdom: Wholesome Bedfellows and More." *Bible Bhashyam: An Indian Biblical Quarterly* 23 (Kottayam 686 010 India; 1997): 151-73.

Scott, R. B. Y. "Introduction." In *Proverbs. Ecclesiastes: Introduction, Translation, and Notes*. Anchor Bible 18. New York: Doubleday, 1965. Pp. 1-30.

————. "Precepts and Proverbs." Chapter 3 in *The Way of Wisdom in the Old Testament*, pp. 48-71. New York: Macmillan, 1971.

Westermann, Claus. "Appendix." In *Roots of Wisdom: The Oldest Proverbs of Israel and Other Peoples*, pp. 140-64. Louisville: Westminster John Knox Press, 1995.

Williams, James G. "The Power of Form: A Study of Biblical Proverbs." In *Gnomic Wisdom*, edited by John Dominic Crossan, pp. 35-58. *Semeia* 17. Chico, Calif.: Scholars Press, 1980.

————. *Those Who Ponder Proverbs: Aphoristic Thinking and Biblical Literature*. Bible and Literature Series. Sheffield: Almond Press, 1981.

6. THE LIBERATING POTENTIAL
OF PROVERB AND PARABLE

Fontaine, Carole R. "Proverbs." In *The Women's Bible Commentary*, edited by Carol A. Newsom and Sharon H. Ringe, pp. 145-55. Louisville: Westminster John Knox Press, 1992.

Fox, Michael V. "Ideas of Wisdom in Proverbs 1-9." *Journal of Biblical Literature* 116 (1997): 613-33.

Freire, Paulo. *Pedagogy of the Oppressed*. Harmondsworth: Penguin Books, 1972.

Herzog, William R. *Parables as Subversive Speech: Jesus as Pedagogue of the Oppressed*. Louisville: Westminster / John Knox Press, 1994.

Johnson, Elizabeth A. *She Who Is: The Mystery of God in Feminist Theological Discourse*. New York: Crossroad, 1992.

Murphy, Roland E. "Lady Wisdom." Chapter 9 in *The Tree of Life*, pp. 133-49.

O'Connor, Kathleen M. "Wisdom Literature and the Experience of the Divine." In *Biblical Theology: Problems and Perspectives. In Honor of J. Christiaan Beker,* edited by S. J. Krafchick, C. Myers, and B. C. Ollenberger, pp. 183-95. Nashville: Abingdon, 1995.

Soares-Prabhu, George M. "The Liberative Pedagogy of Jesus: Lessons for an Indian Theology of Liberation." In *Leave the Temple: Indian Paths to Human Liberation*, edited by Felix Wilfred, pp. 100-115. Maryknoll, N.Y.: Orbis Books, 1992.

Witherington, Ben. "Beginning the Journey: Drinking from the Fount" and "Wisdom in Person: Jesus as Sage." Chapters 1 and 4 in *Jesus the Sage: The Pilgrimage of Wisdom*. Minneapolis: Fortress Press, 1994, pp. 3-74, 147-208.

7 AND 8. THE BOOK OF PROVERBS

Camp, Claudia. *Wisdom and the Feminine in the Book of Proverbs*. Bible and Literature Series 11. Sheffield: Almond Press, 1985.

Ceresko, Anthony R. Chapters 19, 21, 24 in *Introduction to the Old Testament: A Liberation Perspective*.

————. "The Function of 'Order' (*ṣedeq*) and 'Creation' in the Book of Proverbs, with Some Implications for Today." *Indian Theological Studies* 32 (1995): 208-36.

Clifford, Richard J. *The Book of Proverbs and Our Search for Wisdom*. The Père Marquette Lecture in Theology 1995. Milwaukee: Marquette University Press, 1995.

Collins, John J. *Proverbs, Ecclesiastes*. Knox Preaching Guides. Atlanta: John Knox Press, 1980.

Crenshaw, James L. "Proverbs, Book of." In *Anchor Bible Dictionary*, edited by David Noel Freedman, 5:513-20. New York: Doubleday, 1992.

Fontaine, Carol R. "Proverbs." In *The Women's Bible Commentary*, pp. 145-52.

Gottwald, Norman K. *The Hebrew Bible*, pp. 571-75.

———. "Sociology of Ancient Israel." In *Anchor Bible Dictionary*, 6:79-89.

Murphy, Roland E. "The Kerygma of the Book of Proverbs." *Interpretation* 20 (1966): 3-14.

———. "Proverbs." In *Wisdom Literature: Job, Proverbs, Ruth, Canticles, Ecclesiastes and Esther*, pp. 47-82.

———. "Proverbs—The Wisdom of Words" and "Lady Wisdom." Chapters 2 and 9 in *The Tree of Life*, pp. 15-32, 133-49.

———. "Wisdom in the OT." In *Anchor Bible Dictionary*, 6:920-31.

O'Connor, Kathleen M. "How to Cope With Life" and "The Wisdom Woman." Chapters 2 and 3 in *The Wisdom Literature*, pp. 35-85.

———. "Wisdom Literature and the Experience of the Divine." In *Biblical Theology: Problems and Perspectives,* pp. 183-95.

Perdue, Leo G. "Cosmology and Social Order in the Wisdom Tradition." In *The Sage in Israel and the Ancient Near East*, pp. 457-78.

Rad, Gerhard von. *Wisdom in Israel*. Nashville: Abingdon, 1972.

Scott, R. B. Y. *Proverbs, Ecclesiastes*. Anchor Bible 18. Garden City, N.Y.: Doubleday, 1965.

Skehan, Patrick W. "A Single Editor for the Whole Book of Proverbs." In *Studies in Israelite Poetry and Wisdom*, pp. 15-26. Catholic Biblical Quarterly Monograph Series 1. Washington, D.C.: Catholic Biblical Association of America, 1971.

Van Leeuwen, Raymond C. "The Book of Proverbs." In *The New Interpreter's Bible,* 5:17-264.

———. *Context and Meaning in Proverbs 25-27*. SBL Dissertation Series 96. Atlanta: Scholars Press, 1988.

Whybray, R. N. *The Book of Proverbs*. Cambridge Bible Commentary. Cambridge: Cambridge University Press, 1972.

Yee, Gale A. "The Theology of Creation in Proverbs 8:22-31." In *Creation in the Biblical Traditions*, edited by Richard J. Clifford and John J. Collins, pp. 85-96. Catholic Biblical Quarterly Monograph Series 24. Washington, D.C.: Catholic Biblical Association, 1992.

9 AND 10. THE BOOK OF JOB

Albertz, Rainer. "The Sage and Pious Wisdom in the Book of Job: The Friends' Perspective." In *The Sage in Israel and the Ancient Near East*, pp. 243-61.

Cardenal, Ernesto. *The Psalms of Struggle and Liberation*. New York: Herder & Herder, 1971.

Ceresko, Anthony R. "Gustavo Gutiérrez, *On Job*: Some Questions of Method." *Indian Theological Studies* 29 (1992): 223-33. Reprinted in *Psalmists and Sages*, pp. 195-204.

———. "The Option for the Poor in the Book of Job." *Indian Theological Studies* 26 (1989): 105-21. Reprinted in *Psalmists and Sages*, pp. 181-94.

Crenshaw, James L. "Job, Book of." In *Anchor Bible Dictionary*, 3:858-68.

Gottwald, Norman K. *The Hebrew Bible*, pp. 575-79.

Gutiérrez, Gustavo. *On Job: God-Talk and the Suffering of the Innocent*. Maryknoll, N.Y.: Orbis Books, 1987.

Habel, Norman C. *The Book of Job: A Commentary*. Old Testament Library. Philadelphia: Westminster Press, 1985.

Janzen, J. Gerald. "Introduction." In *Job*. Interpretation. Atlanta: John Knox Press, 1985. Pp. 1-24.

MacKenzie, R. A. F. "Job." In *The New Jerome Biblical Commentary*, edited by R. E. Brown, J. A. Fitzmyer, and R. E. Murphy. Englewood Cliffs, N.J.: Prentice-Hall, 1990. P. 466.

McCann, J. Clinton. "Wisdom's Dilemma: The Book of Job, the Final Form of the Book of Psalms, and the Entire Bible." In *Wisdom, You Are My Sister: Studies in Honor of Roland E. Murphy, O.Carm., on the Occasion of His Eightieth Birthday*, edited by Michael L. Barré, S.S., pp. 18-30. Catholic Biblical Quarterly Monograph Series 29. Washington, D.C.: Catholic Biblical Association, 1997.

Murphy, Roland E. "Job." In *Wisdom Literature: Job, Proverbs, Ruth, Canticles, Ecclesiastes, and Esther*, pp. 13-45.

————. "Job the Steadfast." Chapter 3 in *The Tree of Life*, pp. 33-48.

Newsom, Carol A. "The Book of Job." In *The New Interpreter's Bible*, 4:317-637.

————. "Job," In *The Women's Bible Commentary*, pp. 130-36.

O'Connor, Kathleen M. "Job and the Collapse of Relationship." Chapter 4 in *The Wisdom Literature*, pp. 86-113.

Perdue, Leo G. "'You Have Not Spoken Rightly About Me': The Book of Job and the Imagining of God in Human Torment." Chapter 4 in *Wisdom and Creation: The Theology of Wisdom Literature*. Nashville: Abingdon Press, 1994, pp. 123-92.

Pleins, J. David. "Poor, Poverty (Old Testament)." In *Anchor Bible Dictionary*, 5:402-14.

Scott, R. B. Y. "Wisdom in Revolt: Job." Chapter 6 in *The Way of Wisdom in the Old Testament*, pp. 136-64.

11 AND 12. THE BOOK OF ECCLESIASTES

Ceresko, Anthony R. "Commerce and Calculation: The Strategy of the Book of Qoheleth (Ecclesiastes)." *Indian Theological Studies* 30 (1993): 205-19. Reprinted in *Psalmists and Sages*, pp. 222-36.

Crenshaw, James L. "Ecclesiastes, Book of." In *Anchor Bible Dictionary*, 2:271-80.

————. *Ecclesiastes: A Commentary*. Old Testament Library. Philadelphia: Westminster Press, 1987.

Crüsemann, Frank. "The Unchangeable World: The 'Crisis of Wisdom' in Koheleth." In *The God of the Lowly: Socio-Historical Interpretations of the Bible*, edited by W. Schottroff and W. Stegemann, pp. 57-77. Maryknoll, N.Y.: Orbis Books, 1984.

Fox, Michael V. *Qoheleth and His Contradictions*. Journal for the Study of the Old Testament Supplements 71; Bible and Literature Series 18. Sheffield: Almond Press, 1989.

Gottwald, Norman K. *The Hebrew Bible*, pp. 579-82.

Johnston, Robert K. "Confessions of a Workaholic: A Reappraisal of Qoheleth." *Catholic Biblical Quarterly* 38 (1976): 14-28.

Murphy, Roland E. *Ecclesiastes*. Word Biblical Commentary 23A. Dallas: Word Books, 1992.

———. "Ecclesiastes (Qohelet)." In *Wisdom Literature: Job, Proverbs, Ruth, Canticles, Ecclesiastes, Esther*, pp. 125-49.

———. "Qoheleth the Skeptic?" Chapter 4 in *The Tree of Life*, pp. 49- 63.

———. "The Sage in Ecclesiastes and Qoheleth the Sage." In *The Sage in Israel and the Ancient Near East*, pp. 263-71.

O'Connor, Kathleen M. "Qoheleth and the Ambiguity of Life." Chapter 5 in *The Wisdom Literature*, pp. 114-33.

Ogden, Graham. *Qoheleth*. Readings—A New Biblical Commentary. Sheffield: JSOT Press, 1987.

Seow, Choon-Leong. *Ecclesiastes: A New Translation with Introduction and Commentary*. Anchor Bible 18C. New York: Doubleday, 1997.

Towner, W. Sibley. "The Book of Ecclesiastes." In *The New Interpreter's Bible*, 5:265-360.

Walsh, Jerome T. "Despair as a Theological Virtue in the Spirituality of Ecclesiastes." *Biblical Theology Bulletin* 12 (1982): 46-49.

Wright, Addison G. "Additional Numerical Patterns in Qoheleth." *Catholic Biblical Quarterly* 45 (1983): 32-43.

———. "Ecclesiastes (Qoheleth)." In *The New Jerome Biblical Commentary*, pp. 489-95.

———. "'For Everything There is a Season': The Structure and Meaning of the Fourteen Opposites (Ecclesiastes 3:2-8)." In *De La Torah au Messie: Mélanges Henri Cazelles*, edited by J. Doré et al., 321-28. Paris: Desclée, 1981.

———. "The Riddle of the Sphinx." *Catholic Biblical Quarterly* 30 (1968): 313-34.

———. "The Riddle of the Sphinx Revisited: Numerical Patterns in the Book of Qoheleth." *Catholic Biblical Quarterly* 42 (1980): 35-51.

13 AND 14. THE WISDOM OF BEN SIRA

Albertz, Rainer. "A Prospect on the History of Religion in the Hellenistic Period." Part 6 of *A History of Israelite Religion in the Old Testament Period*, pp. 534-97.

Ceresko, Anthony R. "The Liberative Strategy of Ben Sira: The Sage as Prophet." *Toronto Journal of Theology* 13 (1997): 169-85.

Chatnanatt, John. "Christian Spirituality and Justice: Towards a Socio- relational Spirituality." *Vidyajyoti: Journal of Theological Reflection* 59 (Delhi 110054 India, 1995): 319-31.

Crenshaw, James L. "The Book of Sirach." In *The New Interpreter's Bible*, 5:601-867.

Di Lella, Alexander A. "Sirach." In *The New Jerome Biblical Commentary*, pp. 496-509.

———. "Wisdom of Ben Sira." In *Anchor Bible Dictionary*, 6:931-45.

Gammie, John G. "The Sage in Sirach." In *The Sage in Israel and the Ancient Near East*, pp. 355-72.

Hengel, Martin. *Judaism and Hellenism: Studies in Their Encounter in Palestine during the Early Hellenistic Period,* volume 1. London: SCM Press, 1974.

Mack, Burton L. *Wisdom and the Hebrew Epic: Ben Sira's Praise of the Fathers.* Chicago Studies in the History of Judaism. Chicago: University of Chicago Press, 1965.

Murphy, Roland E. "Ben Sira—Wisdom's Traditionalist." Chapter 5 in *The Tree of Life*, pp. 65-81.

O'Connor, Kathleen M. "Sirach and Communion with God." Chapter 6 in *The Wisdom Literature*, pp. 134-59.

Perdue, Leo G. "'I Covered the Earth Like a Mist': Cosmos and History in Ben Sira." Chapter 6 in *Wisdom and Creation: The Theology of Wisdom Literature*, pp. 243-90.

Rad, Gerhard von. "The Wisdom of Jesus Sirach." Chapter 13 in *Wisdom in Israel*, pp. 240-62.

Skehan, Patrick W., and Alexander A. Di Lella. *The Wisdom of Ben Sira*, A New Translation with Notes by Patrick W. Skehan, Introduction and Commentary by Alexander A. Di Lella. Anchor Bible 39. New York: Doubleday, 1987.

Witherington, Ben. "Wisdom at a Turning Point: From Ben Sira to the Wisdom of Solomon" and "Final Reflections on Wisdom's Journey." Chapters 2 and 9 in *Jesus the Sage: The Pilgrimage of Wisdom,* pp. 75-116, 381-87.

15 AND 16. THE BOOK OF WISDOM

Clarke, Ernest G. *The Wisdom of Solomon.* Cambridge Bible Commentary. Cambridge: Cambridge University Press, 1973.

Kolarcik, Michael. "The Book of Wisdom." In *The New Interpreter's Bible*, 5:435-600.

———. "Creation and Salvation in the Book of Wisdom." In *Creation in the Biblical Traditions*, pp. 97-107.

Murphy, Roland E. "The Wisdom of Solomon—A View from the Diaspora." Chapter 6 in *The Tree of Life*, pp. 83-96.

O'Connor, Kathleen M. "The Wisdom of Solomon and the Fullness of Life." Chapter 7 in *The Wisdom Literature*, pp. 160-84.

Perdue, Leo G. "'Wisdom, the Artificer of All, Instructed Me': Creation and Redemption in the Wisdom of Solomon." Chapter 7 in *Wisdom and Creation: The Theology of Wisdom Literature*, pp. 291-322.

Rad, Gerhard von. "The Polemic Against Idols." Chapter 10 in *Wisdom in Israel*, pp. 177-85.

Reese, James M. *The Book of Wisdom, Song of Songs.* Old Testament Message 20. Wilmington, Del.: Michael Glazier, 1983.

———. *Hellenistic Influence on the Book of Wisdom and its Consequences.* Analecta Biblica 41. Rome: Biblical Institute Press, 1970.

Scott, R. B. Y. "Wisdom Piety." Chapter 8 in *The Way of Wisdom in the Old Testament*, pp. 190-222.

√ Winston, David. "The Sage as Mystic in the Wisdom of Solomon." In *The Sage in Israel and the Ancient Near East*, pp. 383-97.

———. "Solomon, Wisdom of." In *Anchor Bible Dictionary*, 6:120-27.

———. *The Wisdom of Solomon: A New Translation with Introduction and Commentary*. Anchor Bible 43. New York: Doubleday, 1979.

Witherington, Ben. "Wisdom at a Turning Point: From Ben Sira to the Wisdom of Solomon." Chapter 2 in *Jesus the Sage: The Pilgrimage of Wisdom*, pp. 75-116.

√ Wright, Addison G. "Wisdom." In *The New Jerome Biblical Commentary*, pp. 510-22.

17. WISDOM OUTSIDE THE "WISDOM BOOKS"

Bergant, Dianne. "Psalms" and "Song of Songs." Chapters 3 and 6 in *Israel's Wisdom Literature: A Liberation-Critical Reading*, pp. 52-77, 124-41.

Cardenal, Ernesto. *The Psalms of Struggle and Liberation*. New York: Herder & Herder, 1971.

Ceresko, Anthony R. "The Sage in the Psalms." In *The Sage in Israel and the Ancient Near East*, pp. 217-30.

Murphy, Roland E. "Song of Songs, Book of." In *Anchor Bible Dictionary*, 6:150-55.

———. "Wisdom's Echoes." Chapter 7 in *The Tree of Life*, pp. 97-110.

Reese, James M. *The Book of Wisdom, Song of Songs*. Old Testament Message 20. Wilmington, Del.: Michael Glazier, 1983.

Scott, R. B. Y. "Prophecy and Wisdom" and "Wisdom Piety." Chapters 5 and 8 in *The Way of Wisdom in the Old Testament*, pp. 101-35, 190-222.

Weems, Renita J. "Song of Songs." In *The Women's Bible Commentary*, pp. 156-60.

———. "The Song of Songs." In *The New Interpreter's Bible*, 5:361-434.

18. OLD TESTAMENT WISDOM
AND THE NEW TESTAMENT

Borg, Marcus J. "Jesus, Teaching of." In *Anchor Bible Dictionary*, 3:804-12.

Brown, Raymond E. *The Gospel According to John*. Translated with an introduction and notes. Anchor Bible 29. New York: Doubleday, 1966. See the "Introduction," Part D "Wisdom Motifs," pp. cxxii-cxxviii.

Dunn, J. D. G. *Christology in the Making*. Philadelphia: Westminster, 1980.

Johnson, Elizabeth A. "Jesus, the Wisdom of God: A Biblical Basis for Non-Androcentric Christology." *Ephemerides Theologicae Lovanienses* 61 (1985): 261-94.

McKinlay, Judith E. *Gendering Wisdom the Host: Biblical Invitations to Eat and Drink*. Journal for the Study of the Old Testament Supplement Series 216; Gender, Culture, Theory 4. Sheffield: Sheffield Academic Press, 1996.

O'Connor, Kathleen M. "Epilogue: Wisdom in the New Testament." In *The Wisdom Literature*, pp. 185-92.

Schüssler Fiorenza, Elisabeth. *In Memory of Her: A Feminist Theological Reconstruction of Christian Origins.* London: SCM Press, 1983.

———. *Jesus: Miriam's Child, Sophia's Prophet: Critical Issues in Feminist Christology.* New York: Continuum, 1994.

Scott, Bernard Brandon. "Jesus as Sage: An Innovating Voice in Common Wisdom." In *The Sage in Israel and the Ancient Near East,* pp. 399-415.

Williams, James G. *Those Who Ponder Proverbs: Aphoristic Thinking and Biblical Literature.* Bible and Literature Series. Sheffield: Almond Press, 1981.

Witherington, Ben. *Jesus the Sage: The Pilgrimage of Wisdom.* Minneapolis: Fortress Press, 1994.

19. CONCLUSION

Murphy, Roland E. *The Tree of Life: An Exploration of Biblical Wisdom Literature.* Anchor Bible Reference Library. New York: Doubleday, 1990.

Newsom, Carol A. "Job." In *The Women's Bible Commentary,* pp. 130-36.

Index of Scripture References

HEBREW BIBLE

NEW TESTAMENT

General Index

Admonitions: as literary form of wisdom literature, 35
Albertz, Rainer, 68
Alexander, Jon, 2, 7
Alexander the Great, 28-29, 140
Alexandria, 140-41, 152, 154
Amos: wisdom and, 168-69
Autobiographical narrative: as literary form of wisdom literature, 33

Babylonian exile, 25: court scribes and, 22
Ben Sira: compared with Jesus, 172-75; as priest-scribe, 23
Bergant, Dianne, 162

Camp, Claudia, 59
Canticle. *See* Song of Solomon
Capable woman, 64-65. *See also* Woman of Worth
Cardenal, Ernesto, 73-74, 162-64
Christological hymns, 175-76. *See also* Hymn
Covenant: Israelite society and, 4
Creation: in book of Ecclesiastes, 98-99; in book of Wisdom, 156-58; Wisdom Woman and, in Proverbs, 58-59

Deuteronomic school: wisdom and, 22
Deuteronomistic History, 16, 22: Exodus experience and, 16; "first edition of," 26-27
Di Lella, Alexander A., 123
Dispute over Suicide, A, 11-12, 66

Ecclesiastes, book of (Qoheleth), 91-114: author of, 103; commercial character of, 95-96; dialectic in,

93-94; God in, 98-100; historical setting of, 92-93; *mashal* in, 104; numerical patterns in, 96-97; theme of death in, 100-101; theme of profit in, 104-5; theme of suffering in, 108-9; theme of time in, 106-8; theme of toil in, 103-8; theme of vanity in, 100-101, 103; wisdom and, 97-98; youth and old age in, 111-13
Ecclesiasticus. *See* Wisdom of Ben Sira
Education: book of Proverbs and, 17, 51-52; scribal schools and, 19; structure of, 96-97; women and, 12-13
Elders: context of wisdom and, 17
Epic of Gilgamesh, 11
Exodus: story of, 3-5; book of Wisdom and, 154, 156-58; Deuteronomistic History and, 16; as paradigm story of liberation, 24; wisdom writings and, 4
Experience: as basis for wisdom, 1-2, 66, 67, 97-98, 181-82

Folly: in Proverbs, 59
Fontaine, Carole, 36, 45, 64

Gandhi, Mahatma, 1-2: as model of wisdom spirituality, 2-4
Genesis, book of: relation to wisdom literature, 168
Good Samaritan, parable of, 2, 4, 174: raising of awareness and, 42
Gospels: John, 177-79; Matthew, 176-77; wisdom and, 174. *See also* Jesus; New Testament; "Q" document
Gunkel, Hermann, 160